New Dramatists 2001

About New Dramatists

Founded in 1949 by a playwright, Michaela O'Harra, New Dramatists is a unique resource for the American theater. The company is dedicated to the playwright and serves as an artistic home, theater laboratory, and a national writers' colony. The company finds and nurtures new talent through a competitive, selection process and a seven-year playwright residency tailored to the writers' individual needs.

New Dramatists gives writers the tools that they need — time, generous theater space, a pool of talented and experienced actors and directors, writing equipment, meeting space, and a gifted peer community — to grow artistically and strengthen their commitment to theater. The company augments this central focus on artistic growth through programs that advocate and distribute each writer's work to theater producers, through grants and fellowships, international exchanges, and with annual playwriting retreats in Lake Placid, New York, and Key West, Florida.

Writers pay nothing to join and participate in New Dramatists. The program is made possible through contributions from the theater and entertainment community. In return for this gift of time and resources, resident playwrights write and create new works for the theater. New Dramatists organizes more than seventy-five readings and workshops of new plays and musicals by its writing company each season.

Resident playwrights and alumni have won eleven Pulitzer Prizes, including the 2002 Pulitzer Prize for Drama to alumna Suzan-Lori Parks, twenty-two Tony Awards, fifty-one Obie Awards, seventeen Drama Desk Awards, and ten Susan Smith Blackburn Awards.

New Dramatists' founding committee included Michaela O'Harra, Howard Lindsay, Russel Crouse, Richard Rodgers, Oscar Hammerstein 2nd, John Golden, Moss Hart, Maxwell Anderson, John Wharton, and Elmer Rice.

SMITH AND KRAUS PUBLISHERS
Contemporary Playwrights / Collections

Act One Festival '95
Act One Festival '95
EST Marathon '94: The One-Act Plays
EST Marathon '95: The One-Act Plays
EST Marathon '96: The One-Act Plays
EST Marathon '97: The One-Act Plays
EST Marathon '98: The One-Act Plays
Humana Festival: 20 One-Acts Plays 1976–1996
Humana Festival '93: The Complete Plays
Humana Festival '94: The Complete Plays
Humana Festival '95: The Complete Plays
Humana Festival '96: The Complete Plays
Humana Festival '97: The Complete Plays
Humana Festival '98: The Complete Plays
Humana Festival '99: The Complete Plays
Humana Festival 2000: The Complete Plays
Humana Festival 2001: The Complete Plays
Humana Festival 2002: The Complete Plays
New Dramatists 2000: Best Plays from the Graduating Class
New Playwrights: The Best Plays of 1998
New Playwrights: The Best Plays of 1999
New Playwrights: The Best Plays of 2000
New Playwrights: The Best Plays of 2001
Women Playwrights: The Best Plays of 1992
Women Playwrights: The Best Plays of 1993
Women Playwrights: The Best Plays of 1994
Women Playwrights: The Best Plays of 1995
Women Playwrights: The Best Plays of 1996
Women Playwrights: The Best Plays of 1997
Women Playwrights: The Best Plays of 1998
Women Playwrights: The Best Plays of 1999
Women Playwrights: The Best Plays of 2000
Women Playwrights: The Best Plays of 2001

If you require pre-publication information about upcoming Smith and Kraus books, you may receive our semi-annual catalogue free of charge, by sending your name and address to *Smith and Kraus Catalogue, PO Box 127, Lyme NH 03768*. Or call us at (603) 643-6431, fax (603) 643-1831. *www.SmithKraus.com*.

New Dramatists
2001

Best Plays by the Graduating Class

Edited by Todd London,
Artistic Director

CONTEMPORARY PLAYWRIGHTS SERIES

A Smith and Kraus Book

A Smith and Kraus Book
Published by Smith and Kraus, Inc.
177 Lyme Road, Hanover, NH 03755
www.SmithKraus.com

Copyright © 2002 by New Dramatists
All rights reserved

CAUTION: Professionals and amateurs are hereby warned that the plays represented in this book are subject to a royalty. They are fully protected under the copyright laws of the United States of America, and of all countries covered by the International Copyright Union (including the Dominion of Canada and the rest of the British Commonwealth), and of all countries covered by the Pan-American Copyright Convention and the Universal Copyright Convention, and of all countries with which the United States has reciprocal copyright relations. All rights, including professional, amateur, motion picture, recitation, lecturing, public reading, radio broadcasting, television, video or sound taping, all other forms of mechanical or electronic reproduction such as CD-ROM and CD-I, information storage and retrieval systems and photocopying, and the rights of translation into foreign languages, are strictly reserved. Particular emphasis is laid upon the question of public readings, permission for which must be secured from the Author's agent in writing. See page 309 for individual contact information.

First Edition: December 2002
10 9 8 7 6 5 4 3 2 1
Manufactured in the United States of America

Cover and text design by Julia Hill Gignoux, Freedom Hill Design
Cover art drawn and donated to New Dramatists by
R. Miles Parker, artist and preservationist

ISBN 1-57525-298-8
Contemporary Playwrights Series
ISSN 1067-9510

Contents

Preface by Robert Anderson vii

Introduction by Todd London xi

Skitaletz ("The Wanderer") by Dmitry Lipkin 1

Boxcar by Silvia Gonzalez S. 61

A Bicycle Country by Nilo Cruz 113

The Negro of Peter the Great by Carlyle Brown 151

The Women of Lockerbie by Deborah Brevoort 199

Millennium 7 by Edgar Nkosi White 267

2001–2002 Resident Playwrights

Liz Duffy Adams
Luis Alfaro
Mark Bazzone
Neena Beber
John Belluso
Glen Berger
Deborah Brevoort *
Carlyle Brown *
Bridget Carpenter
Lonnie Carter
Kia Corthron
Nilo Cruz *
Gordon Dahlquist
Lisa D'Amour
Herman Daniel Farrell III
Catherine Filloux
Stephanie Fleischmann
Karl Gajdusek
Anne García-Romero
Melissa James Gibson
Keith Glover
Joseph Goodrich
Silvia Gonzalez S. *
David Greenspan
Karen Hartman

Julie Hébert
Sander Hicks
Michael Hollinger
Arlene Hutton
Naomi Iizuka
Honour Kane
David Lindsay-Abaire
Dmitry Lipkin *
Ruth Margraff
Rogelio Martinez
Murray Mednick
Alejandro Morales
Lynn Nottage
Kate Robin
Edwin Sanchez
Christopher Shinn
Octavio Solis
Diana Son
Caridad Svich
Dominic Taylor
Edgar Nkosi White *
Doug Wright
Chay Yew
Paul Zimet

* Graduating Class

Preface

There's a sign over my desk that reads, "Nobody asked you to be a playwright." I put it there almost forty years ago to stop my bitching.

Although the message is still lamentably true — talented playwrights are wooed by television and movie producers, but rarely hear "How are you doing?" from theater producers — there was a time, soon after we all came back from World War II, when people were asking us to be playwrights.

The honorable and venerable Theatre Guild had a group of young playwrights meeting under the guidance of John Gassner and Theresa Helburn. Theatre Incorporated, a new producing firm, gathered some of us with Theodore Apstein keeping order. The American Theater Wing, which had been so active during the war with projects such as The Stage Door Canteen, set up a whole "academy" where they sponsored refresher courses for returning veterans.

Mary Hunter, who was the academic head of this Professional Training Program, approached me to teach the playwriting courses. Barely a playwright myself (I had had one off-Broadway production), I started the courses and taught myself and a fair number of other young playwrights. I can still see myself rushing into class full of enthusiasm about what I had just found out that morning about writing plays.

Distinguished guests such as Howard Lindsay, Elia Kazan, Arthur Miller, and Moss Hart came to share their experiences and wisdom with us. And once a week the students' plays were read aloud by a group of neophyte actors including Eileen Heckart, Jean Stapleton, and Harry Belafonte. The Wing also received free tickets to the theater.

At the same time a young playwright, Michaela O'Harra, with one Broadway production to her credit, felt the theater industry itself should offer some "growing ground for *all* qualified new dramatists." Since Howard Lindsay had been extraordinarily supportive of my program at The Theatre Wing, I suggested to Michaela that she solicit his advice and help. Her passion for the idea was contagious, and she persuaded Howard to become the godfather of her venture.

And so with the support of Howard Lindsay and Russel Crouse, The Dramatists Guild, The Playwrights Company, Richard Rodgers and Oscar Hammerstein, and John Golden, the New Dramatists was started in 1949.

For some years the dedicated Michaela ran the organization almost single-handedly, with occasional help from other New Dramatists like Eva Wolas. Our office was the small cloakroom in the Hudson Theatre (owned by Lindsay and Crouse), and we met in a large, dimly lit conference room five flights up at the top of the theater. There, week after week, we neophytes gathered to listen to the likes of Howard Lindsay, Robert Sherwood, Maxwell Anderson, Elia Kazan, S.M. Behrman, Moss Hart, and others. Those early New Dramatists eager for every word included William Inge, Paddy Chayefsky, William Gibson, Horton Foote, Joe Kramm, Ronald Alexander, and Sumner Locke Elliot among others. They would, in due time, return to talk to new generations of New Dramatists, including James Goldman, Michael Stewart, Max Wilk, Joe Masteroff, Arnold Schulman, Jack Gelber, Lanford Wilson, who would in due time . . .

When someone had a play ready, he or she would read it to us and bravely listen to the comments. Thanks to the producers, we went to the theater free. We felt appreciated.

Over the years we grew out of the cloakroom to the offices in City Center with Michaela still firmly at the helm but aided now by such administrators as the late George Hamlin and the casting and production wizard Robert Colson.

Now we have our own building, an old church, which contains two theaters and is located on the same block as the old church housing the Actors Studio. (It's a nice picture, the playwrights and actors developing side by side.) The nature of the group has shifted over the years. The playwrights are more sophisticated, many of them having had productions in regional, Broadway, off- and off-off-Broadway theaters.

The New Dramatists is still a place for talented playwrights to develop, to grow, and to work in a theater with fine actors and directors with no production pressures. In the years since New Dramatists was founded, many valuable nurturing grounds have sprung up around the country. All are doing notable work. The New Dramatists, however, is unique. Upon admittance, the writer becomes a member for seven years — seven years to hear his or her plays read, see them workshopped, listen, learn from others, see theater, enjoy the support and companionship of other playwrights and the services of a trained staff of people who are there to help the playwright grow and develop. There is no charge for all this. The only requirements are talent and a willingness to pursue a goal.

We point with pride to the work of the member playwrights who over the years have shared their talents, wisdom, and caring and who have emerged — if not Pulitzer Prize–winners, as eleven of our members have — at least to a better understanding of their art and craft.

    Robert Anderson
    Resident Playwright, Original Class
    New Dramatists Board of Directors

Introduction

One of the fascinations of working with playwrights is the way what you know about the writer as a person plays off of what you find in their work. It's a process of constant comparison, like gazing at a new friend while you thumb through an album filled with photos from her past. Sometimes the resemblance never wavers — the child, the teenager, the unfortunately dressed product of an earlier era are all plainly evident in the current, dimensional person. And sometimes you have to squint. Sometimes the images before you and the person before you seem like distant cousins at best, or growths from wholly different seedpods.

Likewise, plays can look and feel like their creators and they can also feel as if they were penned by an evil twin — the soft-spoken rationalist becomes the mad-eyed stage anarchist, the city cat writes about the country mouse. Who is the realer self: the written persona or the person in the world?

The writers anthologized here have completed seven-year residencies at New Dramatists, a fifty-three-year-young center dedicated to serving the creative, professional, and human needs of playwrights. Each of these writers has generated extensive bodies of work, and these plays are the tip of those creative icebergs or (to change metaphors in mid-stream) one of the faces they show the world.

Dmitry Lipkin (*Skitaletz*) is one of the most surprising playwrights I know. This surprise began when I met him. I knew he'd been born in the USSR and hadn't come to the States until he was ten or eleven. I'd read some of his plays — at that point notable for the voluble violence of the characters and the monstrous, overt cruelty within families. I had an image of some bearded Dostoevskian character, angry and argumentative, vengeful and unpredictable. And what I found, what everyone finds, is this lovely, kind, thoughtful guy, outwardly boyish American, with a warm laugh, tentative manner, and constitutional inability to spit out a whole sentence. There is no trace of Russia in his voice and no sign of monstrosity in his being, as if it had all been expelled in his writing.

Dmitry once described the difference between plays that feel like plays and plays that feel like living things. Living things: That's an apt description of his work. His plays are so rich, so varied, so full of felt life — especially the dense tangled life of families — that it's hard to categorize them. In this way they remind me most of his countryman Chekhov's plays. There is cruelty in them, and intense love. They are strange things and funny, full of longing for worlds that were hateful to begin with and full of joy about worlds that are hateful now. They are populated not by characters so much as by people who go through life as characters.

His tragicomedies also recall a great tradition of the writing of immigrant sons and daughters — especially Jewish immigrants — who look at America with double vision. In this way Dmitry as a writer seems always to be both intensely connected with his Russian-Jewish heritage and fully assimilated — in the sense that assimilation is always a kind of disconnection, a way of being cut off. He understands what it's like to be both inside and outside of life, of culture, of history. He attunes us intensely to the beautiful, lonely, cruel, crackpot texture of this inside-outside life.

There's something essential in Dmitry's portrait of Pasha in *Skitaletz*, the story of a spirit or time wanderer, a kind of angel who falls to earth on the boardwalk of Brighton Beach, Brooklyn. He becomes part of every other character's life — transforming Zelig-like in ways that help everyone else find some small fulfillment of promise that both the iron fist of the Soviet Union and the golden grasp of America deny. In the end, though, he can't participate in the lives he helps enrich.

Silvia Gonzalez S., on the other hand, is one of those writers whose personality and work seem continuous: She writes as she talks — with vivacity, spontaneity, and speed. I've pictured Silvia out in the wilds of the Northwest, where she lives, banging out plays, channeling her wild imaginings directly to the page.

Because she's so prolific, because her imagination is so gusty and free, it's hard to sum up her work. There's so much of it and it's so varied. Some examples from recent years: *Boxcar*, anthologized here, is her staggering depiction of a group of illegal Mexican immigrants slowly dying in a locked boxcar as they wait for their "Coyote" to transport them into the United States *The Death of the Social Security Benefit*, by contrast, reveals a flair for the farcical, as an elderly woman tries to preserve, mummify, and prop up her new husband for nine months, after which she'll become eligible for his social security check. *Raw Deals and Some Satisfaction* includes four contemporary one acts about moments of trial — a man forcing a doctor at gunpoint to disconnect his comatose wife from life support, a woman waiting for the surrogate birth of her child.

I first met Silvia at the Kennedy Center, where her adventurous cross-cultural Alice play, *Alicia in Wonder Tierra*, was being workshopped. It introduced me to the abandon of her fantasy and her singular insights into cultural passage, as a young girl swirls in a mad landscape of Mexican souvenirs and artifacts come to life. This embodiment of the mythical — humorous or nightmarish, always theatrical — recurs throughout her work.

There are so many kinds of playwrights and some would never even describe themselves as artists. For Nilo Cruz, though, I would guess that being an artist precedes being a writer. One of his influences is the artist Joseph Cornell, whose famous boxes conjure whole worlds with small objects. Before writing, Nilo investigates his own plays sculpturally, fashioning boxes of his own — idea collages. His painful and beautiful *Two Sisters and a Piano* encapsulates his belief in art. At the end of the play, two Cuban sisters, having lived for too long under house arrest, are finally stripped of the last possession that makes their lives palatable: their family piano. They stand, starved and isolated in their empty living room, listening to the strains of a piano they hear or think they hear from next door. "Just listen," one of them says as their captor pounds on the door, "Just listen." And the music swells. Art is the thing that counts — whether real, imagined, or remembered — in a world of deprivation and cruelty. Art is antidote and balm for the pain of the actual.

This belief in the power of art and the imagination can be seen in the games two abused children play in the graveyard in *Night Train to Bolina* or in his recent works on Federico Garcia Lorca, where Nilo meets Lorca on his own ground: one poet making art out of another poet's life. In the following pages, in *A Bicycle Country*, you'll see this desperate, inspiring elevation of art as rafters in the ocean between Cuba and Florida play music on a metal cup and the boards of their makeshift boat.

As much as personality, lives lived seem to shape the writer's vision. Carlyle Brown has traveled the globe many times as a sailor and has trained young people in the wilds of America as a leader in the Outward Bound program. Along the way, he's learned to carry his home with him and cultivated a profound empathy for others.

You can see this empathy in his sense of character. His creations, while trapped or delineated or defined from the outside by social status, skin color, local custom, or political history, are largely fluid, complex, capacious human beings, many times more full of possibility than any category or cultural frame that determines their course in the world. This fluidity and human size comes,

I believe, from Carlyle's core belief in and pursuit of freedom. It comes, too, I think, from his own rare freedom of mind and heart and imagination.

Carlyle is steeped in history, in the dramatic human details of the untold — African-American history (*Buffalo Hair*), the history of global exploration (*Big Blue Nail*), the history of the theater and literature — and he trains his sights on the attempts of people, especially people of African descent, to locate the freedom within themselves within restraints history and politics forge for them. In his now-famous *The African Company Presents Richard the Third*, a troupe of free northern blacks — mostly servants — stage the first black public performances of Shakespeare in defiance of just about everybody. When the "woolly-headed" waiter playing Richard asks the African Company's confrontational producer where he can find a little freedom, he's answered: "You have it. It's there in your head and here in your heart and in your hands." In *The Negro of Peter the Great,* the black godson of the Russian Czar works to keep his honor and his own moral compass as society boxes him in. "I have my own laws," he tells the Czar at gunpoint, teaching the ruler how to live even as his lesson means his death.

Through my eyes, Deborah Brevoort's life looks like a study in contrasts. After growing up in New Jersey, she moved to Alaska, where she spent a dozen years as producing director of Perseverance Theatre, a professional, community-based theater in Douglas. She became a playwright there and changed course, leaving producing to study with Paula Vogel at Brown before obtaining a second graduate degree as a writer of musical theater. I don't know of another writer who achieves the kind of fusion Deborah does, as she brings together—fuses together—the most unlikely opposites. She's written a Noh drama about Elvis Presley, a musical comedy based on indigenous creation myths and, now, as you'll read here, a Greek tragedy about contemporary life in the aftermath of terrorism.

More than merely contrary ideas, though, Deborah's work melds her almost esoteric interest in theatrical structure with a populist accessibility. She writes in forms that only scholars care about in a way that reaches everyone, young and old, working class or wealthy, Alaskan or New Jersey suburban. She makes it work because she understands the profound power of storytelling. "We'll tell you a story," a chorus of carolers sings at the beginning of *King Island Christmas*, the oratorio she's written with David Friedman, and the population of this isolated island in Alaska begins to enact and then to recount story after story. Or in the play you're about to read, personal telling becomes an antidote to grief: "Talk to us. Please./Tell us your story./Tell us where you were/ and what you were doing. . . . /We need to hear it." And the story that

Deborah tells, in every instance, is one of community and transformation. Because the most radical belief among Debbie's many iconoclastic ideas is her belief in change.

Edgar Nkosi White's life, as it appears to me, has been one of border crossings and personal engagements with the world. While at New Dramatists, Edgar wrote essays as well as plays, his own idiosyncratic travelogue. His dispatches came from the wide world: his native Montserrat, after volcanic eruptions leveled most of the island; from prison, where he consistently works with inmates; from the Appalachian Trail — on which he, a solitary black man, must have cut a strange figure (I imagine him with a backpack complementing his usual garb: beret, navy blazer, black knit collarless shirt); and from the New Haven of the 1970s, before and after he left (or, as he detailed it, was booted out of) Yale. This early departure led to equally early successes at Joseph Papp's Public Theatre in New York and in London.

Now Edgar straddles two other connected, disparate worlds — the church and the theater — as he follows a double calling as a writer and minister. His plays, likewise, straddle the polarities of world and home or, as one of his characters puts it, "the rhythm of the world; and the mind of God . . . "

In *When Night Turn Day*, a family gathering serves as a congregation for characters from all corners of the African diaspora. In *East of the Sun, West of the Moon,* he not only portrays Langston Hughes the poet and man, he gives us the man in the world — Harlem, Mexico, Africa, Russia, the American South, Cuba, Spain, and Paris. You can see it for yourself in *Millennium 7.* Two lonely old ladies — one a God-fearing, African-American, former phone company manager, and one a Jewish world-cranky, Upper East–side cynic — trapped in a nursing home become stand-ins for their cultures and, as they connect against all odds, for their forgotten generation.

Every important play contains mysteries. These mysteries are the reason we return, reread, rehearse. One of the most provocative mysteries is the relationship between the art and the person who gives birth to it. These secrets are revealed (and concealed) over a writer's lifetime. Their enigmatic fascination is our pleasure.

Todd London
Artistic Director
New Dramatists

Skitaletz
("The Wanderer")

———≫●≪———

Dmitry Lipkin

To Colette, for getting me to write about gangsters.

When you fall into a trance
Sitting on a sofa playing games of chance
With your folded arms and history books you glance
Into the eyes of Madame George
                            — Van Morrison

BIOGRAPHY

Dmitry Lipkin was born in Moscow and emigrated to Louisiana at age eleven. His plays include *Cranes* (produced by the New Group, 1999), *Skitaletz, "The Wanderer"* (O'Neill National Playwrights Conference, 2000), *The Poet's Hour* (A Contemporary Theatre, Seattle, 2000), *Baton Rouge (EST), The Elephant Play* (Playwrights' Collective, Printer's Devil Theatre), *A Forest of Stone, Pithecus, I Am Laika* and *The Tightwad* (last three at HB Playwrights), *My Job Is My Life* ("Chekhov Now" Festival, 2000) as well as *Incident at Dental Clinic #44*, a screenplay for Fox/Searchlight. Dmitry is a recent alumnus of New Dramatists, an MFA graduate from NYU, a past Van Lier fellow at Manhattan Theater Club and the 2000 Bug 'n' Bob award winner from Primary Stages. He has taught at NYU and is a co-founder of The Playwrights' Collective, with whom he produced a ton of new work off-off-Broadway. After leaving New York City, Lipkin has spent the last six months in Mexico, where he finished a new play, *Total America*, and ate a lot of avocadoes.

ORIGINAL PRODUCTION

Skitaletz received a workshop at the O'Neill National Playwrights Conference. It was directed by Judy Minor with the following cast:

PASHA	Anthony Arkin
SHURA	Amelia Campbell
LUBOV	Anne Pitoniak
BOBA	David Warshofsky
JACKSON	Steven Singer
ANDREI	Jef Whitty
THE BOSS	David Margulies
MUSICIAN	Brian Gottesman

CHARACTERS
> LUBOV BORISOVNA EISENSTEIN: A Russian Jewish woman in her seventies. Tough, smart, wistful.
> PASHA, "THE WANDERER" (AKA Pashenka): A man in his thirties. Nice, clean-cut, peculiar.
> SHURA KORNISHEV (AKA Shurka, Shurchick, Shurochka, Alexa Alexeyevna): A woman in her late twenties. Pretty, a bit zaftig. A dermatologist working as a manicurist at a Brooklyn beauty salon.
> BOBA EISENSTEIN (AKA Bobachka, Borish Michailovich, et al.): Lubov Borisovna's grandson, Shura's boyfriend. A tough muscular guy in his thirties. Used to be a paratrooper in the former USSR, now makes his living as a thug.
> "JACKSON" (AKA Semyon Ignatievich): A soft-spoken man in his late forties. Used to be a nuclear physicist, now works as Boba's "associate." The mind behind the muscle.
> "THE BOSS" (AKA Anton Savelyevich): A man in his fifties or sixties. Very charismatic, though a bit unstable.
> ANDREI EISENSTEIN (AKA Andrushenka): Boba's younger brother. A good-looking kid of twenty. Well-intentioned, a bit naïve.
> STREET MUSICIAN: A man of any age. The street musician sits to the side, scoring the play on a synthesizer.

SETTING/TIME
The play is set in the Russian/Jewish immigrant enclave of Brighton Beach, Brooklyn, and takes place in the present, in the course of one day. The scenes shift between the Eisenstein apartment and the street and, later, between a Russian restaurant and the Brighton boardwalk.

INTRODUCTION
Wilhelmina took no pity but the author will. Play — yes, introduction — nyet.

SKITALETZ
("THE WANDERER")

ACT I

In the dark, we hear a sound of a body falling out of the sky, then, as it hits the ground, a thud. A man's voice grumbles — at first as only a collage of disjointed syllables, then morphing in and out of different languages — Greek, Urdu, Mandarin . . . A romantic slavic melody drifts in as the voice settles into Russian. The lone accordion is soon joined by some guitars, a drum, a balalaika . . .

A MAN'S VOICE: Who am I *now* . . . ?
(Music turns upbeat as lights rise up on Brooklyn's Brighton Avenue. A street musician, downstage right, is feverishly at work on a Yamaha synthesizer, squeezing out of it a whole medley of kitschy standards — Russian, Jewish, Pop . . . He wears an old coat, mittens, tattered rabbit hat — so bundled up we cannot see his face. As he plays, Lubov Borisovna, seventies, enters from the opposite end, similarly bundled up. She walks to her designated corner, scopes out what she can see of the street, and passionately yells —)
LUBOV BORISOVNA: Five bucks a pop! . . . Five bucks a pop! . . . Valakardin five bucks a pop!
(The fallen man crawls onto the stage from the opposite end. He is, most likely, in his early thirties, not striking but of pleasant wholesome appearance. Lubov Borisovna turns, straining to see him.)
LUBOV BORISOVNA: . . . Valakardin, young man? Relieves the pressure. Cleans your blood.
(The man — let's call him "Pasha" — moans, pulling himself along with his hands, his coat and hat covered in snow.)
PASHA: Valakar — what . . . ?
LUBOV BORISOVNA: Young man — let me tell you about Russian drugs. From time primeval and primordial, I've been incurring strange pains in my joints. So? — not to worry. Little analginchik in the morning, little more at night, and everything was fine, and could still be fine! — had I not come down to this forsaken country with their ways of medicine and pharmacology! . . . "Go. Have it looked at" — Grandson said — "They're wizards here, these doctors in America!" . . . And so, I go. Show them

my Medicare, my Medicaid, show them my green card — show them everything! What do they do? — They put me in a hospital. Beth Israel. "I'm not Israeli" — I tell them. They look at me like I'm an idiot. *(She laughs. He watches her, intrigued.)* Then all the doctors come — like the United Nations all these doctors are! The first comes in — looks at my ears, second — eyes, a third takes X-rays, then a fourth, a fifth. Then nurses, dietitians, experts in I don't know what! I tell them in plain Russian — *(As if to a child.)* "Pain in joints" . . . Again, they look at me like I'm an idiot. Then finally, a Russian doctor comes. "Doctor," — I tell him — "Stop the torturing!" "You know what you need? Analgin." . . . After a day of being poked and prodded by the foreigners, the only thing I need . . . is analgin! . . . Of course they do not have *our* analgin. *Their* so-called "analgin" is pink, and long, and horrible . . . And that is when I said — "Enough" . . . "Enough is enough" young man! We've seen their wizardry. We know the tricks they pull and we say — that's enough! Yes, Russian medicine had problems, but at least there was a common understanding. When you told them "pain in the joints," they didn't check your ears. They knew their ears — and knew their joints — and knew the difference!

PASHA: . . . I see.

(Silence. She looks at him more closely.)

LUBOV BORISOVNA: But what is wrong with *you?*

PASHA: Oh babushka. I've fallen very far . . . and very hard.

(He points a finger to the sky.)

LUBOV BORISOVNA: So have we all, young man. No use to gripe about it. *(She studies him, then looks around.)* But where exactly *have* you fallen from?

(He looks around, a little caught.)

PASHA: I uh. . . . *(He points.)* . . . I'd venture to say from that scaffolding.

(She looks.)

LUBOV BORISOVNA: Are you some kind of acrobat . . . ?

PASHA: An acrobat?

LUBOV BORISOVNA: Young man, that scaffolding is three full blocks away . . . !

PASHA: . . . Indeed . . . A freak occurrence if I do say so myself.

(She looks at him suspiciously.)

LUBOV BORISOVNA: Who are you then?

(Pasha looks at himself, opens his coat, discovering a pair of splattered overalls.)

PASHA: . . . A painter, I believe . . .

LUBOV BORISOVNA: . . . An artist of some sort?
PASHA: *(Observing himself.)* No . . . No. More like a painter . . . of the house.
LUBOV BORISOVNA: I see . . .
   (He shuffles stiffly in the snow, tries to get up as his right leg begins to twitch.)
LUBOV BORISOVNA: . . . My God. You look completely out of sorts.
PASHA: I am . . . completely out of whack.
   (She offers her hand.)
LUBOV BORISOVNA: Here. Let us get you up.
PASHA: Oh. Babushka.
LUBOV BORISOVNA: You have to fool your legs, young man. Lift with your left but let it think you're lifting with your right. *(He obeys.)* You see?
   (He lifts his right leg, gets up, wobbling.)
PASHA: It is a miracle.
LUBOV BORISOVNA: A minor one. What you need is some solid dermitol. *(She produces the drug.)* Here. Take it daily for the next two weeks.
PASHA: Oh, babushka. I thank you from the bottom of my heart.
LUBOV BORISOVNA: Don't thank me. Pay me. Seven bucks a pop.
   (He searches in his pockets for the cash.)
PASHA: It . . . must have fallen on the way.
LUBOV BORISOVNA: *(Suspiciously.)* When you fell from that scaffolding?
PASHA: That's right.
   (He wobbles, nearly falling down again. She helps him, then looks at him, sadly.)
LUBOV BORISOVNA: It doesn't pay too well, does it young man?
PASHA: Not from the looks of it.
LUBOV BORISOVNA: And you do all this "scaffolding" by choice?
PASHA: Oh, what is choice and what's necessity? What does it matter in this world?
LUBOV BORISOVNA: Alas, that is the first sane thing you've said . . . *(She sighs, in sympathy.)* Though I do hear there's money to be made.
PASHA: Really? In what?
LUBOV BORISOVNA: Well, many things. Take baking goods. Money like hotcakes — left and right.
PASHA: Money like hotcakes?
LUBOV BORISOVNA: Sure. If you're in the right neighborhood. It is the latest craze, you know. You ought to give a try yourself — take out a little loan, put up a baking business of your own . . .
PASHA: *(Thinks, dreamily.)* A baking business of my own . . . Well . . . Maybe in another lifetime then.

LUBOV BORISOVNA: "Another lifetime." Lazy like them all . . .
(He starts to limp away.)
LUBOV BORISOVNA: Here. Here . . . Dermitol for free.
PASHA: Oh, babushka. You are my savior.
LUBOV BORISOVNA: "Your savior." Get out before the others see me doing this!
(He shakes her hand vigorously.)
PASHA: I thank you, from the bottom of my heart.
LUBOV BORISOVNA: Go on, young man. Go make a life . . . !
(Pasha limps away with the drug. She looks into her hand, finding a mangled piece of paper he had left in it. Baffled, she unfolds the paper, reads the scribbled writing with difficulty —)
LUBOV BORISOVNA: "To whom it may concern. Please let this woman off . . . the hook" . . . ?
PASHA: *(Limping away.)* . . . A note like that may come in handy . . . if you're ever in some trouble with authorities . . .
(He is gone.)
LUBOV BORISOVNA: *(Under her breath.)* Poor crazy idiot . . . *(She pockets the note. The musician strikes up a tune.)* Five bucks a pop! Valakardin five bucks a pop! *(She freezes momentarily as the music keeps on. Lights dim on the street downstage and rise on the Eisenstein apartment. The living room is in the center, with a portion of the bedroom to the right and a part of an outside hallway visible on its left. It is an ordinary, somewhat gaudy Brooklyn apartment.)*
(In the living room, Shura, late twenties, lies on the couch watching TV. She looks pretty, but a little tacky — made up and dressed with "Flash." Voice of a TV announcer is heard, speaking in a Russian accent, in a theatrical, mannered tone.)
TV ANNOUNCER'S VOICE: We will return to the serial "The Wild Rose of Rio Pecco" after these words from our sponsor — *(Very theatrical, lush.)* — the elite discotheque and diner's club, "The Palace"!
(Lush harps fill the air as "The Palace" commercial begins.)
THE SAME ANNOUNCER'S VOICE: Tired of the every day? No time to just relax and play? Need a romantic spark to light your night? . . . Come to "The Palace"! *(More harps and violins.)* Our chefs, straight from the finest restaurants of Paris, will indulge your sense with a delicately prepared Continental eight-course feast. "No. It is not your mother's blintzes" — critics rave. And when you're done indulging in our fine cuisine, indulge your legs and while the night away upon our dance floor — *(Now the harps are replaced by a disco beat.)* — where our Emcee, super DJ Vanya Pos-

torukhin, plays the top hits and combines the best mixes from the old world and the new . . . So give your life a break, and come to "The Palace." And remember — you may be a monk at home but at "The Palace," we treat you like a tsar! All major credit cards accepted.

(Shura sighs, as music fades.)

TV ANNOUNCER'S VOICE: We now return to our Mexican serial "The Wild Rose of Rio Pecco." *("Rio Pecco" music fades in; a woman sings in Spanish.)* "The Wild Rose of Rio Pecco"! (translated from the Spanish by Andrei Surkov.) *("Rio Pecco" music continues to play as Boba, thirties, and Jackson, forties, appear in the outside hallway. Both wear stonewashed jeans, black gloves, threequarter length black leather jackets. Boba, a big man with a crewcut, seems to belong in the clothes. His "Associate," Jackson, clearly does not, and looks more like a professor of nuclear physics than a thug. Boba unlocks the front door with his keys.)*

BOBA: Ey, Jackson. Guard the door.

JACKSON: Yes. Will be done, Boris Michailovich.

(He remains in the hallway as Boba enters.)

TV ANNOUNCER'S VOICE: *(Theatrical.)* Part fifty-four: "The Black Heart of Eduardo."

BOBA: Shurka! How's the barbershop?

(She waves, her eyes glued to the TV.)

SHURA: Beauty salon . . .

(Boba crosses into the bedroom, takes out a ring box, briefly looks at the ring inside, puts it away. He then steps back into the living room and takes off his coat, revealing a tight T-shirt that accentuates his physique. A tattoo of a snake adorns his arm.)

BOBA: Shur-ka . . .

(Eyes on the TV, she vaguely waves him off.)

BOBA: Shurka, c'mon. Take off your pants.

SHURA: I'm watching Rio Pecco, Boba.

BOBA: So?

SHURA: — So I am watching it.

(He sits next to her. Pause.)

BOBA: Oh yeah, the rerun. It's the part "el stranger" shows.

SHURA: Bastard.

BOBA: . . . You knew he was responsible. Who killed the gaucho? Who burned all the evidence?

SHURA: Boba, I'm watching it! You hear me? — I am watching it! *(She turns back to the TV. Silence.)* So Isabella sees "el stranger"?

(Pause. Boba lights a cig.)
BOBA: Yep.
SHURA: Who is he?
BOBA: No one knows. He takes his mask off, but beneath it — there's another one. Tells her he is "Eduardo" from the coast — but sounds like he might be American.
(Pause. Boba smokes nonchalantly. Shura frowns into the TV, processing the info.)
SHURA: . . . So then . . . he knows who took the baby?
BOBA: Yeah he knows. *He* took the baby. Hid him in his rancho by the sea.
(Silence.)
SHURA: Bastard . . . You didn't have to tell me that.
BOBA: Shurka, c'mon. The kid had "ransom" on his head. Now let me see your legs.
SHURA: Forget it. I am mad at you.
(He puts out his cigarette, begins to put his moves on her. She stares at the TV.)
BOBA: Ey . . . Shurochka . . . I'm on my lunch break.
SHURA: You're not eating lunch.
BOBA: I ate my lunch . . . Now I am on my other lunch break.
(He pinches her behind.)
SHURA: Pig.
BOBA: Don't call me pig. I'm not a pig.
(She snorts, pig-like, attacking him.)
SHURA: Pig — pig — pig — pig . . .
(He tickles her back. They laugh. She lifts up his T-shirt and suddenly stops, staring at something in shock. Silence.)
BOBA: Look what I got.
(He rolls up his T-shirt, revealing a newly etched U.S. Marines logo on his chest.)
SHURA: The few . . . The proud . . . The . . .
BOBA: Marines. United States Marines . . . You like it?
SHURA: *(Forced.)* . . . Yeah, it's nice.
BOBA: What's wrong? . . . What? You don't like it?
SHURA: . . . No. I said I did . . . I like it.
BOBA: See — this is the logo that they wear. The eagle, and the planet Earth . . . And this is what they say. If someone asks them who they are, they say — "We are the few, the proud, the marines" . . . !
(He laughs, rolling back the shirt. She looks at him, concerned.)

SHURA: But . . . Boba.
BOBA: What?
   (*Pause.*)
SHURA: *You* were never a marine.
BOBA: So?
SHURA: So it's like . . . you're saying you were a marine, and you were not.
BOBA: . . . So what? . . . Because I'm from an evil land that didn't have marines, but only had the iron fist that squeezed you, and your balls and mind — does that mean I can't be marine at heart!? . . . "The Semper Fi" is in the heart!
SHURA: The what?
BOBA: The Semper Fi. It's like "good evening," or "hello."
SHURA: The . . . "Semper Fi" . . . ?
BOBA: And they have other words they say. In Latin, like a code. I'm gonna learn and then tattoo it — the entire code.
SHURA: But Boba . . . why?
BOBA: Because I'm proud to be an American, that's why! If you don't like it, go back where you came from! Ha-ha-ha!
   (*He slaps her behind, laughing obnoxiously. She moves away from him, obviously upset.*)
BOBA: Shurka. I'm kidding . . . That's not what I meant . . .
SHURA: Yeah yeah.
   (*She stares out at the TV. He tries to put a move on her. No luck. Silence.*)
BOBA: What? . . . What's the matter now?
SHURA: . . . I don't know . . .
BOBA: What?
SHURA: . . . I'm not happy, Boba.
BOBA: You're not happy . . . ? Why?
   (*She shrugs.*)
SHURA: I don't know . . . I don't mean to be . . . Maybe I'm eating too much fat. You know, it's all this fat that isn't good for you. All of these toxins in the food . . . ?
BOBA: Why don't you go on a diet?
SHURA: I *am* on a diet. (*Pause.*) But I keep on slipping. Everybody on TV is thin, but everybody in reality, like in the beauty shop, is fat. Just fat and ugly . . . And, you know, I keep on slipping. Going back and forth between the beauty shop and all those models on TV . . . Just back and forth like some . . . I don't know, like a ship that never makes it from the sea.
   (*Silence.*)

BOBA: What, like a big ship?
SHURA: . . . Like a what?
BOBA: Like a big cruiser? . . . Or an aircraft carrier?
SHURA: Boba, I'm trying to tell you something.
BOBA: And so, it's important what kind of a ship. Because a carrier can carry aircraft and you can sneak and hit your enemies. But with a cruiser — that's vacation time.
(He laughs.)
SHURA: But how does that apply to me?
BOBA: To you? What do you mean — "to you"?
SHURA: What does it have to do with what I'm telling you . . . !
(Silence.)
BOBA: I gotta take a leak.
(He goes to the bathroom. She looks out the window, in thought. He begins to pee.)
SHURA: Boba . . . ?
BOBA: *(Offstage.)* Yeah . . . ?
SHURA: . . . I am thinking . . . maybe it is for the best . . .
BOBA: *(Offstage.)* . . . What's for the best?
SHURA: That I go back . . . you know . . . ?
(Silence. The peeing stops. Boba reappears, concerned, zipping up.)
BOBA: Again you threaten me?
SHURA: It's not a threat . . .
BOBA: What kind of commie move is that?
SHURA: Boba, the commie fell ten years ago.
BOBA: So . . . ?
SHURA: . . . So maybe I'm not meant to come to port.
BOBA: To what?
SHURA: Maybe I should go back. I mean, I'm stuck in shitty work. And you come home and beat these people up for like, a buck . . . What kind of life is that? *(She looks away.)* At least at home you know what you have got.
(He glances back, defensively.)
BOBA: Well where am I supposed to beat them — It's my job!
SHURA: So?
BOBA: So you do your job and I do mine.
SHURA: But Boba, I don't wanna "do my job." I wanna quit and live a life. I want to be a human being.

BOBA: . . . And if you want, that's what you do. See, that's the beauty of free enterprise . . . !

SHURA: So why don't you quit yours?

(Silence. He looks away in avoidance.)

BOBA: I can't . . . Savelyevich will have me by the balls.

SHURA: "Savelyevich" . . .

(She sighs in frustration. He looks off, embarrassed.)

BOBA: . . . C'mon Shurka . . . You'll stay, right?

SHURA: Why, you are gonna marry me?

(She laughs, then stops, looks at him, gradually softening . . .)

BOBA: . . . I could.

SHURA: "You could," huh?

BOBA: Yeah. Just when you're least suspecting it. *(Pause.)* Maybe tonight . . . Then. Maybe not.

(She approaches, taking hold of his crotch.)

SHURA: Is that how he has got you . . . ?

BOBA: . . . Yeah.

SHURA: I'll have you by the balls if you would like.

BOBA: . . . Oh yeah?

(She backs away, seductively. He lunges for her, as she eludes his grasp.)

(A phone rings in the outside hallway. Jackson shuffles in his pockets, then pulls out his cell.)

JACKSON: "Boba's Mufflers and Repair." How may I help you?

(Jackson listens, growing businesslike. In the living room, Boba stalks Shura around the dining table.)

BOBA: Shurka . . . C'mon.

SHURA: You know you want it.

BOBA: Yeah. I know.

SHURA: So you will quit . . . ?

BOBA: First chance I get.

(He tries to grab her, unsuccessfully.)

SHURA: . . . And that's when you are getting it.

JACKSON: Hold on Anton Savelyevich . . .

(Knocks on the door.)

BOBA: I'm busy, Jackson!

SHURA: Say it then.

BOBA: Okay. Okay . . . I'm gonna quit.

SHURA: Are you?

(Jackson knocks again, then timidly opens the door.)

BOBA: I'm busy damn it!!
(Jackson covers up the receiver.)
JACKSON: Uhm . . . Boris Michailich. It's the boss.
(Boba looks at Shura, then at the phone.)
BOBA: Soon, Shurka. Oath of Red Chief Vinnitu . . . Not right this minute though.
(Boba goes to the phone. Shura walks to the window, sad. He opens his mouth to answer the boss as we hear the Musician's medley.)
(Lights dim on the apartment and rise on the street. Lubov Borisovna is in her spot.)
LUBOV BORISOVNA: Five bucks a pop! Valakardin five bucks a pop!
(Andrei, a good-looking kid of twenty, enters from left. He sports a stylish haircut, and wears a leather jacket like his older brother Boba.)
ANDREI: Hi babushka.
LUBOV BORISOVNA: Andrushenka. Put on your hat.
ANDREI: I do not want to, babushka. I'll get a "hat head" if I do.
LUBOV BORISOVNA: You'll get a "meningitis" if you don't. Your brain will freeze. And then, no agency will like you, even with this brand new haircut. Put on your hat . . . Put on your hat!
(He does, reluctantly.)
Where did you go today?
ANDREI: Elite.
LUBOV BORISOVNA: Elite! Ho-ho! Creme de la creme! What did they say?
ANDREI: The same thing Wilhelmina said. And Ford. And Click.
LUBOV BORISOVNA: They didn't like your pictures on the boardwalk?
ANDREI: *(Dejected.)* No.
LUBOV BORISOVNA: Not even the romantic one, where you are staring at the stormy sea?
ANDREI: They said I need "professional portfolio" . . . But I don't get it. I'm right there in the flesh. They see how good *I* look, you know? . . . I would be perfect for an MTV campaign, or *Dawson's Creek*, or Calvin ads . . . But they don't even look at me. Just watch my Polaroid's like I'm not even in the room.
LUBOV BORISOVNA: What hypocrites!
ANDREI: I know. I'll show them though. I'll get their stupid ass "professional portfolio" . . . How was your day?
LUBOV BORISOVNA: Not too bad for an off-peak Wednesday. *(Takes out some bills, counts them.)* Sold mostly valedol. Five ampules. Mariya Ivanna came by for some permidon. Her legs are swelling up, and so we griped a lit-

tle bit . . . *(She laughs, then, serious —)* Valakardin is still quite slow. I don't know why. I even tried to sell some to that kid on second floor, but he kept asking for a thing he called a "dime bag." "I don't have it" — I told him — "And if I did I wouldn't sell it for a dime." *(She laughs.)* Perhaps the hearts are pounding well, and so I'm taking solace in the health of all our neighbors.

ANDREI: Good for hearts, not so good for business, huh.
(She thinks.)

LUBOV BORISOVNA: . . . And then, there was this . . . other man.

ANDREI: A who?

LUBOV BORISOVNA: A funny, limping man, who told me he fell "very far" and "very hard" . . . Claimed to be worker on the scaffolding, but I'm not sure I believe him . . .

ANDREI: So who was he then?

LUBOV BORISOVNA: Who knows. *(Takes out the crumpled note, shows it.)* Gave me this little note.

ANDREI: *(Reading.)* "Please let this woman off the hook"?

LUBOV BORISOVNA: I know. It takes all kinds of loonies to make up the world. *(She laughs. A police siren is heard, growing louder. Andrei quickly hides the money and covers up the drugs. She looks around, unaffected, as the siren fades. Andrei looks at her, concerned.)*

ANDREI: Babushka. Cover up at least when the police rides by.

LUBOV BORISOVNA: Why should I? These are fine proven medicines. They heal, they soothe. They make us better as a human race!

ANDREI: But they are not exactly legal, are they?

LUBOV BORISOVNA: . . . What *is* "legal"?

ANDREI: Legal is "The Law." *(Pause.)* You're in their country. You should . . . well, at least pretend.

LUBOV BORISOVNA: "The Law." *(She scoffs.)* The law like retarded child, Andrushenka. In every country, every place — walking on edge of life, completely out of step with us. Somebody needs to push the child to its death. Push the retarded one to the precipice. *(Hands Andrei some bills.)* Here. Put it in your modeling career. Stun all those hypocrites with your charisma and your brilliance.
(He takes the money, gives her a kiss. Boba and Jackson enter stage right, remain at a distance so as not to be seen.)

BOBA: Ey, Andrei! . . . Psst!
(Andrei looks out, much too obvious. Lubov Borisovna notices.)

LUBOV BORISOVNA: Bo-bachka? . . . Who you're hiding from?

(They approach. Boba kisses Lubov Borisovna.)
BOBA: Lubov Borisovna.
LUBOV BORISOVNA: Semyon Ignaievich. Always a pleasure.
BOBA: *(Quiet.)* We have job to do. Nothing too hard for you.
ANDREI: A job?
BOBA: Say it a little louder, idiot.
LUBOV BORISOVNA: Pork chops for dinner?
JACKSON: Pork chops would be splendid.
BOBA: *(To Jackson.)* Who invited you?
LUBOV BORISOVNA: Fou, Boba. Where's the tact?
BOBA: I'm kidding, babushka. You know we kid . . . We gotta go.
LUBOV BORISOVNA: Already? Where you off to like a hurricane?
ANDREI: *(To Boba, oblivious.)* What kind of job we're gonna do?
LUBOV BORISOVNA: A job . . . ?!
  (She looks at Boba, hurt. Boba grows pale.)
BOBA: . . . I uh . . . I mean . . .
JACKSON: *(Stepping in.)* Your grandson doesn't want to get your hopes up. He's applying for a business loan. He only said it was a "job," because for him, to beg for money from Americans is just about the hardest "job" there is.
LUBOV BORISOVNA: . . . Is that true, Bobachka?
  (Boba looks at Jackson, uncomfortable.)
BOBA: . . . Exactly, just like Jackson said.
LUBOV BORISOVNA: *(Dreamy.)* A business loan . . . ! And I thought . . . Well. You were never one to break your promises . . . But then, the hard reality can . . . twist and change the human soul . . . And it looks good the loan?
BOBA: Oh . . . Yeah! . . . I mean, I'm past the first stage, where they take out all the . . . bad eggs. You know, all the . . .
JACKSON: . . . "Undesirables." So you could say he's "good egg," El Borisovna.
LUBOV BORISOVNA: A "good egg"! My grandson! My Bobachka!
JACKSON: Yes, and it's time to be that egg once more.
  (Boba and Jackson exchange a look.)
BOBA: . . . Yes. Time for me to be the good egg, babushka.
  (Kisses her.)
LUBOV BORISOVNA: Good luck to you.
JACKSON: *(Kissing her hand.)* Good luck to *you*, Lubov Borisovna. With trafficking of fine medicines, that is . . . In fact I'll take an ampule of that savory permidon of yours.
LUBOV BORISOVNA: Of course, Semyon Ignatievich.
  (He pays and takes the drug.)

ANDREI: Be careful, all right?

LUBOV BORISOVNA: You too, Andrushenka . . . Good-bye, my doves. I'll see you in the evening . . . ?

ALL THREE: Good-bye babushka.

(They wave and leave. She looks out, in thought.)

LUBOV BORISOVNA: "A business loan" . . .

(Street musician begins a quiet tune . . .)

LUBOV BORISOVNA: . . . Should I believe him? *(She thinks.)* Do I have a choice . . . ? *(She shrugs.)* And if I had a choice what would I choose? . . . *(She sings:)*
What was the point, where was the hook
Why did I come here on my tired feet . . . ?
Mistook a sign, misread a book
I skipped and I flipped and arrived on this street

My life in Lvov was full of love
But lacking for what's needed
No heat, no meat, gray sky above
But soul I had and food to feed it . . .

My daughter dead, my son a drunk
So at the mercy of young ones
I hopped a plane, unpacked my trunk
And pinned my hope on my grandsons . . .

(She continues to hum the tune, as three shadows appear upstage. They are of Boba and Jackson, holding Pasha by the arms, half-dragging him as he vaguely resists. Andrei's shadow follows, meandering behind.)

PASHA: I . . . I . . . I . . . I . . . !

BOBA: Shut up.

LUBOV BORISOVNA: *I help them live, they help me eat*
 But this is such an odd place
 Plenty of meat, plenty of heat
 But every window holds a strange face . . .
 And so I shout and so I yell
 Selling the pills I've treasured
 For after all you must control
 What you've known and seen and measured . . .

(Boba and Jackson drag Pasha off. Andrei follows, dropping a few coins into the street musician's coffee can.)

LUBOV BORISOVNA: For after all you must control
The years you lived and loved and treasured.

(Music ends. Blackout. In the dark, we hear a couple punches, thrown rhythmically, with a bit of an "Oh!" and an "Ah!")
(Lights up on the Eisenstein apartment. In the bedroom, Pasha sits tied to a chair. He now wears a baker's outfit and looks different from the "scaffolding worker" of Scene One. Boba holds his fist, in pain. Jackson stands nearby, holding some sort of ledger. Andrei's in the living room, on the "lookout.")
BOBA: *(To Jackson.)* Why did you start that crap about the business loan?
JACKSON: You looked like you were in jam, Boris Michailich . . . And I saw a flicker of lost hope inside her eyes.
BOBA: Lost hope . . . ?
JACKSON: Well. We did manage to extinguish it.
BOBA: And now I feel like shit . . . My babushka, my innocence . . .
(He punches a wall, shakes his fist, hurt.)
JACKSON: Try to get over it.
BOBA: I'm on the bottom of a moral pyramid, Jackson. Goddamn my wretched lying soul! *(He hits himself, then turns to Pasha, who stares back at him, oddly placid and smug.)* And you — what are you looking at you shit? Where's the money?
PASHA: . . . "Money"?
BOBA: Where's the money?!
PASHA: "Money"?
BOBA: Where's the fucking money?!
(He's about to hit him as the cell phone rings. Boba stops as Jackson puts a finger to his mouth.)
JACKSON: Hello. "Boba's Mufflers and Repair." How may I help you? . . . No. We don't have mufflers . . . No . . . No no. We don't repair. *(He hangs up.)* Some joker thought that we repair.
(The two share a laugh, as Pasha joins in, laughing as if on cue. There is a strangeness about him, as if he had found himself in a skit, the rules of which he is now trying to decipher. Both men glare as Pasha gradually quiets. Meanwhile, in the living room —)
ANDREI: *(On phone.)* Yes. E-Z Models please. Long Island City.
(Waits to be connected.)

BOBA: You think it's funny, funny boy? *(Pause. Pasha shrugs.)* I didn't hear you?
PASHA: No . . . No no.
   (Pause.)
BOBA: All right . . . So where is it?
   (Silence.)
PASHA: . . . By "it," you mean . . . ?
JACKSON: . . . The twenty thousand, young man, you borrowed from your kind and gentle friend, Anton Savelyevich.
PASHA: Right . . . I . . . don't have it . . . ?
BOBA: I will kill him.
JACKSON: *(Playing the "good cop.")* Restraint is a virtue now, Boris Michailovich. Our Mister Pasha's telling us he "doesn't have the money." Let's accept that as an option . . . a hypothesis. Let us assume he doesn't have the money. *(Pause.)* Where then, could the money be?
   (Jackson and Boba look at Pasha, waiting for an answer. Pasha stares back, smiling. Meanwhile, in the living room —)
ANDREI: Hi. Do you do *professional* portfolios? . . . You do? That's great . . . !
   (Boba and Jackson go off to the side.)
JACKSON: I don't think he's all there, Boris Michailovich. Not too much mind left in that man.
BOBA: He's playing dumb. I know his type.
   (Living room —)
ANDREI: Yeah. I can make the five o'clock today.
   (He hangs up, filled with hope, as in the bedroom, Jackson approaches Pasha, looks at him, kindly —)
JACKSON: Pasha. Have you been making profit from your bakery, like you had sworn Anton Savelyevich you would?
PASHA: . . . My what . . . ?
JACKSON: Your bakery. The reason for your loan . . . ?
   (Pause. Pasha looks at himself, discovering the baker's outfit.)
PASHA: I see . . . Well, I don't recollect the swearing, but . . . if I'm to take a guess, I'd say there's not a penny earned . . . ?
   (Pause. Jackson throws Boba a private look.)
JACKSON: And, there is nothing wrong with that. If you aren't making money, that's okay. Your strategy of business isn't a concern to us . . . See . . . what is a concern to us is that you aren't paying money back. You missed three payments —
BOBA: Three. One two three — count them. Count the payments shmuck!
PASHA: One, two, three . . .

18   DMITRY LIPKIN

JACKSON: — Pasha! How many payments do you plan to miss?
(Pause. Pasha looks at them, earnest.)
PASHA: Dear sirs, I wish to be of help. But this is just the question I would ask myself . . . !
(Silence. Jackson and Boba exchange a look.)
JACKSON: None, Pasha. None.
PASHA: . . . Okay.
JACKSON: *(Barely keeping his cool.)* . . . Pasha. Do you have any grasp on — just — what — kind — of trouble — you — are — in?
PASHA: . . . Not yet, but dear sir I'm beginning to . . . And what you say is of enormous help . . . !
JACKSON: *(To Boba, quiet.)* I'm telling you. He isn't right.
PASHA: Like at the present moment I have total grasp on myself as a baker . . . And that . . . I have borrowed money, parts of which you now seek returned . . . ?
JACKSON: Look Pasha —
BOBA: *(Exploding.)* — This is not a fucking interview, all right!! Stop talking crap and tell us where the money went!!
(Pasha cowers as Boba goes to punch him. Jackson pulls him back. Pasha looks at them, oddly surprised by his own emotion.)
PASHA: And that I grasp that I am scared . . . And that my life's in shambles . . . as I look into the future . . . knowing not of what will come . . .
(The new emotion overwhelms him and he begins to cry. Boba and Jackson look at each other, taken aback, feeling bad.)
JACKSON: What. What's the matter now.
PASHA: I don't know . . .
JACKSON: . . . It's coming back now?
PASHA: . . . Some of it . . .
BOBA: Look, we don't wanna hurt you, man. Just tell us where the money is and you'll go home, all right?
PASHA: My gentle captors. Don't you think I'd tell you where the money is, if I indeed knew where it was? Clearly my gentle captors, I do not . . .
JACKSON: You mean . . . ?
PASHA: . . . I mean, I don't.
BOBA: What did you do with it?
PASHA: I don't know what I did with it! . . . But I know I don't have it! I just don't . . . !
(He cries, in deep despair. Boba hangs his head. Jackson takes a deep breath.)

PASHA: I mean, I *want* to make the payments! It is obvious — it *should* be obvious I want to make the payments . . .

JACKSON: . . . Look, Pasha. Look . . . Boris Michailovich and I perceive your willingness to pay. We understand your problem and we do, to some extent, feel bad for you . . . None of us want to be here, in this room . . . Doing what we don't want to do . . . what maybe, we weren't meant to do . . . *(Glances at Boba.)* . . . Boris Michailich, for example, was a paratrooper in the other life. And not a lowly private, but an officer. A highly decorated hero of the former land . . . ! He soared through heights the likes of us cannot imagine . . . and received a Lenin's medal on account of saving his platoon along with an Uzbeki village filled with screaming kids . . . ! *(Pause.)* I, lowly as I am, did not grow up for this. I was a physicist — tenured professor in The Moscow University. No — I was not an Einstein or a Sakharov . . . But I conceived. I too had notions of the universe . . . Some of the students even called me "genius" . . . ! *(He laughs.)* Yes, sure — it was the students who did not know quasars from the hole inside their ass! . . . But socially speaking, I had status . . . And I had a wife . . . who loved me, as she claimed. Who said I was the most important human cell form in her life . . . !

BOBA: *(Concerned.)* Jackson . . .

JACKSON: What I am trying to tell you, Pasha — is that this is not so easy for the lot of us! — Is that it's hard and there's no end in sight! — No light in tunnel's end but for the coming of a train . . . ! But we must all bite down and bear the beast of burden we call —

(A loud buzzer sounds in the living room, drowning out Jackson's sentence. All three look toward the noise as Andrei, long having abandoned his position as "lookout" and reading Penthouse, *jumps up, tucks the mag under the sofa, runs in panic to the kitchen, then to the bedroom —)*

ANDREI: Guys . . . grandma.

BOBA: What . . . ?!

ANDREI: I think . . . grandma.

(Pause. They look at each other, then grab the chair and begin to move Pasha into the closet. We hear another loud buzzer sound.)

BOBA: There's no time . . . Jackson, you deal with it.

(Panicked, Boba lets go of the chair and runs with Andrei to the living room. As they check their clothes and hair, we hear a third more insistent buzzer sound. They look at each other, run out the front door.)

(In the bedroom, Jackson drags Pasha's chair, trying to stuff him in the closet.)

PASHA: The closet is too small, Semyon Ignatievich. I'll never fit.

(Jackson stops, taken aback.)

JACKSON: What did you say?

PASHA: . . . "The closet is too small."

JACKSON: But then you said my name.

PASHA: . . . I did? . . . I must have overheard it, I suppose.

JACKSON: . . . Look, Pasha —

PASHA: — Yes, Semyon Ignatievich?

(Jackson, strangely affected, looks away. Finding no other hiding place, he grabs a white sheet and a piece of masking tape, as Pasha looks on, concerned . . .)

PASHA: But —

JACKSON: — What? What do you want young man?!

PASHA: You really think there is no "end in sight"?

JACKSON: — What do you think?

PASHA: I think the "beast of burden" could be slain. So your wife left you. So big deal. So the funding was revoked . . . *(Pause. Jackson stares at him, taken aback.)* If I may give you some advice I'd say probe deeper. Jump the groove. The future holds a wealth of opportunity, but opportunity is wasted if you do not probe . . . !

JACKSON: — Young man. I don't know who you are but you have crossed the line!

PASHA: And life unprobed is life unlived. While life unlived hardly resembles life at all. *(Pause. He looks at Jackson.)* Besides, a lot of your sub-quantum notions are quite sound, and good . . . !

(Silence. Jackson, about to put masking tape over Pasha's mouth, stops, hesitates.)

JACKSON: You think?

PASHA: I do . . . And there's a man in Frisco who'd love to fund a mind like yours.

(Pause.)

JACKSON: Should I . . . Should I send a resume . . . ?

PASHA: He's reading it, Semyon Ignatievich.

JACKSON: . . . He *is* . . . ?

PASHA: . . . As we speak.

(Silence. Jackson looks at him, confused, unable to process it all. Pasha looks back, placidly. Confounded, he covers Pasha's mouth with masking tape, as Boba and Andrei enter, carrying groceries.)

BOBA: I thought you said it's grandma.

ANDREI: I . . . I thought it's grandma . . .

(Shura enters with a couple of bags.)

BOBA: You're supposed to be on the lookout, idiot.

SHURA: What's going on?

BOBA: Nothing.

(She looks at him, then at the bedroom.)

BOBA: *(Guilty.)* . . . Nothing . . . !

(Growing suspicious, she steps toward the bedroom, as Boba quickly blocks her way.)

BOBA: . . . I wouldn't . . . if you know what I mean . . . ?

(She turns away from him, pissed off. In the bedroom, Jackson watches Pasha — eyeing him, his mouth taped — then covers the chair and Pasha with the white sheet.)

BOBA: C'mon Shurka . . . I didn't think he'd take so long, I swear.

SHURA: I stayed out like you asked.

BOBA: I know . . . but then the boss . . .

SHURA: *(Snapping.)* "The Boss." Always — "The Boss" . . . !

BOBA: . . . Look. I'll be finished soon. This guy's a real nut. Brain of pea . . . skull of a coconut.

SHURA: I do not want to hear it, Boba. I just don't . . .

BOBA: Come out, Jackson. It's okay . . . !

(Jackson remains in the bedroom. Shura sits down on the sofa, sees the Penthouse, *sticking out of the cushions.)*

SHURA: What's this?

BOBA: *(To Andrei.)* This what you're on the "lookout" for, you shit?

ANDREI: I . . . don't know what you mean.

SHURA: Don't try to pin this on your little brother, Boba. We all know you like big tits. *(Leafs through.)* You like these "Penthouse Pets"? . . . You think they're hot stuff for marines like you?

BOBA: Tell her it's yours.

ANDREI: I've never . . . in my life . . .

(She laughs, as Jackson comes out of the bedroom. All three look at him as he laughs out of context, an emotional wreck.)

BOBA: . . . Are you all right?

(Silence.)

JACKSON: I dare say I am not . . . Boris Michailovich.

(Pause. Andrei looks out the window, spots something in the distance and —)

ANDREI: She's walking up the street!

(Boba runs to the window.)

ANDREI: Two hundred meters. Course unchanged . . . I didn't screw it up, did I . . . ?

BOBA: *(To Jackson.)* You shoved him in the closet . . . ?
JACKSON: It's too small.
  (Boba looks around, beginning to panic.)
BOBA: . . . Shurka, get in and lock the door.
SHURA: What?
BOBA: In the bedroom. On the double.
SHURA: "On the double"? — Who do you think I am?
BOBA: Shurka don't fuck with me!
SHURA: Boba, forget it. I'm not part of this.
BOBA: You think this is a game? I said go get in there!
SHURA: Fuck you . . . !
BOBA: Fuck you . . . !
ANDREI: *(Looking out the window.)* She's heading straight for the entrance.
BOBA: Shurka I need you. She finds out — she'll never speak to me.
  (Gets down on one knee.)
  Love of my life. The guiding star that shines above my gutter . . . Red Chief Vinnitu is begging you . . . ! I'll make it up to you tonight! I swear to you!
SHURA: — All right, Boba. Shut up.
  (He hurries her into the bedroom.)
BOBA: Good, now get in and lock the door. Don't look at him. Don't touch him. Don't do anything. Anyone knocks — just say you're changing, understood?
SHURA: *(Playing retarded.)* No. I don't get it. I'm an idiot!
  (She shuts and locks the door.)
ANDREI: Still . . . Wait . . . I think she has a customer . . . *(Looks closer in, confused.)* . . . What's that police car doing . . . Guys!
  (Andrei stares out, his mouth agape, then runs out. Boba and Jackson run up to and open the window, as a police siren is suddenly heard from outside. Silence.)
BOBA: *(Stunned.)* They are arresting her . . .
LUBOV BORISOVNA'S DISTANT VOICE: Help me! . . . Help me!
BOBA: Don't run, grandma!
LUBOV BORISOVNA'S DISTANT VOICE: Help me! . . . Help me!
JACKSON: Lubov Borisovna! . . . Do not resist arrest!
  (They wince, as a distant noise is heard. Shura — the bedroom window being closed — remains oblivious.)
BOBA: Oh God . . . Don't hit him, grandma! He is a policeman!
JACKSON: Lubov Borisovna! He has a gun!

(Jackson runs out.)
LUBOV BORISOVNA'S DISTANT VOICE: Help me! . . . Help me!
BOBA: Grandma, do not resist arrest!!
(More noise is heard. Boba moves to go, but now sees that he is the only one left.)
BOBA: *(Cursing.)* . . . Yob tvoyu mat . . . !
(He goes to the bedroom door, bangs on it.)
SHURA: I'm changing!
BOBA: Shurka don't go anywhere! We'll be right back!
SHURA: You're leaving me alone with him . . . ?
BOBA: We're coming back! Stop being a monkey on my back, all right? . . .
(He runs out the door.)
SHURA: "Monkey on your back" . . . What happened to the guiding star above your gutter, Bobachka?
(Silence. Glancing at the draped chair apprehensively, she walks up to the bedroom window, opens up the drapes.)
SHURA: Oh God . . .
(She lifts the window open, as various sounds of street commotion enter the room.)
SHURA: Lubov Borisovna . . . !
LUBOV BORISOVNA'S DISTANT VOICE: Andrushenka, tell them it's only permidon!
ANDREI'S DISTANT VOICE: We'll meet you at the station, babushka. Do not despair!
(A police siren is heard, drowning out all the other noise, then slowly fades into the distance . . . silence.)
SHURA: *(Looking out, sad.)* I guess we can't all be a guiding star . . . Some of us have to be a meteor . . . Some maybe . . . just a piece of cosmic dust.
(She closes the window, then turns and looks at the chair, becoming aware of the living breathing being beneath the drape. She watches it a moment.)
SHURA: Do you think I'm cosmic dust?
(Pause. Shura watches as the drape goes up and down a bit with Pasha's breath.)
SHURA: I'm sorry . . . God. Why am I asking you? You've plenty problems of your own. *(Silence.)* Well . . . I am gonna go and . . . watch TV . . .
(She backs up, fascinated, watching him closely. Then, breaking off, walks to the living room, sits down, flips on the TV.)
TV ANNOUNCER'S VOICE: And remember — you may be a monk at home but at "The Palace," we treat you like a tsar! All major credit cards accepted. *("The Palace" music fades.)* We now return to our Mexican serial, "The

Wild Rose of Rio Pecco." *("Rio Pecco" music fades in. The same woman sings in Spanish.)* "The Wild Rose of Rio Pecco"! — (translated from Spanish by Andrei Surkov).

SHURA: Oh Isabella Isabella. What are we to do?

TV ANNOUNCER'S VOICE: Part fifty-five: "The Search for Little Rohelito."

(She turns down the volume, thinking, as if unable to shake something off, then gets up, walks to the window, looks out, turns, makes her way back to the bedroom, slowly approaches the draped chair, picks up the edge of the sheet, begins to lift it apprehensively . . . hesitates . . . then goes on, gradually revealing Pasha underneath the drape. He stares at her — oddly different from how he seemed with the men. Silence.)

SHURA: *(Holding the sheet.)* I'm sorry . . . I should cover you back up. *(He shakes his head, grunting.)* I'm sorry — but I have to . . . This is unprofessional. *(He grunts, looking at her pleadingly.)* All right. Just stop the sorry attitude.

(She takes off the sheet. They look at each other. She runs to the window. He grunts.)

SHURA: It's okay. You don't have to thank me. *(He grunts evocatively.)* . . . What? *(More evocative grunts.)* I don't know what you mean.

(He motions expressively with his head, trying to squish the masking tape.)

SHURA: The tape? No way . . . If I undo your mouth, you'll start on and on about . . . I don't know. Like how you didn't do what you did . . . Trying to get me to untie you — which I'll never do! *(Pasha grunts defensively.)* You will! . . . You know you will. It'll be like that whole thing with the forbidden fruit. *(A serpent's voice.)* "Come. Try the apple, Shurochka." *(He grunts, quite disappointed.)*

SHURA: Look . . . If I take your tape off, you must promise not to talk to me. *(Pause.)* I mean, you know — you can talk to me, but not about your problems. Like . . . Your problems are your own. *(Pause. Pasha grunts.)* You have to promise. If you start up with your bullshit, I am putting it back on . . . And draping you as well! No sunlight — nothing! *(He grunts, in promise. She looks at him.)* Upon your mother's health? *(Pasha grunts, sadly.)* . . . Your mother's dead . . . ? *(He nods.)* Okay. Upon your father's health! *(Pasha grunts again, very sad.)* Your father's dead as well? . . . Oh . . . God. You . . . you poor thing . . .

(She gently removes the tape from his mouth, then runs up to the window to check if it's safe.)

PASHA: They're dead to me at least. They're communists.

SHURA: Liar. You haven't said a word and you already lied to me.

SKITALETZ ("THE WANDERER") 25

PASHA: "Go Pashenka" — they said — "Go get devoured by the sharks of venture capital." Now I'm devoured here in Brooklyn and they're starving back in Peterburg.
SHURA: Oh yeah? I'm from Peterburg . . .
PASHA: What part you're from?
SHURA: Parnasskaya.
PASHA: Me too.
 (Pause.)
SHURA: Really?
PASHA: Yeah . . . Near . . .
SHURA: The Lakes.
PASHA: Yeah. Ozerki.
 (She studies him, a little apprehensive.)
SHURA: Wow . . . So we're neighbors.
PASHA: Yeah . . . Bedfellows, practically.
SHURA: Hey! Hey! What's with this fellow shit!
 (She lets out a burst of sudden laughter. He observes her, studying her face.)
PASHA: Hey . . . What's your name?
SHURA: . . . Shura . . . Why?
PASHA: Nothing . . .
SHURA: . . . What?
PASHA: Forget it. This is totally absurd.
SHURA: What?!
PASHA: . . . What school did you go to?
SHURA: . . . Forty-four.
 (He smiles at this, nodding.)
PASHA: And in sixth grade, you were in . . .
SHURA: Polina Yakovna's class . . . ! Homeroom . . . !
PASHA: *(Smiling.)* Uh-huh . . .
 (Pause. They observe each other, now with this wholly other, newly found excitement.)
SHURA: You sat behind me, didn't you?
 (Pause. Pasha nods . . .)
PASHA: I think so . . . Pasha.
SHURA: . . . Pasha . . . Yeah . . .
PASHA: Of course my hair was different.
SHURA: You hair?! Entire you was different! My God. Entire me was different . . . Sixth grade. My God . . .
 (She smiles, in thought.)

PASHA: I actually . . . I think I had a crush on you back then.
SHURA: No shit. You followed me around like a puppy dog!
   (She laughs, then stops. They look at each other. An uncomfortable pause.)
SHURA: And then . . . we kissed . . . I mean, did we . . . ?
PASHA: I think we did.
SHURA: . . . Back on the lake . . . behind the school . . . ?
PASHA: . . . Yeah. Near the hockey rink.
   (She watches him.)
SHURA: Yeah . . . I remember. And the ice was really thin . . . And I said . . . What was it I said . . . ?
PASHA: You didn't want to go. You thought the ice would crack.
SHURA: That's right . . . And you said . . .
PASHA: . . . I said, "It will be all right."
SHURA: Yeah. "It will be all right." *(She looks at him, remembering.)* And we walked out on the ice.
   (Silence.)
SHURA: So . . . How are you?
PASHA: Seen better times.
   (Glances at the ropes.)
SHURA: . . . I bet . . . And you have been in Brooklyn . . . ?
PASHA: For three years. Will be three — *(Spits thrice across his shoulder for luck.)* tfu tfu tfu — in March.
SHURA: . . . I'm only here two . . . Boba, my boyfriend . . . he and I met, like my first week in the States. And it was like, his second week . . . ! My parents are still back in Peterburg . . .
PASHA: Back in Parnasskaya . . . ?
SHURA: Uh-huh . . . How's your English?
PASHA: . . . Pretty good. I manage.
SHURA: Yeah. Me too . . . But I wish I knew more. I don't think I'm learning, I'm . . . I'm closing myself off.
PASHA: Sometimes. I wish I studied more when I attended Touro College.
SHURA: You attended Touro College too?!
PASHA: Yeah. But for two semesters. So my English isn't great.
SHURA: I couldn't understand a word they said. And all those tapes! *(Monotone.)* "How are you? I'm fine. How are you? I'm fine. How are you? I'm fine" — Over and over, like a drill into your head! . . . Or — "If he wants to 'get ahead' in business, Sven must work 'around the clock.'" *(She scoffs.)* . . . "Around the clock." Who do they think we are?
PASHA: We aren't Sven.

SKITALETZ ("THE WANDERER")

(They laugh.)

SHURA: So I dropped out . . . Anyway . . . *(She looks at him.)* You aren't doing all that great yourself. What did you do?

PASHA: Borrowed some money.

SHURA: Yeah? . . . I guess you didn't borrow from the bank. *(Laughs, then stops, guilty.)* You borrowed it from . . . Boba's "boss"?

PASHA: That's right.

SHURA: . . . You know, I've never seen "The Boss" . . . I've tried to figure out who he was . . . like at some parties . . . but to no avail. And Boba never tells . . . Maybe tonight.

PASHA: Why, what is going on tonight?

SHURA: We're going to "The Palace."

PASHA: Oh.

SHURA: I picture him a bald man, with a pony tail and lots of scars. And somehow, very large, like Peter — not the saint, but emperor. A couple sizes larger than the rest of us.

PASHA: I've seen the boss. He's balding, but extremely small. *(She looks at him, impressed.)* He used to be an engineer in Kuybishev. They say he used to peddle some industrial size nut.

SHURA: Like . . . nuts and bolts . . . ?

PASHA: Uh-huh. Made a huge fortune on that nut way back before The Perestroika . . . Then came here, started peddling all kinds of . . . "nuts."

SHURA: To think what money you can make in "nuts," huh?

PASHA: Yeah. I should have peddled nuts myself. Or been an engineer . . . from Kuybishev.

(He laughs.)

SHURA: . . . What do you mean?

(Silence. He looks at her, a little caught. She waits for a response.)

PASHA: *(Choosing his words.)* I mean . . . If I were blessed with like, another "go at it" . . .

SHURA: A "go at it"?

PASHA: Say like, another lifetime.

SHURA: Oh.

(He looks at her, then at the ropes, sadly.)

PASHA: But clearly, I don't have another "go at it." Clearly, I am a baker. And a baker, in this lifetime, I will sink or swim.

SHURA: *(Concerned.)* . . . What happened?

PASHA: *(Perplexed.)* Well. I think I bake well. I have the things a Russian bakery should have. All the desserts a Russian likes to have after his meal . . .

But there's a problem. I'm not in a Russian neighborhood. I am enveloped by Italians, and what they want — I do not have . . . ! And I have tried to bake canole or whatever they have called that shit — but I am not the person for the job . . . *(He looks at her, his tone slowly shifting.)* "Location is the king" — the pundits say. It's where you are . . . and who, and when . . . The great successes catch the wave, riding the zeitgeist of their time, at one with everything around them. But who am I? A baker out of synch. A human out of touch. Floating around the world, without a home . . . without a face . . . A person out of time, and out of place . . .

SHURA: . . . A wanderer?

PASHA: I am a wanderer.

(They look at each other, intensely. Pasha breaks it off.)

PASHA: And so, a wanderer, I've wandered into "Boba's Mufflers and Repair" . . . discovering the hard way, that in life — there are no mufflers . . . and that "Boba" never did, nor ever will . . . repair.

(She smiles, then, growing sad, walks to the window. Silence. He watches her.)

PASHA: What's wrong?

(She shrugs, looking out.)

SHURA: Nothing . . . That's how I also feel, you know.

PASHA: That Boba never did repair?

SHURA: No . . . No. A wanderer . . .

PASHA: Surely you jest.

(She shakes her head.)

SHURA: Like coming to a new land, all alone . . . Then meeting Boba first week into it . . . It was fantastic . . . It was fun. *(She smiles.)* We had this plan that I was gonna take my dermatology exams and he was gonna get a bank loan, and start up his "Health Emporium" . . . And then, once the Emporium is running, we'd move out to Fort Lee and get a big estate with like . . . two Dobermans . . . ! *(She laughs.)* And a horny cat named Vlad.

PASHA: A horny cat . . . ?

SHURA: Yeah . . . It was fun to dream.

(Silence.)

PASHA: You don't think this will come to be . . . ?

(She shrugs.)

SHURA: "A dream's a dream, but fact's a fact" . . . That's what they say at least. *(Pause.)* He's grown hard . . . When we first met, he was so sensitive, you know? I know it's weird, since he was like a "commando," but he was really the most gentle gentle man . . . Then I don't know what happened. He got these ideas in his head — how he's gonna be this new American —

the cowboy, the marine, the thug. *(She shakes her head.)* And I got kind of down after the language tapes . . . And never went for my exams . . . *(Silence.)* So I don't know . . . Right now there's no Dobermans, no Health Emporium, no Vlad . . . *(She looks out, sad.)* And then my job . . . ! I am a dermatologist and what do I do? Pedicures and facials. Women wanting hair pulled out of their lips . . . And always bitching how it hurts. "Well, lady, stop growing a mustache then! Don't bitch at me about it" . . . *(Looks out.)* Sometimes I think — "What am I doing here . . . in this place?" *(She looks at Pasha. Pause.)* A dream's a dream, but fact's a fact — well maybe they are right, you know . . . ?

(Pause. She lights another cigarette.)

PASHA: Give me a smoke, will you?

(She approaches, extending her extremely long cigarette, holding it as he smokes.)

PASHA: What kind are these?

SHURA: They're "Max." I like them . . .

(Takes a drag herself.)

I used to smoke "Mores Menthol," but . . .

PASHA: They weren't long enough . . . ?

(She looks at him. Silence.)

SHURA: So Pasha . . . ?

PASHA: Yeah . . . ?

SHURA: . . . What do you think . . . ?

(He smiles at her, mischievously . . .)

PASHA: You're asking me, Alexa Alexeyevna . . . ?

(She shrugs.)

SHURA: . . . I guess.

PASHA: Well . . . I think I would not pay too much heed to "them" . . . If I were you, I'd pitch a tent.

SHURA: . . . You mean . . . ?

PASHA: I mean . . . I'd stay.

(She looks at him, unsure.)

SHURA: You would . . . ?

PASHA: If I were you, I would.

(Silence. Pasha breaks the tension with a smile.)

SHURA: How did you know I wanted.

PASHA: . . . Lucky guess.

(Pause.)

SHURA: Pasha . . . ?

PASHA: Yeah . . . ?
SHURA: Can I kiss you?
(Silence. He looks at her, quite touched.)
PASHA: Alexa Alexeyevna. I thought you'd never ask.
(Almost magnetically, she moves in and kisses him, long and deep. Silence.)
(A noise is heard outside. Shura pulls back as if from a dream, goes to the window.)
SHURA: Shit. They're coming . . .
(Grabs the masking tape, tries to unfold it as it stubbornly sticks to itself.)
SHURA: . . . Damn this tape . . .
(Unfolds the tape.)
I'm sorry.
PASHA: Life is not a hockey rink.
(They look at each other briefly. She puts the tape over his mouth, then unfolds the sheet draping it over him. She airs out the smoke, straightens the drapes, picks up the ashtray and leaves, closing the door behind herself. In the living room, Shura sits down on the sofa, straightens herself, turns on the TV. "Isabella," heroine of "Wild Rose of Rio Pecco" is now on a search for her son.)
"ISABELLA": *(Distant.)* Rohelito? Rohelito? . . . Where are you, my little Rohelito?
(In the bedroom, Pasha's hands come out from behind the chair, untied. He rises, as the drape falls off him, steps to the doorway, looks with longing through a crack at Shura's frozen figure.)
"EDUARDO": *(Shrill.)* Walk with me, little Rohelito. It will be all right.
(Lights fade.)

END OF ACT I

ACT II

In the dark, after a couple of notes from the street musician's synthesizer, we hear —

JACKSON: He's gone.
(Lights go up on the Eisenstein apartment — Boba, Jackson, and Shura stare at the white drape covering Pasha's empty chair. In the living room, the plot of "Wild Rose of Rio Pecco" continues to unwind. It is less than fifteen minutes after the end of Act One.)
SHURA: He was right there. I swear to you.
BOBA: You let him go?
SHURA: What? . . . No!
BOBA: Yeah — don't play dumb. You let him go?
SHURA: What are you talking about?
(Jackson pulls back the drape, sees an open window, leading to the fire escape.)
JACKSON: Boris Michailich, look at this.
(Boba goes to the window, stares out.)
JACKSON: He must have sneaked out through the fire escape.
(Shura looks around, confused.)
SHURA: I didn't touch him . . . like you said!
BOBA: Yeah well . . . he's Houdini then.
(Silence. They think. Jackson's cell phone begins to ring. Both look around, unsure of what to do, beginning to panic.)
BOBA: Don't answer it. *(The phone continues to ring.)* I said don't answer it . . . !
JACKSON: Boris Michailovich —
BOBA: Alright . . . Alright, go answer it.
JACKSON: *(Quiet.)* Uhm. Boba's mufflers and repair.
(He listens, growing a little scared, as Boba chases Shura out of the room. She crouches by the door listening in. Jackson hands Boba the phone.)
BOBA: Good afternoon, Anton Savelyevich. No, can't complain . . . Progress? Of course. There's been some regress earlier, but now — right back on the stallion as they say. *(A forced laugh.)* Ha-ha! . . . No. No, Anton Savelyevich . . .
(He listens, his features growing serious, his voice remaining upbeat.)
BOBA: Yes . . . *Yes*, Anton Savelyevich. Of course . . . !
(He laughs again, hangs up, grows somber. Shura crouches closer, trying to listen.)

JACKSON: You didn't tell him . . . did you?

BOBA: Didn't have the guts.

(Pause. Boba picks up the open ring box, looks at it. His ring is missing.)

BOBA: Bastard. The ring is gone.

JACKSON: The ring?

BOBA: It was my mother's, may she rest in peace. I planned to give it to my love tonight.

(He looks down, sad, the weight of the world almost overwhelming him . . .)

BOBA: My babushka's locked up . . . Now this . . . *(Silence.)* All right. Let's get the little shit. *(He goes to the cabinet, takes out two pistols.)*

JACKSON: Oh God . . . !

(Jackson recoils as Boba tries to tuck one of the guns under Jackson's belt.)

JACKSON: Boris Michalich I don't think —

BOBA: — Stop wiggling! It's semper fi, man. Seize the day!

JACKSON: It's semper what?

BOBA: It is America, Jackson! *(He tucks it in, observes.)* That's right . . . Just like Goodfella! Ey! *(Doing the "Taxi Driver," with his gun.)* "You're talking to me? Ey? Do you talk to me?!"

JACKSON: Boris Michalich . . . I am lost . . . !

(Pause. Boba looks at him, then turns away.)

BOBA: "Lost lost" — Go find yourself!

(He opens the door, as Shura dashes away from it.)

BOBA: Don't think I'm through with you.

SHURA: Where are you going?

BOBA: Tzatz . . . !

(They walk out. Shura follows them to the landing.)

SHURA: Boba . . . ! Come back . . . !

JACKSON: I'm sorry . . . I'm so sorry for the stress, Alexa Alexeyevna . . .

(They disappear. Long silence. Shura goes to bedroom, stares at the chair, then at the open window, trying to understand what has occurred. In the living room —)

TV ANNOUNCER'S VOICE: — where our MC super DJ Vanya Postorukhin plays the top hits and combines the best mixes from the old world and the new . . . So give your life a break and come to "The Palace." And remember, you may be a monk at home, but at "The Palace" —

(Lubov Borisovna opens the front door.)

LUBOV BORISOVNA: — we treat you like tsar. Yeah yeah. We've heard it all before. The monk has drowned, the tsar was shot, but we must still be treated to their legacy . . .

(*She turns on the kettle, lights one of Shura's cigarettes, then goes to the living room. Distracted, Shura does not hear her.*)

TV ANNOUNCER'S VOICE: Part fifty-six: "The search goes on."

LUBOV BORISOVNA: The search for little Rohelito . . . Some sangria Roselita . . .

(*Suspense music swells as Lubov Borisovna sits down on the couch. In the bedroom, Shura touches, then lifts the draped sheet, but finds no Pasha underneath.*)

LUBOV BORISOVNA: Shurochka . . . ! The "search" is on!

(*Shura steps out, surprised.*)

SHURA: . . . Lubov Borisovna . . . ? But you were . . .

LUBOV BORISOVNA: In a prison cell. Released on bail for good behavior.

(*She laughs.*)

SHURA: Really?

LUBOV BORISOVNA: I'm kidding Shurochka.

SHURA: . . . They dropped the charges?

LUBOV BORISOVNA: "Dropped the charges" — they put me with hookers and the pimps! The junkies with their eyes crisscrossed from crack or smack or whack or what they're doing nowadays. The junkies and the pimps, and me . . . And why? For selling permidon? A proven drug that eases pain! They dropped the charges, yes.

SHURA: That's great.

LUBOV BORISOVNA: I knew that man was shifty when he asked — (*Imitating an American.*) "Does madam po-ssess per-mi-don?" — But then I thought — how nice there's an American who knows wisdom — of our medicine! . . . A fool I was to trust his accent. Shurochka.

SHURA: That's great they dropped the charges though.

LUBOV BORISOVNA: "They dropped the charges" — Please. They took my week's supply! Valakardin and Analgin, and Permidon, and Valedol . . . (*She thinks, dragging in the smoke.*) Still, maybe the note helped.

SHURA: . . . The note, Lubov Borisovna?

LUBOV BORISOVNA: Oh Shurochka, don't ask . . . I cannot make a head or tail of it. A lunatic gave me this note. A crazy limping man without a sane thought in his head. "Please let this woman off the hook" — it said.

SHURA: Please let this woman off the hook?

LUBOV BORISOVNA: That's all it said! In chicken scratch! But when they read it, I was off the hook!

(*She shrugs, thinking.*)

SHURA: . . . Maybe the crazy man had influence.

LUBOV BORISOVNA: On who? On what?

SHURA: Maybe he knows the judge . . . Maybe, he had connections to the underworld.

(They laugh as the tea kettle begins to whistle. Shura goes to the kitchen, gets the kettle and two cups.)

LUBOV BORISOVNA: Maybe he did . . . at any rate, all's well that ends without a fine, or hours of service to community.

(She smiles, then looks out at TV.)

"ISABELLA": Rohelito . . . ? Rohelito . . . ?

"EDUARDO": Swallow the hard pill senora. Or you'll never see your son again.

"ISABELLA": My baby? Rohelito? It is you?

LUBOV BORISOVNA: It's him, mama. It's him.

"ROHELITO": Ma-ma! It's me!

(Shura returns with the tea.)

LUBOV BORISOVNA: *(Watching TV.)* What I don't understand is that a half-wit with no clue would know that it's a trap, and yet, she's walking plainly into it.

SHURA: It is their way, Lubov Borisovna. To make us feel we're in the know.

LUBOV BORISOVNA: But why? It's lunacy!

(The suspense music swells . . . then stops.)

LUBOV BORISOVNA: Cut off as always, at the moment of suspense.

(Shura pours the tea.)

SHURA: . . . So now?

LUBOV BORISOVNA: What?

SHURA: . . . What will you do?

LUBOV BORISOVNA: Well, surely as I'm sitting now, I'll never sell a bit of permidon to an American.

SHURA: And to a Russian?

LUBOV BORISOVNA: Well . . . *(She shrugs.)* My neighbors need me. How can I abandon them? *(She looks off, wistful —)* Each week, I get a parcel from my niece in Lvov. Each week, my neighbors know I have the things they're looking for. If I will not provide for them, who will?

(As she continues, Jackson and Boba appear downstage, guns in hand. They stealthily walk up to a rickety door above which hangs a crooked sign, displaying a badly drawn pie and some cyrillic letters. This is Pasha's "bakery.")

LUBOV BORISOVNA: If no one meets the needs of the community, then the community is lost. Then the community is forced into a strange world of unknown pharmacies, a world that doesn't care about who they are . . . The sweet souls that I cater to need me, and the stability I offer them . . . *(She looks off, sad.)* For life has turned them upside down and they're lost . . . And being lost on foreign shore is not an easy burden for the human heart.

(Silence. They drink tea, as downstage —)

BOBA: Ey Jackson, cover me. I'm going in.

JACKSON: I . . . don't know what . . . you mean . . .

(Jackson makes a vague attempt to stop him, as Boba kicks open the door and goes in commando style. Jackson winces as horrible clamor is heard from within the bakery then, silence . . . Boba reappears, grim and sad, his head and face covered in flour.)

JACKSON: That was my point, Boris Michalich. It seems his own bakery would be the last place he would hide.

BOBA: He's around somewhere.

JACKSON: He's gone . . . I don't know where else we can look.

(The cell phone begins to ring.)

BOBA: Don't answer it.

JACKSON: We have to answer it.

BOBA: We can't . . . !

(Silence. Boba looks around, desperate. The phone continues to ring.)

LUBOV BORISOVNA: Besides, I need them too. Maybe the crazy man is here to take care of me. I'll get arrested — he will get me off the hook . . . !

SHURA: I wouldn't count on it, Lubov Borisovna.

LUBOV BORISOVNA: Oh, I don't know. Much stranger things have happened in the world.

(The cell phone stops ringing.)

BOBA: We cannot answer it.

JACKSON: Are you alright?

(Boba shakes his head, then, frustrated, kicks a large UPS box sitting by the side of the door. The box falls apart as strange, almost deformed-looking toys fall out of it. Boba takes out a toy, looks at it, smiling at the absurdity.)

BOBA: Oh but to hell with it.

(Defeated, he sits down, sinking into the box. Jackson disappears into the bakery. In the living room, Lubov Borisovna gets up, looks out the window, worried. Shura sneaks a glance at the bedroom.)

LUBOV BORISOVNA: I hope Andrushenka's alright, the poor boy . . .

SHURA: Where is he?

LUBOV BORISOVNA: Long Island City. Went to have his pictures taken at a place called E-Z models. Spending hard-earned money on his dream. *(She lifts up the teacup for a toast.)* Here's hoping E-Z does him well . . . !

(She drinks, then, noticing that Shura is distracted, looks at her, concerned.)

LUBOV BORISOVNA: Did I upset you, Shurochka? . . . With all my talk of "the community" . . . ?
SHURA: Oh no Lubov Borisovna . . . I'm only thinking.
LUBOV BORISOVNA: What about?
SHURA: *(Shrugs.)* Life . . .
LUBOV BORISOVNA: Life?!
SHURA: Yeah . . . The twists and turns of it.
LUBOV BORISOVNA: Oh yes, the twists and turns . . . The bumps, the bruises, the acceleration and the slow crawl, to oblivion . . . *(She smiles. Pause.)* You feel like you are at a bump, or at a bruise?
SHURA: I . . . I don't know . . . How can you tell?
LUBOV BORISOVNA: Well with a bump, you hit and go. But with a bruise it bleeds, and festers till there's nothing left of you. But you've time. Entire life ahead of you.
SHURA: Is it?
LUBOV BORISOVNA: Of course it is. The world is full of endless possibilities.
SHURA: . . . I know. That's how I should be seeing it.
LUBOV BORISOVNA: . . . And yet, you don't . . . ?
(Shura looks at her, a bit embarrassed.)
SHURA: I feel a little stuck, I guess . . .
LUBOV BORISOVNA: . . . Stuck with my Bobachka?
SHURA: . . . Oh . . . No. He's . . . wonderful.
LUBOV BORISOVNA: Well, he has problems. His hot temper. His bull-headedness. Then, ever since his unit dissolved, he's been more anti-Russian than the Chechnyans. The "evil empire" this, the "evil empire" that — quoting this Ronald Reagan like some testament. I tell him — "Bobachka. You were a hero of the 'evil land' " . . . And then that job of his. What kind of job is beating people to a pulp . . . ?
SHURA: *(Shocked.)* . . . You know about it?
LUBOV BORISOVNA: I'm not entirely blind, my dear one . . . Beating poor people and for what? And always sneaking so I wouldn't register . . . He'll never get to Fort Lee at this rate . . . *(She thinks.)* But he's got a good heart, Shurochka. He really does.
SHURA: I know he does, Lubov Borisovna.
LUBOV BORISOVNA: At least you'll unwind tonight. Like the commercial says, you know — to "give your life a break"?
SHURA: I guess.
LUBOV BORISOVNA: . . . You love each other?
SHURA: Undisputably.

LUBOV BOROSOVNA: That's good. It's good to love somebody undisputably. My husband and I loved each other, but "disputably." *(She laughs.)* But those were times of stress. The purges and what not.
SHURA: We wouldn't . . . No, Lubov Borisovna. Your grandson. I think he's the one for me.
LUBOV BORISOVNA: The one for you, huh?
SHURA: Yeah.
(Pause. She looks at Shura, playfully.)
LUBOV BORISOVNA: So, who's the other guy?
(She steals a cigarette, lights it, smiles at Shura, who is a bit in shock.)
SHURA: . . . What do you mean?
LUBOV BORISOVNA: I mean — "who's the other guy"?
SHURA: . . . There is . . . no other guy, Lubov Borisovna.
LUBOV BORISOVNA: Come, Shurochka, I wasn't born the other day. Nor in the day *before* the other one. Believe me, I can tell. *(Looks at her, kindly.)* Besides, it's perfectly okay.
SHURA: It is?
LUBOV BORISOVNA: Of course! It's not like you are married to the imbecile.
SHURA: That's true.
LUBOV BORISOVNA: . . . Ah-ha! So then I'm right . . . !
(Shura sighs, caught.)
LUBOV BORISOVNA: — I knew it! Who is he, a Russian?
SHURA: Uhm . . .
LUBOV BORISOVNA: American?
SHURA: Lubov Borisovna . . .
LUBOV BORISOVNA: A Jew or not a Jew?
SHURA: Lubov Borisovna . . . It isn't what you think.
LUBOV BORISOVNA: . . . What do you mean?
SHURA: I mean . . . Boba is wonderful . . .
LUBOV BORISOVNA: . . . Uh-huh . . .
SHURA: But this is . . .
(She looks to the bedroom, stops herself.)
SHURA: . . . I don't know.
(She goes to the window, still totally disconcerted. Lubov Borisovna watches her.)
SHURA: I mean . . . I knew this boy when I was twelve . . . who had like a big crush on me . . . And then one day out on this lake . . . I kissed him.
LUBOV BORISOVNA: . . . Out on the lake . . . ?

SHURA: That's right. *(She thinks.)* And now, so many years down the road, I meet this boy again . . . Here in America.
LUBOV BORISOVNA: . . . So what is wrong with that?
SHURA: Nothing . . . Except it all feels very strange to me.
(Silence. She looks out the window, in thought.)
LUBOV BORISOVNA: It seems that he has taken you for quite a ride, this "other guy."
SHURA: . . . I guess.
LUBOV BORISOVNA: *(Suggestively.)* . . . So you and him are "très intime"?
SHURA: Lubov Borisovna, it really isn't what you think . . . Believe me, this is something else.
(Lubov Borisovna approaches her.)
LUBOV BORISOVNA: What kind of . . . "something else" . . . my dear one?
SHURA: I wish I knew. *(Silence.)* It's like . . . just seeing him again made me believe in things . . . you know? In things behind the boring, and the regular . . . As if . . . there was some hand behind me . . . pushing me along . . . !
LUBOV BORISOVNA: Ah, yes. I think I understand . . . !
(She smiles at her. Silence. Downstage, Jackson returns holding a bound notebook.)
JACKSON: Boris Michalich, look at this.
(He shows him the book.)
BOBA: A diary?
JACKSON: His diary.
(He sits next to Boba. Both read the book.)
LUBOV BORISOVNA: So now . . . ?
SHURA: . . . Now he's gone.
LUBOV BORISOVNA: You don't know where he is?
SHURA: In truth Lubov Borisovna, I don't think . . . I know anything.
(Lights dim on the living room as, downstage, Jackson begins to read —)
JACKSON: Dear diary. I am a failure, an utter failure. I've taken out a loan I can't repay, and now all is lost. *(Pause.)* Where did I go so wrong? I think I bake quite well. I have the things a Russian bakery should have. All the desserts a Russian likes to have after his meal . . . But diary, there's a problem. I'm not in a Russian neighborhood. I am enveloped by Italians, and what they want — I do not have . . . ! And I have tried to bake canole or whatever they have called that shit — but I am not the person for the job . . . . "Location is the king" — the pundits say. Successes catch the wave. But who am I? A baker out of synch. A human out of touch . . .

A failure, an utter failure. *(Pause.)* My bakery has failed. My other venture is a bust. Perhaps tonight will be the night. I'll have my supper at 8:30 at "The Palace" and then come what may.

(Silence. They sit, visibly affected.)

BOBA: What is the date on that?

JACKSON: The entry's today.

(Silence. They sit. Boba looks at his gun, then at the ugly deformed toy in his hand.)

BOBA: I don't know how long I can do it, Jackson, beating these poor shmucks for cash. I want to be the good egg. Not a criminal.

JACKSON: He took your mother's ring.

BOBA: . . . Maybe he needed it.

(Silence. Boba looks at himself.)

BOBA: And then these codes and snakes I painted on myself . . . I don't know what is in my heart. *(Silence.)* But it is not a semper fi. *(He looks at Jackson. Pause.)*

JACKSON: The snakes and daggers that we paint. The skits and dances that we do . . . to mark the time among our fellow men.

(The cell phone rings again.)

BOBA: I'll answer it.

(Jackson hands him the phone.)

BOBA: Hello. *(Boba listens, somber.)* . . . I understand, Anton Savelyevich.

(He hangs up, sits without uttering a word.)

JACKSON: . . . What did he say?

BOBA: He wants the money by tonight . . . Something about his son arriving. Needing a solarium.

JACKSON: Oh my . . . But we . . . What if . . . ?

(Pause. Boba looks at his gun, then at Jackson, ominously.)

JACKSON: Oh . . . my . . .

(Both sit, in thought.)

JACKSON: Boris Michalich, I don't think . . . I'm that kind of a man . . . !

BOBA: You think *I'm* that kind of a man?

JACKSON: Well you . . . the war experience . . .

(Silence.)

BOBA: 8:30 at "The Palace" then?

(Jackson looks fearfully at his gun.)

JACKSON: 8:30 on the dot.

(Boba gets up, wipes off the flour, puts the ugly toy back into the box; then, rechecks his gun.)

BOBA: I'm sorry, friend. I'm lost as well.

JACKSON: It is all right, Boris Michailovich.

(Boba leaves. Jackson sits, staring off, in thought. His cell phone rings again, he picks it up, annoyed.)

JACKSON: Hello Boba's mufflers and repair. Sir, I have told you — we do not have mufflers. No! We don't — repair! *(Pause. He furls his brow, trying to understand.)* . . . Yes. This is him. How do you know my name? *(Silence. He freezes momentarily.)* . . . Oh . . . From the résumé . . . ?

(Blackout. In the dark we hear a melancholy synthesizer melody, accompanied by the sound of ocean waves. A couple of seagulls screech somewhere in the distance. Lights up on Andrei, standing on the boardwalk, looking out to sea. The street musician with his coffee can and synthesizer becomes dimly visible stage right.)

(Silence. Andrei listens to the waves, smoking a cigarette. He sits down on the railing, sighs . . .)

ANDREI: Ah Andrei Andrei . . . A lunkhead you are, a lunkhead you will be, Andrei . . . *(He takes a drag.)* "We work with *Rolling Stone*, we do Versace ads" . . . I should have known that cross-eyed freak was no photographer. *(He spits.)* Now all the money's gone and where are you? Not quite as easy as you thought, is it Andrei — you show-biz wanna-be . . . *(Stares out to the sea.)* A grain of sand you are, my friend. A grain of sand in this enormous sea of life . . . Don't you forget it now. *(Stubs out his cig, lights another one.)* Look at Volodya, Mira Yakovna's son — computer scientist. Got full tuition scholarship into Cornell and now pulling sixty thousand at *Reader's Digest*. Moving his family into a new house in Fort Lee — same age as you — now that is a good son . . . And you? Where are you moving *your* entire family? . . . "Actor slash model" — *(Scoffing.)* — lunkhead's all you are! . . . Without a penny to your name . . . *(He thinks.)* And you had that Volodya beat. You used to help him with his homework — solve his integers, decline his nouns . . . True, it was many years ago . . . And not the same Volodya . . . Still. *(He smokes.)* Face it Andrei. It's not the Polaroids — it's you. You just don't have the chops for supermodeling. "He's beautiful but for the face" — the saying goes . . . and it applies, in this case, right to you . . . That's what they have been trying to tell you, all those agencies — "You're beautiful, but for the face." Ford said it, Wilhelmina said it. Even Click . . . A Van der Beek you're not, my friend. *(He sighs, then spits, puts out his cig, looks for another, but the cigs are gone.)* Now all the cigarettes are gone. Can't even smoke my life away. Can't even have a jailbird's luxury.

(Dejected, he crumples up the pack and tosses it away upstage. Just then, a Blind Man with a cane walks by, bends down and picks up the crumpled pack. A moment later, as the Man continues on his way, Andrei stops him.)

ANDREI: Hey mister, have you got a cigarette?

(The Blind Man stops.)

THE MAN: What kind you smoke?

ANDREI: Camel unfilters ultra wide.

(The Blind Man turns, approaches, fishes in his coat, takes out a brand new pack.)

THE MAN: Well then, today's your lucky day, my friend.

(He tosses Andrei the pack — the brand requested, nothing less.)

ANDREI: Thanks man.

THE MAN: Don't mention it.

(Andrei lights one, turns to give back the pack.)

THE MAN: Nah, I don't smoke . . . Asthma.

ANDREI: . . . I . . . see.

THE MAN: So what's all that about being a lunkhead, huh?

ANDREI: There's no use in denying it . . .

THE MAN: Then why?

ANDREI: Why what?

THE MAN: Deny it, man.

(The street musician strikes up on his synthesizer, softly playing what is to become "Andrei's Song" — a bluesy kind of thing — as the Blind Man, who is indeed Pasha, begins —)

PASHA: Shine it. Embrace it. Love it. Use it. Mm-mm . . .

(He sings, softly at first.)

Wilhelmina took no pity

Shmuck Volodya sitting pretty

Got rejected by the world at large

Never saw the ones in charge

Oh Andrei Andrei

Your life's in disarray

Andrei Andrei

Your life's in disarray.

ANDREI: I like that. It's catchy.

PASHA: Yeah? . . . Well, catch the wave. *(Sings.)*

Wilhelmina took no pity . . .

ANDREI: *. . . so you go out to Long Island City*

PASHA: *Filled with dreams and looking good*

ANDREI: . . . *on my way to Hollywood*
PASHA: *(He joins in a bit hesitant.) Oh Andrei Andrei*
   Your life's in disarray
   Andrei Andrei
   Your life's in disarray
PASHA: *Once you're out in L.I. City*
ANDREI: *Things ain't turning out so pretty*
PASHA: *E-Z swiped your every dime*
ANDREI: *(More confident now.) What he did should be a crime!*
BOTH: *Oh Andrei Andrei*
   Your life's in disarray
   Andrei Andrei
   Your life's in disarray
PASHA: *Now you're stuck without a paddle*
ANDREI: *Got no book — can't be a model*
PASHA: *Got no cash no options left*
ANDREI: *Time for crime and petty theft*
BOTH: *Oh Andrei Andrei*
   Your life's in disarray
   Andrei Andrei
   Your life's in disarray
PASHA: *But you know, it doesn't matter*
   All the ads and idle chatter.
   (He comes closer, secretly —)
   They're just jealous of your looks
   That's why others need their "books"
   (Andrei nods, getting it.)
BOTH: *Oh Andrei Andrei*
   Your life's in disarray
   Andrei Andrei
   Your life's in disarray
   (The music turns upbeat. Andrei, happier, begins to move about, doing a crazy sort of soft-shoe, making strange noises as he lets himself go. Pasha reciprocates, making wild animal noises, etc.: unhinging bit by bit, as the absurdity and the visceral joy of it all takes over.)
PASHA: *Wil-hel-mina took no pi-ty . . . !*
ANDREI: *Shmuck Vo-lo-dya sit-ting pretty . . . !*
PASHA: *Got re-jected by the world at large . . . !*
ANDREI: *(Idea crossing his mind.) But soon I will be in charge . . . !*

BOTH: *Oh Andrei! Andrei! Your life's in disarra-ay!*
Andrei! Andrei! Hey-hey-hey . . .
(Swinging about wildly.)
Wil-hel-mina took no pi-ty . . . !
Shmuck Vo-lo-dya's in Ta-hi-ti . . . !
Damn the world at large . . . !
And we're gonna be in charge . . . !
Hey hey-hey! Andrei!
Your life's in disarra-a-ay!
Andrei! Hey-hey! Your life's . . . in . . . dis . . . aah . . .
(A momentary freeze. Silence. Pasha is gone. Sound of the ocean. Andrei smiles.)

ANDREI: *(Softly.) Your life's in disarray.*
(In an instant, lights change dramatically. Andrei is gone. The street musicians throws off his coat and hat, revealing a head of slicked back hair and an Armani suit. He is now a very nordic looking "Super DJ Vanya Postorukhin." Enveloped by the dizzying effects of club lighting, Vanya kicks into his techno rap version of "I Will Survive." We are now in "The Palace.")

SUPER DJ VANYA POSTORUKHIN: *(Surly and flamboyant.) Oh no, not I . . . I will survive . . . As long as I know how to love/I know I'll stay alive . . . 'Cause I got all my life to live/And I got all my love to give/And I'll survive . . . I will survive! . . . Yeah yeah . . . !*
(As Postorukhin keeps on with his shtick, we see Boba, walking through the audience, checking out people's faces — eyeing some closer than others, then walking away.)
(Shura sits off to the side, at a table filled with continental treats, wearing a green sequin dress, which wondrously accentuates her figure. There's a suggestion of a dance floor in the middle and neighboring tables on the periphery. She watches him, annoyed; then gets up, taking her purse. Boba checks his watch —)

BOBA: Where the hell is Jackson?
SHURA: *(Over the music.)* I am leaving, Boba.
BOBA: What?
SHURA: I said I'm leaving! Bye!
(Boba runs back to the table, stopping her.)
BOBA: Where you going? We just got inside!
SHURA: Yeah like you give a shit.
BOBA: I give a shit. I said we'll have a good time so we are!
(She looks at him.)

SHURA: . . . He isn't here you know.

BOBA: Who?

SHURA: "Who." He's not an idiot. This is the last place he would show.

BOBA: You wanna bet?

(She looks at him, hurt, begins to walk away.)

BOBA: Shurka! C'mon! That isn't what I meant! I'm here for *you*!

SHURA: Bullshit.

BOBA: It's true! I . . . Never mind.

(She looks back at him, vulnerable.)

SHURA: What, Boba.

BOBA: . . . Do you wanna meet the DJ? He's really cool.

SHURA: I . . . I don't know.

BOBA: C'mon. I'll introduce.

(Trying to be the man, Boba pulls Shura toward Postorukhin, who is now sampling pioneer songs, Le Marseilles, etc. The effect is a shocking dance-techno gumbo.)

BOBA: Vanya, my friend! What's all that super heavy shit you're sampling? *(Postorukhin ignores him.)* Hey, Vanka! . . . Vanya, my friend . . . ! You phat? *(Postorukhin continues to ignore him. Boba goes to tug his shoulder, then thinks better of it. As they return to their table, the music fades.)*

BOBA: He's busy with his licks. I'll introduce when he's on a break.

SHURA: You know Boba, you do not have to blow this dust into my eyes.

BOBA: Dust? Who's blowing dust? Vanya and I we go way back.

SHURA: Back to where?

BOBA: Way . . . just way back.

(He looks off, embarrassed.)

SHURA: I am impressed by you, if you know Vanya or do not.

BOBA: You are?

(She nods. Boba smiles. Both sit down.)

BOBA: So like . . . you think I am a prince to you.

SHURA: I wouldn't go that far.

BOBA: But you think . . . I am pretty cool.

SHURA: *(Warm.)* Yeah . . . You're alright.

(Silence. He is touched.)

BOBA: You know Shurka, I know I haven't been the best of men.

SHURA: You what . . .

BOBA: — I know I've made mistakes. Fucked up for lifetime and a half . . . But Shurka, I'm human, flesh and bone . . . And I can change . . . *(Looks down, sad.)* You see, there's something that I planned to ask of you tonight . . .

SHURA: Uh-huh . . .

BOBA: Because I thought it long and hard, and I thought, if not now, then when? Or if not here, in this way . . . ? And then . . . it all got fucked. *(Takes out the empty ring box, looks at it.)* I lost the prop . . . Then you got mad at me. And now The Boss is eating at my soul . . .

(Suddenly, a small and lively Armani-clad bald man appears and begins to sneak toward him. Shura sees him, but finds herself unable to say anything. Boba clears his throat.)

BOBA: So maybe what I'll say will be a shock. But Shurka I am hoping it's a shock of pleasure. And not pity, or disgust . . .

(The man puts a finger to the back of Boba's head.)

THE BOSS: Move and I'll blow your head!!

(They freeze. Then, his instincts kicking in, Boba spins, attacking his assailant.)

BOBA: You . . . mother! —

(The man steps back, laughing uproariously. Boba, seeing who it is, stops just short of smashing him.)

BOBA: An . . . ton Savelyevich . . .

THE BOSS: Got you! Got Boba good!

(The Boss laughs wildly, out of proportion with the stunt. Boba is pissed off but laughs along. The Boss goes on, and on . . .)

THE BOSS: I got you!

BOBA: You . . . you got me . . .

(The Boss goes in hysterics, slapping Boba on the back, imitating the stunt, etc. . . . then rather abruptly, stops, grows somber.)

THE BOSS: Good instincts, Bolobai Vasilyevich.

BOBA: Boris Michailovich . . .

THE BOSS: I know. And way to stab a friend in the back!

SHURA: I . . .

THE BOSS: It's alright. Backstabbing is the highest form of flattery and first rule of defense, my personal opinion, how are you?

(An uncomfortable pause.)

BOBA: We are . . . Good. We're good.

THE BOSS: You do not plan to introduce me to your . . . "friend"?

BOBA: I . . . yes of course . . . Alexa Alexeyevna . . . An . . . ton Savelyevich.

SHURA: *(Grasping who this is.)* . . . Ant . . . A . . .

THE BOSS: *(Kissing her hand.)* Perhaps you have heard of me?

SHURA: I . . . uh . . .

46 DMITRY LIPKIN

THE BOSS: Good things I hope.

SHURA: Good. Only good . . . !

THE BOSS: That's good. It's nice to hear only good things about yourself.
(He laughs again, again too much, as Shura looks back and nearly gasps in horror. On the other side of the club, smoking and wandering aimlessly, she sees Pasha.)

BOBA: What brings you to "The Palace," dear Savelyevich?

THE BOSS: "Brings me"? I own the fucking place! . . . Or part of it. The part we're in right now — *not* the part where Postorukhin stands. *(He laughs, throwing the DJ a cold glance.)* The shval . . . But kids like it, so what am I to do? *(Pause. He looks around apprehensively.)* Listen. Can I . . . join you?

BOBA: . . . Join? — yes, of course . . .

THE BOSS: Thank you.

SHURA: Excuse me please.

BOBA: Shur-ka . . .

(But Shura is already off. The Boss sits down, grabs a pork chop. Then, hiding —)

THE BOSS: My relatives are visiting from Kuybishev and they are driving me insane . . . ! "Tosha, when do we go to Tiffany's? Tosha, when do we go to Disney World? Tosha, when do we go to Hollywood?" *(Dark.)* . . . When do we go to hell — is what I want to know. When do we go to hell. *(Devours a piece of shishkebab.)* Except my son. Light of my life. The only one who understands.

BOBA: . . . Your son is here?

THE BOSS: My only son. Just finished polytechnic back at home — straight A's across the board. Now visiting his dad. My son . . .

(He looks off lovingly, proudly, at someone offstage. Meanwhile, upstage, Shura approaches Pasha, trying to shield him from being seen —)

SHURA: What are you doing here?

PASHA: *(Unclear.)* What?

SHURA: This is the last place you should be . . . !

PASHA: Excuse me. I . . . don't understand.

SHURA: Get out of here . . . ! Go!

(She tries to pull Pasha away, as —)

THE BOSS: I'm trying to get him to stay here for good. We'll fix the visas, passports, fix it all . . . ! Then maybe, he can help me with the business, take it over inch by inch with his new . . . polytechnic skills!

(He laughs.)

SHURA: Get out of here. Go . . . ! Go . . . !
(But it is too late. The Boss' eyes land on Pasha . . .)
THE BOSS: My son . . . Come . . . ! Come my son . . . ! *(He waves him on.)* Come. Do not be afraid . . . That's right, come come . . . !
(Shura looks around, believing The Boss to be addressing someone else. But it is Pasha who responds, approaching the table, waving shyly — oddly dignified and aloof.)
PASHA: Hi, Papa . . . What is it?
(As he gets to the table, Shura gasps. Boba does not seem to register anything odd.)
THE BOSS: *(Proudly.)* My son. Come meet my friends, my son.
PASHA: Always a pleasure to meet good friends of my papa's. *(Extends his hand to Boba.)* You would be . . . ?
BOBA: Boris Michalich. Pleasure's all mine.
THE BOSS: As it should be! *(The Boss laughs.)*
PASHA: Papa. Please. *(To Shura.)* And you would be . . . ?
(Shura stares back, at a loss.)
SHURA: . . . Your son . . . ?
BOBA: Shur-ka . . .
THE BOSS: My son. May I present — Alexa Alexeyevna.
PASHA: Alexa Alexeyevna. A pleasure.
SHURA: *(Confused.)* . . . pleasure . . . yes . . .
(She weakly extends her hand as Pasha kisses it. An awkward pause.)
BOBA: So you are fresh from polytechnic, uh . . . ?
PASHA: I am.
THE BOSS: His first time in America! My ex-wife Mashka, may she rot in hell, insisted he not come until he graduates with a degree! So now, there he is! — My son, the engineer! Like I was once an engineer! —
(He tussles Pasha.) — My little boy, my little boy . . .
PASHA: *(Resisting.)* Papa. I'm not your little boy . . .
THE BOSS: You are! You are my baby little boy . . . !
(He tussles Pasha to no end, pinching his cheeks, mussing his hair. Boba nods along.)
PASHA: Papa, c'mon.
THE BOSS: Sit down, damn it! Join us! *(Feeling his ribs.)* You are skinny as a corpse!!
PASHA: I'd like to, but —
THE BOSS: — The relatives?
(Pasha looks offstage.)

PASHA: Aunt Sveta's calling me away. She is a monster, but she's still my aunt.
THE BOSS: And that's the dirty truth . . . All right. Go then . . . Tell them I'll see them all in kingdom come . . . And son . . . ?
PASHA: . . . Yes, papa?
THE BOSS: *(Pleading.)* Eat. You need to eat.
(Pasha smiles.)
PASHA: I will, papa. I will. *(He turns to the table, cordially.)* A pleasure meeting you.
(He departs. Shura stands, at a loss.)
THE BOSS: So, what you think?
BOBA: A carbon copy of yourself, Anton Savelyevich.
THE BOSS: And smarter too . . . My son . . .
(He looks off, watching Pasha, as tears suddenly appear on his face.)
THE BOSS: He almost died, you know. As a kid . . . ?
BOBA: He did . . . ?
(The Boss sobs, then wipes off his tears.)
THE BOSS: But then . . . perhaps that is a story for another day.
SHURA: Excuse me please.
BOBA: Shur-ka . . .
(He glares at her.)
SHURA: What? Bathroom . . . Heard of bathrooms, Bobachka?
(As she departs upstage, Pasha, having apparently left "the relatives," appears just outside "The Palace," downstage. He lights a cigarette, staring into the sky.)
THE BOSS: Nice woman you have there, Bobrui Kondratievich. Nice woman, that can't be denied.
BOBA: It is . . it is "Boris Michailovich."
THE BOSS: "Bobrui," "Boris" — what does it matter in this world of animals and thieves . . . ?
BOBA: It doesn't, except . . . I'm Boris.
THE BOSS: *(He laughs, slapping Boba on the back.)* I know, I know you are, Boriska. You are gonna marry her?
BOBA: That is . . . what I intend.
THE BOSS: Well intend harder then. *(Spits out a pickled tomato into a napkin.)* Too fucking salty. Vanka! Play us something good!
(Postorukhin nods, but continues as he was.)
SUPER DJ VANYA POSTORUKHIN: Who got the threads/And who got it cookin' One name's the game/Super DJ Vanya Postorukhin/MIR *(Spins, giving a flamboyant peace sign.)* MIR, baby, MIR . . .

SKITALETZ ("THE WANDERER") 49

(Shura appears downstage, approaching Pasha from behind. Lights dim a bit on the men as she reaches out, touching his shoulder.)

SHURA: His son, huh . . . ?

PASHA: Pardon me?

SHURA: It's me . . . Don't you remember me?

PASHA: From . . . from the table, yes. Alexa Alexeyevna.

SHURA: No. Not the table. From . . . you know.

(She puts her hand over her mouth, grunting evocatively, like he had done in Act One.)

SHURA: I still don't understand why you were . . . if you are his son! But I'm glad you're safe . . . And I guess . . . I guess the bakery's alright . . . ?

(He looks at her, unsure.)

PASHA: I . . . do not understand.

SHURA: That you are not in trouble! And that everything's alright . . . !

(She touches him.)

PASHA: . . . What . . . kind of trouble was I in . . . ?

SHURA: . . . What do you mean?

PASHA: Well. You are saying that I was in trouble, and so, I am asking.

(Pause.)

SHURA: You . . . don't remember me . . . ?

PASHA: Alexa Alexeyevna, I only met you. How could I remember you?

SHURA: . . . But . . .

PASHA: . . . Yes?

SHURA: We didn't only meet. We've met before.

PASHA: We have . . . ?

(Silence.)

SHURA: Back in my room . . . ? You were . . . tied up . . . ?

PASHA: I was . . . ? *(She smirks.)* That must have been a sight.

SHURA: You . . . you do not remember this.

(Pause. Pasha shrugs.)

PASHA: I'm sorry, but it's news to me . . . How did I get to be in such a state?

SHURA: You owed a lot of money to . . . Anton Savelyevich . . . The Boss.

PASHA: . . . I owed a lot of money to my dad?

(Shura nods uncertainly as Pasha laughs.)

PASHA: And I suppose he is the one who tied me up.

SHURA: No . . . Boba did . . .

PASHA: *(Pointing to "The Palace.")* Boris . . . Michailovich?

SHURA: Uh-huh . . .

PASHA: Well. Now the plot thickens doesn't it.

SHURA: It's not a plot!
PASHA: It's not?
SHURA: No. It's the truth!
(He continues to laugh. She looks at him, something crossing her mind.)
PASHA: Have we met in the polytechnic maybe? . . . Back in Kuybishev?
SHURA: You're fucking with me, aren't you.
PASHA: Alexa Alexeyevna. It seems you're doing very well in fucking me . . . ! Did my dad talk you into this? *(She looks at him, unsure.)* To pull a stunt on me like this. Or was it my aunt Sveta? She's capable . . . C'mon, Alexa Alexeyevna. Who put you up to it?
SHURA: Pasha. Nobody "put me up to it." . . . !
PASHA: Who's Pasha?
(Silence. She grows pale, upset.)
SHURA: No one. Forget it all.
PASHA: Oh . . . You mean . . . ? You really thought that I was him. *(Silence. Shura grows more and more upset.)* In that case, I'm sorry to upset you so . . . I really am . . .
SHURA: So like . . . you're saying you have never baked . . . ?
PASHA: Baked?
SHURA: Owned a bakery.
PASHA: *(Genuine.)* Well, I . . . I like to *eat* baked goods, if that is what you mean . . . *(He looks at her, sadly.)* But no. I am an engineer.
SHURA: And you are not from Petersburg . . . ?
PASHA: No. I'm from Kuybishev.
SHURA: And you . . . you haven't been to Touro college.
PASHA: . . . Touro what?
(Silence. She looks at the street, at the sky . . .)
PASHA: I'm sorry to upset you . . . I thought you were merely playing. Some kind of a joke.
(She looks at him.)
SHURA: Pasha.
PASHA: Alexa Alexeyevna. I'm sorry . . . But I am not him. . . . You are confusing me with someone else.
SHURA: *(Looks at him.)* How could I be? It's you . . . !
PASHA: *(Genuine.)* Well . . . it is me. And yet, not quite what you mean by the word . . . *(Silence. She cries a bit.)* Perhaps a misplaced face . . . ? Some kind of grim . . . coincidence . . . ?
SHURA: A "grim . . . coincidence" . . . ?
PASHA: A face that you had known and loved that stuck with you. Face of a

friend, perhaps an angel, in the image of your making. A reflection of yourself ad infinitum, to the core of what's inside of you. *(Silence. He smiles at her.)* But dear Alexa Alexeyevna, that mute reflection is not me. And I'm not him.

SHURA: You're not . . . ?

PASHA: No, I'm not him. I am the son of a prominent Mafia Boss . . . *(He smiles at her kindly.)* Now do we have an understanding here?

SHURA: Understanding . . . ?

PASHA: Are we seeing . . . eye to eye?

(Pause. She looks at him, then nods, lost. Slowly wanders back into "The Palace." Pasha sighs, looking up at the sky, lights up another cigarette. A moment of stillness. Then, Shura cranes her head back out of the doorway . . . steps out, gradually.)

SHURA: Who *are* you then?

(Pause. He doesn't turn around.)

PASHA: Alexa Alexeyevna, I thought that we established —

(He chuckles, a bit forced, points to "The Palace" —)

SHURA: — Yeah . . . But who are you for real . . . ?

PASHA: Who am I . . . for . . . ?

SHURA: . . . Who are you . . . when all is said and done?

(Silence. He doesn't turn back.)

PASHA: Alexa . . . Alexeyevna . . .

(She takes a step forward, then back.)

SHURA: . . . You see . . . I *know* it's you. *(Silence.)* Maybe right now . . . you are saying that you're not . . . and maybe . . . you have reason to be saying this, but — I still know it's you . . . *(Silence.)* I . . . cannot tell you how or why, but I still know . . . Like, I knew the first time I kissed you, on that ice . . . I knew exactly who you were . . . And that, I've known you all my life . . . And when the ice below us didn't break . . . *(She smiles.)* In truth I wasn't surprised . . . I knew it wouldn't break . . . like I knew two and two is four . . . ! *(Silence.)* So, I am onto you, you see . . . The places that you hide . . . The corners of the world you roam . . . *(Silence.)* And in the corner of *my* world . . . you're caught.

(Silence. She stands, waiting for a response. He smokes, without turning back to look at her.)

PASHA: An interesting analysis . . . For a beginner may I add.

(Pause.)

SHURA: So . . . ?

PASHA: "So . . . ?" *(Silence.)* So what do you propose? . . . I can just "flick you off" you know.
SHURA: You can . . . ?
(A suspenseful pause. He shrugs.)
SHURA: I do not think it's what you want . . .
PASHA: Oh yeah? . . . How do you know what I want?
SHURA: I think you like me.
PASHA: Do I?
(Pause.)
SHURA: I think you do.
(Silence. He turns toward her, betraying a tiny smile.)
PASHA: Fair enough.
(He flicks his cigarette, then looks at her . . . extends his hand.)
PASHA: . . . You want to join me for a dance . . . ?
(She looks at his extended hand, the impact of it all becoming finally too much . . .)
SHURA: . . . Up in "The Palace"?
PASHA: Where else would we dance . . . Alexa Alexeyevna . . . ?
(She takes his hand, wobbles a bit, as he keeps her on her feet.)
SHURA: I am a little . . . woozy . . . I guess.
PASHA: I am sure you are.
(They walk inside, slowly, as lights shift, and music from the club rises, magically. Postorukhin is now in his slow phase, playing his version of Van Morrison's "Madame George." We fade up on the men, still at their table. Boba, restless, is listening to the Boss, drunkenly recounting an apparently endless tale.)
THE BOSS: The doctors said it was pneumonia, but we know what it was. Just malnutrition, that was all. A lack of vitamins, of calcium and zinc . . . of all the things a little body needs to feed on, and survive out there . . . in that swamp . . . *(He buries his head, distressed.)* And when they laid him down in the hospital . . . my little one was all but skin and bones . . . *(He cries.)* . . . and they said . . . that it was too late . . .
BOBA: . . . Yet clearly, it was not, Anton Savelyevich.
THE BOSS: Clearly, my friend. Clearly as crystal bell. For when my baby didn't die . . . it was a miracle. *(Smiles, wiping off tears, raises his glass.)* And I said thank you to the heavens for the gift that was all life.
BOBA: *(Raising his glass.)* To your son's health, Anton Savelyevich.
THE BOSS: To my small baby's health.
BOBA: And health in general.
(They clink glasses, drink.)

THE BOSS: *(Suddenly mean.)* Fuck health in general! Health in particular — is what I'm trying to say. Health in particular. Not general!
(Boba takes a breath, getting up his nerve.)
BOBA: Anton Savelyevich. About the baker. There's something I need to —
THE BOSS: — Discuss? There's nothing to discuss!
(Shura and Pasha appear and begin to slow dance — near Postorukhin, on the other side of the stage. The Boss looks across —)
THE BOSS: And now, there he is . . . my son. So rosy, so alive. Dancing so closely with your future wife . . .
(Boba, flushed with jealousy, tries to get up. The Boss pulls him back down.)
THE BOSS: You do not mind, do you Bobrui Efremovich? *(He laughs.)* Better watch out for him though. Back in the polytechnic he was quite a ladies' man . . . quite, quite a ladies' man . . .
(Boss laughs, slapping Boba on the back, as Shura and Pasha continue to dance . . .)
SHURA: So they can't even tell . . . ?
PASHA: Tell what?
SHURA: That . . . it is you . . . !
(He dips her, gracefully.)
PASHA: Again — with "you," Alexa Alexeyevna . . . Who *am* I, after all? . . . An engineer without a home . . . ? *(A dip.)* . . . A human out of touch . . . ?
SHURA: A wanderer?
(He shrugs, spinning her slowly.)
PASHA: . . . Maybe I am, what you would call, a wanderer . . . But then . . . what of it? And what value is a wanderer to them? *(They spin.)* My dad is happy — that I am alive. And I am glad to be of help, but it is not "the wanderer" he likes. *(They spin.)* It's not the wanderer they hold — but someone in particular . . . A man, a woman, little girl or boy . . . even a screaming baby once or twice.
SHURA: And me . . . ?
PASHA: . . . Well, clearly you're a special case.
SHURA: . . . I am?
PASHA: You know you are, Alexa Alexeyevna. *(He looks away, a little hesitant.)* I knew it all along.
SHURA: You did . . . ?
(He nods.)
PASHA: . . . The very first time that that whiner kissed you on the lake.
(Silence. She smiles as they dance . . .)
SHURA: Why do you call him that?

PASHA: Because he was. A total whiner with no self-esteem . . . Stared at your back for years, trying to get the nerve.

SHURA: But then . . . he did . . . ?

PASHA: Well, he had help . . . You miss him, I suppose . . . ?

SHURA: A little bit. *(She smiles.)* I miss . . .

PASHA: The cheat sheet on the desk?

SHURA: How he would slip it, and I'd never know from who . . . !

PASHA: And there it'd be — the inert gases right in front of you.

SHURA: "Argon, Radon, Neon . . . Not Oxygen

PASHA: . . . for Oxygen we breathe . . .

SHURA: . . . and what we breathe —

BOTH: — is not inert."

(Silence.)

SHURA: And how he'd look at me — just as the teacher handed out the test — and whisper that —

PASHA: — immortal phrase, imbedded for eternity in all of us.

(They look at each other, whispering.)

SHURA: "Remember Shura —"

BOTH: *(Whispering, Pasha slightly behind.)* "Every Hunter Yearns to Know Where Pheasant Sits."

(They laugh.)

PASHA: *(Musing.)* EHYKPS . . . Known in this world as ROYGBIV.

SHURA: The color spectrum of the universe.

(Silence.)

PASHA: Poor sap. Went on to sell insurance in some bank . . . Still selling it, I think. Somewhere in Novgorod.

SHURA: . . . You mean . . . he is not a baker . . . ?

(Pasha laughs at the notion, dipping her.)

PASHA: "A baker" — Please . . . ! *(Then, turning serious . . .)* The baker is with us now. Getting . . . how you say? — "the hang of things" . . . ?

SHURA: *(Unsure.)* . . . I . . . see . . .

PASHA: Trust me, Alexa Alexeyevna — the whiner is the whiner, and the baker is the baker, but in truth, none of it really matters in the end. *(They spin.)* Enjoy. Be happy. That is all it takes.

SHURA: . . . But . . .

PASHA: You are still afraid . . . ?

(She looks at him.)

SHURA: . . . A little bit.

PASHA: Of what?

SHURA: *(She shrugs.)* . . . I don't know. Maybe of the way things are. *(They dance.)* See, now I'm here, dancing in this place with you . . . And everything is right. And everything — I understand. *(She looks at him.)* . . . But what will happen when you leave? The dance will end. You'll say goodbye, put on your coat, become that engineer, or baker, or whatever you have been. And where will *I* be after that? Still stuck with all my problems, with my stupid job and ladies with their hairy lips . . . Still stuck with all my dreams . . . ? When you are gone, will I still think my life is special? . . . You see, I don't want this to be a dream . . . !

PASHA: . . . It's not a dream, Alexa Alexeyevna.

(He looks at her, warmly. They stop dancing.)

PASHA: But how you see your life is up to you . . . Yes I can coax, keep passing crumpled notes, sending unwritten résumés . . . *(Gently touches her face.)* But it is you who lives, and you who kisses, and who walks, and laughs, and smiles, and loves . . . It's you who dreams and only you . . . *(Smiles, at his most vulnerable.)* . . . who keeps on walking on that ice.

(They go on. The men sit at the table —)

THE BOSS: *(Blurting.)* The baker's dead. Just killed himself.

BOBA: He . . . ?

THE BOSS: Dead. Done. Dead. Came here for supper less than hour ago. But shmuck did not have reservation, so they turned him back . . . I had him followed. Drove out to Pulaski Skyway, 15E. Jumped in the Hackensack and bul-bul-bul. Poor shmuck. A borrower must not a taker be.

(Pause. Boba looks at him, shaken.)

BOBA: . . . Did he . . . ?

THE BOSS: Say why? Of course he did. Left a long note, blaming his woes on free economy. Used up the rest of my loan to buy these "Freaky Toys," these cripple little toys that he was gonna turn a profit on. Only the shipment got lost in the mail — and the day he jumps? — *(Reaches in his pocket, producing a toy.)* — They show up at his door. *(Drinks, producing another toy.)* Now he's dead, and I've got boxes full of little freaks. You want it? This is "Humpbacked Herbie." And this — "Two-Toed Tommy." 'Cause he got two toes!

(Boba looks down, distressed, as the Boss begins to sing, drunkenly, playing with the toy, shoving it in Boba's face.)

BOBA: C'mon Anton Savelyevich. Don't wiggle in my face.

THE BOSS: *(Singing.)* *The two-toed Tommy got two toes*
And when you wiggle them he glows . . .

BOBA: Stop it . . . Stop it, Anton Savelyevich.

(He grabs the toy out of the Boss' hands.)

THE BOSS: . . . You threaten me? I'll have you by the balls!

BOBA: Maybe . . . *(He takes a breath.)* But I don't think we should be laughing at his memory. He was a man, Anton Savelyevich, like you and me. A strange man but he had his dreams . . . And now he's dead because of us. How you think that makes me feel?

THE BOSS: *(To the toy.)* Who cares how you feel, Bonzai Karpatovich.

BOBA: It is . . . it is Boris Michailovich, and I care — *I* care — how I feel! *(Boss turns somber, looks up from the toy.)* . . . So. I don't know . . . I don't think I am meant to come here and cause pain and suffering . . .

(Pause. The Boss focuses on him, drunkenly.)

THE BOSS: So . . . what you're saying . . . ?

BOBA: I guess . . . what I'm saying is I quit.

(Pause. The Boss stares at him, enraged.)

THE BOSS: You're quitting me? The bastard's quitting me?!

BOBA: *(Scared.)* . . . I . . . am.

THE BOSS: You're quitting me?! . . . *Who's* quitting me?!

BOBA: *I* am . . . Anton Savelyevich.

(Pause.)

THE BOSS: Just like that. Two bastards quit on me today . . . Your friend the other guy? Flew off to Frisco, like a fucking bird . . .

BOBA: . . . Jackson . . . ?

THE BOSS: Who else. *(Silence, he thinks.)* Well I don't know . . . Maybe to change is good . . . My son, God bless his soul, is trying to have me change as well . . . start up some . . . what you call those things?

BOBA: . . . What things, Anton Savelyevich?

THE BOSS: A charity! Helping the weaklings little bit . . . !

(He drinks, grandiose.)

BOBA: You aren't mad at me?

THE BOSS: Whatever. You are free. Go live a life . . . !

BOBA: *(Raises his glass.)* To freedom then?

THE BOSS: To freedom, sure. And quick apocalypse.

(They drink. The Boss looks grimly at the toys. Boba looks at Shura, takes another drink for courage. Shura and Pasha continue to dance.)

PASHA: I think it's time for me to go . . . Your friend has simmered long enough and if I don't . . . bones may be broken.

SHURA: Yours or his?

PASHA: "Mine" . . . "His" . . .

(He laughs. Boba takes out the empty ring box.)

THE BOSS: . . . Go on, Bashkir Lulukevich. Now I am through with you.
BOBA: . . . I gotta take a leak.
(He runs to the bathroom, leaving the ring box on the table.)
SHURA: Where are you off to?
PASHA: Here and there. Oporto. Bled. Dar es Salaam. If it's not one thing, it's another. Always something. Always trying to stay afloat.
SHURA: . . . And I am sure you manage.
PASHA: Well. I do my best. *(They look at each other. He steps away.)* But anyway . . . "Time waits —"
SHURA: "— for no one."
PASHA: . . . As they say . . . Boris Michalich is about to come ask your hand in marriage, so I better split.
(Kisses her hand.)
SHURA: . . . Should I . . . ?
PASHA: *(Unclear.)* "Should you" . . . ?
SHURA: Get married?
PASHA: *I* don't know . . . Who do you think I am, a counselor of some sort?
(He smiles, moving away from her, walks to the table, picks up Boba's ring box, takes out the missing ring and puts it inside. He then takes off his jacket and hangs it over a chair. She does not see this.)
PASHA: But one thing I can tell you straight, Alexa Alexeyevna.
(Boba comes out of the bathroom, looks at table and sees the missing ring, as Pasha moves farther away . . .)
PASHA: That thing "they" say about time . . . ? A hoax.
(Boba looks at the ring, unsure. It seems like it has been there all along.)
PASHA: Time waits for everyone.
(He smiles. Shura looks out, smiling back, as Pasha disappears. The Boss lightly caresses Pasha's jacket as Boba approaches with the ring, gets down on one knee in front of Shura.)
THE BOSS: *(To Postorukhin.)* Vanka, some ambiance goddamit — friend is getting married!
(Postorukhin begins to play something "ambient." The Boss approaches, motioning for other patrons to gather around as their images and shadows appear everywhere. Boba pulls out the ring.)
BOBA: — Shurka you see, it's all about family. And children running in the yard, squealing like pigs with love and gratitude. *(He laughs, then, pondering —)* A large estate in Fort Lee with two Dobermans and a fat horny cat named Vlad. Just like we planned Shurka, remember? All the things we talked about . . . And we'll show him off at parties to our friends and

they will laugh and toast to us, and our estate, and all our kiddies and the kiddies they will ever have! — Our seed will spread and colonize the earth . . . !

(He laughs, then looks at her, poetically, takes her hand in his as they look at each other, filled with warmth. Andrei and Lubov Borisovna come out from opposite ends, slowly approaching the proposal site. Everyone — alive and projected — looks on in suspense, as Postorukhin milks the moment musically . . .)

BOBA: Will you, my dear and my light, will you my dear one . . .

(And on that, we freeze. In stony silence, Pasha comes out, looks at us.)

PASHA: . . . marry me?

(He walks to the tableau, observing the frozen figures, quite sad.)

PASHA: No . . . I am not the one to colonize the earth. You are. *(He looks at them.)* . . . Nor will I ever be a pop star . . . or a soldier . . . or a physicist. *(He looks at Shura, with longing.)* Nor in the years and centuries not once can I come close and say these words . . . To anyone who'd listen . . . or say "yes," in ways we both can comprehend . . .

(He walks around the frozen figures, touching parts of them, all still in time.)

PASHA: For this is where I live. *(Silence.)*

And when you laugh, and dance, and dream . . .

This is the way I see you . . .

And as close as I will ever come . . .

(He looks at Andrei's pack of cigarettes, at Lubov's crumpled note, at Boba's ring.)

PASHA: And when all the crumpled notes are passed, and all the bakers had their day . . . life goes to the ones who live . . . And what I want the most . . . escapes.

(We begin to hear the sound of a wedding. Then a party, voices, laughter, splashing in a pool, dogs barking — sounds of life continuing, of life beyond the stage . . . Pasha listens to the sounds.)

PASHA: The distant dog bark

And the splashing of the pool

The laughter and the music and the guests

And all the loved ones someone loves . . .

(He sighs.)

The echoes of the living, and the life

(Pasha continues to listen. The sounds of life briefly grow closer, more abundant, then slowly fade with the lights . . .)

END OF PLAY

Boxcar

Silvia Gonzalez S.

To Ambrocio Gonzalez Sandoval
(a constant visitor from the spirit world)

BIOGRAPHY

Silvia enjoys writing in various styles. Her favorite characters to write are women, Hispanics/Latinos, and senior citizens. Productions of her plays include: *The Narcissistic Personality Disorder Radio Show* produced in Chicago by Stockyard Theatre Project; *Don't Promise*, Stockyard Theatre Project; *Alicia in Wonder Tierra*, Theater for Young Folk, Teatro Humildad, Berkeley Rep tour, and The Coterie; *Border*, the American Playwrights of Color II, San Francisco; *Born in the Other Room*, Theatrix Theatre NYC; *Los Matadores*, Paula Productions; *Waiting Women*, Mutt Repertory Theatre, NYC; *Border*, Bilingual Educational Institute and Aquijon Theatre Company. *¡Fiesta!*, John F. Kennedy Center; *La Llorona Llora*, Whole Art Theatre and A Stage of One's Own; *U Got the Look*, The Original Theatre Works; *T (For Torture)*, Aquijon II Theatre Company, A Stage of One's Own.

Awards and Commissions include: The Lila Wallace/Reader's Digest Grant; Oregon Arts Council Theatre Grant Fellowship, Kennedy Center Youth in Education; Lane Arts Council Grant, (Warm Spring Indian Reservation); Lee Korf Playwriting Award with The Original Theatre Works; Barebones Film Festival Screenwriters Competition, Literary Arts Fellowship in Theatre; Leslie Bradshaw Theatre Fellowship; Hispanic Playwright Award at Southwest Rep; *Libros y Familias* Oregon Grant, and New Dramatists' Whitfield Cook Award.

Published works include, *Waiting Women, Alicia in Wonder Tierra (or I Can't Eat Goat Head), The Migrant Farmworker's Son,* and *La Llorona Llora* all with Dramatic Publishing.

She is also a alumna of New Dramatists, Chicago Dramatists, Body Politic Theatre and Central Oregon Artist in Residence program for Central Oregon schools.

EXPLANATION OF NAME

Silvia went to her father's homeland for the Mexican Day of the Dead celebration, which is always a family reunion at the burial site of family members. As her father was recalling relatives who have passed on, Silvia asked why many of the names on the tombstones had the Gonzalez family name with a capital *S* at the end. Her father responded, "You know Spanish names always include the mother's maiden name." Silvia answered. "I know, but why an *S* then a period inscribed on the tombstone?" Her father smiled and said, "Oh, we ran out of room." From then on, Silvia includes the *S* after her name.

CHARACTERS

ROBERTO: of Mexican descent and thoroughly assimilated. Mid-thirties.

BILL: though toxic at times, he's sincere in his arrogance.

AZTEC SKULL DANCER wears a skull mask with an Aztec headdress, an Aztec tunic and sandals. He is illuminate.

MANUEL: extremely good-natured. Always with a Zorba-type personality.

FRANCISCO: slender. He has dark, deep set eyes, and thick eyebrows. Mid-thirties.

NOEL (No-EL): well-dressed. There is a different quality that separates him from the other characters in the boxcar. He carries himself like a typical US boy, even though he is from El Salvador.

HUERO (wher-RRO): young and poorly dressed. He's extremely spunky and very full of life. He is fair with blue/green eyes.

HERNAN (er-NAN): well-dressed, though his clothes may be worn. He wears a leather jacket. His early twenties.

LUIS (Loo-eeze): wearing very tattered clothes. There is a mystical-spiritual quality in him.

PEPE (Peh-peh): wears traditional clothes of old Mexico and carries a Mexican nylon grocery bag. His sixties.

ABUELITA (A-ble-lee-ta): Roberto's grandmother from old Mexico.

Suggested Doubling:
Skull Dancer/ensemble member
Border Patrol Officer with no face/Bill
Undocumented Workers (illegal aliens)/Ensemble

SETTING
Texas. A boxcar in the desert.

TIME
Present

NOTE
The play is based on an actual event.

BOXCAR

PROLOGUE
Bad Dreams

Darkness. Dim lights on a slumbering man. Aztec music. A slight wind. Birds chirping in a distant jungle. A Mexican radio station pushes through the sounds, then all sounds fade away.

The slumbering man is Roberto. A Mexican blanket covers him.

Roberto moves slightly as a mist of fog glides over him. Lying next to him is the Aztec Skull Dancer.

The Skull Dancer stares at Roberto, then gets up and dances through the fog. He then sees the Border Patrol Officer (with no face) emerging from the darkness. The Skull Dancer makes his way toward some sand and digs out stones in the shape of skulls. He places seven carefully aside. He then digs out a black box and raises it ceremoniously above him, then buries it again. He then pulls out a notepad and starts writing.

Several illegals walk hauntingly by. They are strangely illuminated with blank faces.

Abuelita walks from the opposite direction.

The faceless Border Patrol Officer raises a gun and takes aim at all of them in slow motion. He fires several times but there are no sounds, and no reaction from the victims. He then follows the Skull Dancer with his gun.

The Skull Dancer runs into the sound of a door slamming in his face. He turns and looks up.

A festive, Mexican "Day of the Dead," sugar skull is seen above. It then crashes downward.

Shattered sounds.

ROBERTO: **ABUELITA!**
(Roberto awakens, looks around, and covers himself. Blackout.)

END OF PROLOGUE

ACT I
SCENE ONE, 1987

Country music from a radio in the distance. The sound of Bill's footsteps as he walks in, pushes a chair, then stops. After a moment a light switch flips on. Roberto is at a desk. Bill eyes him strangely and notices crunched-up paper balls, and maps spread over on the desk. Bill picks up Roberto's shirt and gives it to him. He then heads to an exit and turns off the lights. At that instant, there is the sound of screeching train wheels, then bright blinding lights.

In the blinding lights, Abuelita and the Aztec Skull Dancer appear again. They face each other, then exit. Roberto thinks he sees them, but then looks into the desert to reality.

Silence. Reality.

The blinding lights subside and Roberto and Bill are seen looking in different directions. A soft sunny glow is behind them, then finally, there is clarity.

BILL: Yep. It's going to break a hundred. Goin' to be a hot one. Yep. Willard Scott said hundred and twenty. *(No answer.)* You know, my wife can't sleep when it's hot like this. I don't mind. Even when it's a hundred at midnight, I can sleep through it. *(Watches Roberto.)* I slept like a baby. *(Long moment.)* You can still hear the cicadas. Some of them just don't know when to quit. *(No answer.)* Come on! Jesus Christ.

ROBERTO: *(Preoccupied in thought.)* Yeah, Jesus Christ.

BILL: You didn't sleep last night? *(Moment.)* Wrap your fingers 'round your pecker real tight now, and jerk it. Didn't you learn anything in junior high?

ROBERTO: What? . . . *(Realizing.)* I don't need to do that!

BILL: You got some stress going on there. Thought I can help with some advice. *(Draws his gun.)* HEY! Look at that!

ROBERTO: What is it, asshole?

BILL: I'll get him.

(Bill aims carefully into the distance.)

ROBERTO: Leave him alone.

BILL: I'm going to get the bastard. *(Moment.)* Hey, Robert. It's your turn. Remember?

ROBERTO: It's not my turn.

BILL: Yes, it is. Come on. He's waiting for you. Shoot him. It's your turn, man.

ROBERTO: It's a mess afterwards.

BOXCAR 65

BILL: The sun dries 'em. Okay. Then I'm gonna to take your turn. You know how I hate cats. Where is he now? *(Pause.)* Ah heck. Damn. He got away.
ROBERTO: Get to work.
(Bill takes out a set of binoculars and begins to scan the audience.)
BILL: Alright. Where are the mice?
ROBERTO: They're not mice.
BILL: Yes, they are Robert. You said so yourself. Remember?
ROBERTO: *(In realized-embarrassment.)* Look by the trees.
BILL: Yes, sir.
ROBERTO: And over there. And there.
BILL: And over there. Just like always. Let's just wait a minute in case there's more. *(Long moment.)* What's eating you? You hating this job already?
ROBERTO: Don't you?
BILL: Always did. Pays the bills, though . . . Hey look . . . *Now?*
ROBERTO: Not yet.
(Long moment.)
BILL: Who died?
ROBERTO: What?
BILL: Who died? The last time you were like this —
ROBERTO: *(Overlapping on "you".)* There was no last time.
BILL: Like hell. When your grandma died, you fool. And you were no fun then either. You told me it bothered you a whole lot 'cause you didn't see her after you grew up. You always knew she was there, but you didn't see her. How come you didn't see grannie?
ROBERTO: What? I never said that.
BILL: Yes, you did. You did. *(Long moment, then he looks through the binoculars.)* There's a few more now. I'm going to — *(Roberto reaches for his pistol and shoots up indicating it's time. Sound: Gun shot.)*
VOICE(S): La Migra! ¡La Migra! ¡CORREN! ¡Pronto! *(Ad-lib.)*
(The characters rise from seats in the audience, shouting, "LA MIGRA" etc.)
BILL: *(In bad Spanish.)* Manos aribas. E-ma-grasion. *(Ad-lib.)*
(Bill jumps off the stage to pursue them in the audience. Some are reluctant to run too far. They know they'll be caught anyway. Manuel is hiding behind an audience member. He then starts toward the opposite direction. Roberto sees him and lifts his gun in the air and shoots. At the sound of the blast, Manuel stops, drops his suitcase, and turns around quickly throwing his hands up in a comical way. He then recognizes Roberto.)
MANUEL: Roberto! Que me lleva la trampa. Look, if you catch me again, they'll think we are dating. Only lovers meet together like this.

ROBERTO: *(Enjoying Manuel's very friendly personality.)* Manuel.

MANUEL: *(Eagerly.)* ¿Si?

ROBERTO: Aye, Manuel. How many times do we have to go through this?

MANUEL: *(Smiling.)* I don't know. How many times? One, two, three, four, five?

ROBERTO: We always find you.

MANUEL: Someday you won't find me. I'll already be gone.

ROBERTO: This is the twentieth time.

MANUEL: Twenty? *(Thinks.)* No, much less.

ROBERTO: No, it's about twenty times.

MANUEL: Well, then, maybe you're right. But the last time you didn't shoot your gun. Are we losing respect for one another?

ROBERTO: No. I have lots of respect for you.

MANUEL: That's when I know you're like us. When, you respect people much older than yourself. Thank you for stopping to say hello.

(He starts to exit.)

ROBERTO: Don't you think you're getting too old for this behavior?

MANUEL: What? Looking for work? Aye Roberto, what education you unfortunately lack! *(Patiently.)* Mira, when a man stops looking for work, it's time for him to die. If you don't work, then you don't deserve life. We learn that over there. Bad schools here, huh?

ROBERTO: They pay you shit.

MANUEL: Easy for you to say. They pay me more shit over there. I even smell it.

ROBERTO: It's illegal for you to come.

MANUEL: I know. *Strange thing.*

ROBERTO: Go toward the jeep like everyone else.

MANUEL: There's nothing over there for me. Just a couple of dollars from the tourists. Even they are getting stingy.

ROBERTO: You work your butt off.

MANUEL: Work is good.

ROBERTO: For low wages.

MANUEL: Work is good.

ROBERTO: In the jeep.

MANUEL: *(Comically.)* You're the boss.

ROBERTO: I'm sending you home.

MANUEL: I am home, Roberto. Someone made a mistake with the history books. This all used to belong to Spain, then Mexico after the rebellion.

ROBERTO: It belonged to the Indians first.

MANUEL: Yes, but they liked us better than the English . . . Whatever you say,

Mr. Part-Americano. It's probably in better hands now. Let me see your hands. Ehg, they're ugly. Go wash them. Let's go. Take me to the jeep, jefe.

ROBERTO: I'm doing my job.

MANUEL: And you're doing it so well.

(Silence. Manuel puts out his hands for the handcuffs.)

ROBERTO: Don't be stupid.

MANUEL: Roberto. Is it stupid to improve your life? Go ahead. You caught me.

ROBERTO: It's my job to return those who were born over there —

MANUEL: *(Overlapping on "over.")* Your grandfather was born over there. *(Pause.)* Aye, my friend. Do your job. I have a job, too. It's to survive in anyway I can. Even to come where I'm not wanted. It's the last possible thing, believe me. I wouldn't do it if it was any better for me. Why humiliate myself? *(Long pause.)* Well, I go to the chariot that awaits me over there. The one that looks like a bus. Oh, you brought the van this time! Nice seat covers. How many of my compadres are you sending home? Hopefully some of them worked at least a day to cover expenses. *(Uncomfortable, yet a kind silence.)* Adios, señor gato. *(Starts to exit.)*

ROBERTO: Manuel, the van is over there.

(Manuel notices weakness from Roberto and continues walking toward the opposite direction.)

ROBERTO: *(Continues.)* Manuel. Manuel! *(He pulls out his gun.)* Freeze, Manuel. FREEZE.

(But Roberto just can't shoot. He covers his face with his hands as Manuel continues to walk offstage. Bill is heard in the distance calling out directions to other Border Patrol Officers. Bill enters.)

BILL: They're all in. All going back home where they belong. You ready? Hey, Look. *(Starts to aim his gun.)*

ROBERTO: Put it away.

BILL: Shit! There he goes! Did he come by here? Didn't you see him? What's wrong with you?

ROBERTO: Bill, let him keep going.

BILL: Why? Give me one reason why I shouldn't shoot for him to stop? Should kill it to end its misery. Alright! But you once said you hated cats . . . Then lets shoot the fucker before he gets too far off. God, I hate 'em. They have those round emotionless eyes. And piss in my flower beds. They bug you?

ROBERTO: Once a cat ate my grandfather's canary. Right there in front of me. I was just a kid.

BILL: Then, hell Robert. It's payback time

(A grin later, they do a fancy spin and shoot.)
(Blackout before guns go off. Two gun blazes are seen.)

SCENE TWO

In Texas, on route to California. Francisco is inside the boxcar. He hears sounds. He then waits for the sounds to pass before he moves. He then fiddles with a cardboard box that contains his belongings. Moments later, the door of the boxcar slides open slowly. It's Noel.

NOEL: *(Looks around, and hesitates.)* Buenos dias.
FRANCISCO: Buenos dias . . . Enter.
(Noel enters cautiously with a gym bag.)
FRANCISCO: *(Continues.)* What's the matter?
NOEL: I'm broke. I can't give you any more until later.
FRANCISCO: You don't owe me anything. I'm here like you.
NOEL: I thought it was you I was supposed to see.
FRANCISCO: No. We're both supposed to wait here. Then later we'll see someone else . . . They've taken most of your money?
NOEL: He took more than I expected, but I should be all right.
FRANCISCO: All right? You have a charge card or something? If you do, you should have taken a plane. Why this?
NOEL: At the time, a plane wasn't a good idea.
(Huero opens the door and stands there with a huge smile.)
HUERO: Mis queridos, companeros!
(Huero throws in a pillowcase filled with his belongings before jumping in.)
HUERO: *(Continues.)* Incredible! No walking, no running. Just put our big butts on the floor and let a great train take us to the stars. Look, I have my Michael Jackson T-shirt, and this cap. With a skull on it. Que feo. And torn-up pants. I'm dressed like an American.
FRANCISCO: Maybe you shouldn't talk so loud, huero.
HUERO: *(Whispers at first, then gets increasingly louder.)* Oh, that's right. I'll be quiet. And you're right about my name. Everyone calls me Huero. For this very light skin I have. There's others who are called Huero, too, but they don't come close to my color. Just look at this skin. I'm so fair, I get bad sunburns. But now I carry this. I won't get burned if I put this on. *(To Noel.)* I'm Huero DeLuna. Aren't you jealous? I can pass for an American much easier than you. They can pick you out in a crowd. Me? I just

blink my green eyes and say "Okay," "all right," and "no problem" and I pass for an American. Lucky skin, eh? That's why I refuse to tan.

NOEL: You still tan with that. That's suntan lotion.

HUERO: What? Oh, no. That would be horrible.

NOEL: You want a *sunblock*. Do you know what that is?

HUERO: *A what?* No, that would ruin my skin. Don't you know this skin is priceless?

FRANCISCO: Your skin reeks of an aristocrat.

HUERO: With a family as poor as mine? I just look it. My mother and sister have the same skin color. Oh, the Spanish went everywhere and made friends with everybody, *including the Indian women.* That is why my father came out brown like coffee. I came out like my grandfather. *(To Noel.)* You are a little of both. Coffee with cream I would say. Almost the coloring of an Italian. *(To Francisco.) And you are too dark* . . . I brought a bathing suit, sunglasses, and toilet paper — I'm going to California. And the most important thing. I have dice. What's in your little bag?

NOEL: Nothing much. Some water, and a book.

HUERO: A book? If you need toilet paper you can use mine.

(Hernan appears, holding an unconscious Luis at the door.)

HERNAN: Help me.

(All help carry Luis into the boxcar.)

HERNAN: *(Continues.)* I think he's supposed to be with us.

NOEL: What's wrong with him?

FRANCISCO: We'll put him over here.

HERNAN: *(Looks around.)* Just the four of us?

FRANCISCO: The more they can stuff in here, the better the profit for them.

HERNAN: Then, there should be more so they can get rich from us. To think they once did it for free . . . *(Motions to Luis.)* He was under the train. I crawled under to ask him if he was going my direction. I must have startled him because he suddenly hit his head and passed out. He didn't make another sound so I pulled him out and carried him with me.

FRANCISCO: Luis. Wake up.

HUERO: Do you know him?

FRANCISCO: Luis. Open your eyes. Look at me, hombre.

HERNAN: Well, if you know him, then it was right to bring him here. To be among friends.

FRANCISCO: Last year, I ran into him in the mountains. He told me he was looking for Mt. Olives. Another time, he said he was looking for Jericho.

HUERO: He's waking up again.

(*Luis opens his eyes and sees Huero, then passes out again.*)

HUERO: What's the matter?

HERNAN: He's acting like he's seen a ghost.

HUERO: I'm not *that white*. I'm just a huero. What's wrong with him?

HERNAN: *(Sternly.)* Yeah! What kind of man are you?

PEPE: *(Off.)* A man fighting for survival . . . Like us.

(*Pepe opens the door. He has black oil all over him. They stare at him.*)

PEPE: *(Continues.)* Well? I'm an old man, help me in.

HUERO: *(Approaches then withdraws.)* "Aye canijo." You smell.

PEPE: You would too if you've been where I just came from.

(*Pepe winces with pain as he tries to get into the boxcar. Huero and Hernan help.*)

PEPE: AYE! Watch the legs!

(*Huero and Hernan struggle in lifting Pepe. Pepe responds by whacking them with his hat.*)

PEPE: *(Continues.)* Aye. Aye! Stop it! You're not helping this old man! Idiots. (*Pepe stares coldly at Hernan and Huero and they laugh at this.*) What do you expect from the young and stupid. I'll get in myself. *(Pepe crawls in slowly.)* If 'el coyote' tells you to hide in a barrel, tell him to eat shit. The border patrol are all over. Twice we had to reroute. Hijos de su shingada madre. How long are we to wait here?

FRANCISCO: We just wait until it's time.

PEPE: That's what I do, wait until it's time. I waited with many last night. El coyote could only take a few of us. He counted eight, then told us to get into barrels. I thought he was crazy, but I knew I had to do it. This method is too expensive, but he promises to keep us from being robbed.

FRANCISCO: He still robs you.

PEPE: *But honestly.* Look at the other choice: doing it yourself. My brother crossed on his own and got his throat cut by a "pollo" before he reached the border. I tried myself before, and that pinche "pollo" took all my money. Then had the audacity to demand my clothes.

HUERO: They wouldn't want them now, they stink.

PEPE: And so do you.

NOEL: Then what happened?

PEPE: I pleaded like a meek Mexicano. I do that in emergencies. I said, "Please señor, you have all my money. Don't take the clothes off my back. This is a terrible thing to ask of someone who could be as old as your father." He said, "I hate my father." . . . Ah, look at me. How am I going to find a job looking like this?

FRANCISCO: Want a cigarette?

PEPE: And blow up from this oil? No thank you. *(Starts cleaning his clothes with a hanky.)* I rather have been strapped to a plane with my tongue.

HUERO: That's worse!

PEPE: I'm kidding. Any foreigners today? I met these men from Arabia last year. They said they are coming this way, too. Then I heard that the Chinese are coming this way. I thought the Chinese were rich.

HERNAN: It's the Japanese.

PEPE: Oh . . . How we all desire the same thing.

HUERO: Like what?

PEPE: A better life, menso! You shouldn't be teasing an old, tired man who is in pain.

(Long moment of all characters settling in.)

NOEL: . . . How much pain are you in?

PEPE: What? Oh, I'm fine.

NOEL: But you said you were in pain.

PEPE: I meant here in my heart. I have pain thinking about one who didn't make it. If I do something, I could jeopardize my own family . . . One of the barrels fell off the truck. I'm sure of it. But when I mentioned it, everyone was too busy with the next part of their journey.

NOEL: Are you sure?

PEPE: They had to use a crowbar to take the lid off *my barrel.* If he fell out in the desert, there is nothing. There were eight of us, altogether. A mother and her two small children. Me, and four other men. I remember their eyes.

HUERO: A mother, two children. Three. You and four other men. That's eight.

PEPE: Only seven arrived.

HERNAN: Then you counted wrong.

PEPE: No I didn't . . . In the barrel, I was swimming in my sweat. When I came out, I was soaked. Completely wet.

HUERO: Well? Aren't you a *wetback?*

(The men all laugh then the door slides open. A man with a fierce look stares at them, then cracks the warmest and largest smile, and pushes in an old suitcase. Manuel is in different clothes than in the first scene. [He may have grayer hair, or a mustache to show time went by.] He will always have a winning personality and a sense of fun throughout the play, even in the bad situations.)

MANUEL: *(Joyful.)* Andale, muchachos, ayudame.

HUERO: Do you smell?

MANUEL: No, do you? . . .

(He jumps in before the boys help him and laughs at their attempt.)

Boy, are you guys ugly. I better go back, right now, before it rubs off on me.

HUERO: You didn't see my face!

MANUEL: Yours is worse!

HUERO: No, I'm cute.

(They all laugh. Sound: Train bells.)

HUERO: *(Continues.)* We're getting ready to go.

MANUEL: I just made it in time. Lottery tickets here I come.

HUERO: Did you hear that the Mexican who won the California lottery was already rich? He didn't need the money.

MANUEL: What else is new? The rich get richer and the poor have a sense of humor. I'm Manuel Felicitas. And you?

FRANCISCO: Francisco Ceja de Fierro.

MANUEL: Let's have a good journey. Who is this baby-face over there?

NOEL: Noel Martin de Cabos.

MANUEL: Good to meet you. How about your name, huero?

HUERO: Huero.

MANUEL: Last name then.

HUERO: DeLuna.

MANUEL: DeLuna? *De la* Luna. Of the moon. White as the moon. *(Laughs.)* Did your mother see a white moon when you were born? I bet the doctor did.

HUERO: Hey, that's my mother you're talking about —

MANUEL: *(Overlapping on "talking.")* Oh, come on Huerito. Your mother had to be white for you to come out like this.

HUERO: Of course, the Spanish are white. I have roots all the way to Northern Spain.

MANUEL: We all do, but who admits it?

FRANCISCO: He's an aristocrat.

HUERO: No, I'm not.

MANUEL: Don't worry, we forgive you.

(Manuel notices Luis and goes to him. He taps him with his foot and gets no response.)

MANUEL: Who is this man? Is he drunk?

FRANCISCO: His name is Luis Antonio del Cruz. He's from near my village. He is a man to be respected.

HERNAN: Respected? Why? Look at him.

FRANCISCO: Because I say so.

BOXCAR 73

MANUEL: Well, you all heard that. We'll respect him in the morning. It's morning!

HERNAN: My name is Hernando Cortez. Call me Hernan.

MANUEL: Are you an explorer?

HERNAN: I am now. I'll be looking for land and riches.

MANUEL: Looking for gold or spice?

HERNAN: Gold.

MANUEL: Cortez borrowed gold from the Aztecs and never returned it.

FRANCISCO: No wonder Mexico is so poor.

MANUEL: Cortez started the tradition. *(They all agree.)* Now that I have all your attention, and I see that you're ready to accept me as your master of ceremonies, let me introduce my humble self to you. My name is —

PEPE: Manuel Felicitas. You're still an asshole. *(Laughs.)*

MANUEL: Pepe? Pepe. *(They hug.)* Is that you? Shingado. How old you look! And you've changed colors. You are now black. What has life done to you?

PEPE: Broken every bone in my body.

MANUEL: And mine, too. But I don't show it. Oh, the good times we had!

PEPE: I don't remember any.

MANUEL: The girls. The dancing. You remember. We only danced with beautiful women.

PEPE: Where?

MANUEL: How could you forget Chicago?

PEPE: I remember Chicago.

MANUEL: Remember when the pollacks chased me? They beat the shit out of me.

PEPE: Now why would they do that to a big mouth?

MANUEL: My mouth wasn't that big, then. Ah, you're beginning to remember.

PEPE: Well a little is coming back to me. But honestly, you had a very, big mouth.

MANUEL: But it took me places. It helped us get into the Aragon Ballroom. It was filled with beautiful girls ready to dance. I danced with all of them. I was able to kiss one, too. Then her boyfriend became very angry. I couldn't help it. I'm a Latin lover. You danced with her, too. Don't you remember? She was so big!

HERNAN: How big was she?

HUERO: Was she this big?

(Huero grabs Hernan's chest and demonstrates breasts.)

MANUEL: More than you can handle. She had big everything. Big eyes, big lips —
HERNAN: Big nose?
HUERO: Big feet?
HERNAN: Big ears?
MANUEL: No. A big —
PEPE: Oh, now I remember.
HUERO: A big what? What?
PEPE: The boyfriend beat you up for stealing his girlfriend. You ran very fast before he got you.
MANUEL: She couldn't help herself with me.
PEPE: You haven't changed. You're still as obnoxious as ever.
MANUEL: The women fought to dance with me.
PEPE: They fought to get away from you.
MANUEL: The women loved my profile.
PEPE: They liked the profile from behind when you left.
(*They all laugh.*)
MANUEL: Pepe, you have a sense of humor.
PEPE: No sense of humor. It was the truth.
MANUEL: (*Eyes Huero's pathetic pillowcase luggage.*) What's in your bag?
HUERO: Sunglasses, a bathing suit, suntan lotion, toilet paper, and dice.
MANUEL: DICE? I lost a woman with dice. She saw my number!
(*Train bells, then a big jolt. The men are thrown to the side. Pepe gets hurt from his fall. Hernan takes a look out of the boxcar.*)
HERNAN: They are reconnecting the cars. Why are they doing that? . . . Quiet. Someone's coming!
(*The men hug the walls and stay very quiet. Long silence.*)
(*Someone on the other side jiggles the boxcar door. Manuel takes a look then goes out. He returns later and closes the door. The door is then latched from outside.*)
MANUEL: He locked the door for our safety.
NOEL: ¿Quien?
MANUEL: El coyote. Don't worry. It's all right. He will open it again when we get further along. We made it this far. *We are in the United States!*
(*The train jerks forward. There is commotion outside the boxcar door as the train begins to move. The men sense that something went wrong, but are unsure what. They look at each other in silence. The train sounds take over.*)

SCENE THREE

Dim lights. The men are lying in pathetic positions on the boxcar floor. Luis rises from his sleep in a ghostlike manner.

LUIS: This must be a dream. Where am I? Am I in hell? Where have I been taken to this time? Oh, my God. Why are you putting me through this? This is a torture. And these men. Who are they? Why are they here? Why have you asked that I remain with them? What deed are you asking from me this time? If you must punish me, punish me with the familiar. What is your plan? Why do you send me like John the Baptist? I have no message. I have only confusion. I have only forced breath and no will to live. Even John the Baptist had a message. I only have fear. I only have death on my mind. I carry the pain of living. Why do you continue to push me toward life when all I know is that I should be seeing death?
(The Aztec Skull Dancer approaches.)
LUIS: *(Continues.)* There. That is more like it.
(They stare at each and circle around.)
LUIS: *(Continues.)* What is my mission? What is the horror that awaits me. You know that I've been waiting for the end. Let God take it, for suicide is not in good taste. Destroying a temple is always in poor judgment. Pleading and waiting for death is more admirable when one has sinned and wishes to caress the heavens, and thereby beg forgiveness from the one and true God . . . For this is what I wait for.
(The Skull Dancer disappears. Luis then takes his place with the men.)
LUIS: *(Continues.)* Then, so be it.
(Luis lies down and closes his eyes. Lights dim out.)

SCENE FOUR

Bill is resting on the ground. Roberto writes on his notepad, then reads a map.

BILL: *(Looks up and watches Roberto.)* What are you looking for?
ROBERTO: My heritage.
BILL: Your heritage? You can't find it. No one really can. It's a figment of the imagination. No one really cares that far back. I have no idea where I came from. Most people, I know, don't.
ROBERTO: I have an idea.

BILL: What's your last name?

ROBERTO: Muñoz.

BILL: That's where your idea came from. It's only an idea.

ROBERTO: A short break, Bill.

BILL: What? Shit. How 'bout you snoozing a bit? Look at your eyes. Aren't you a little bit tired? You don't sleep. That's why you're neurotic. Sleep is sleep. An important element of life.

ROBERTO: I keep having these dreams.

BILL: Wet dreams?

ROBERTO: You're an asshole, you know that. Never mind.

BILL: Alright, go on.

ROBERTO: I hear voices. I see places. I see faces that make me want to "tear up."

BILL: See a therapist.

ROBERTO: This is too complicated for a therapist. The answer is within me. And I'm too freaked out to find the key. Bill, what if we are doing something real wrong. I mean, look at who we are.

BILL: I know who I am. I'm a handsome cowboy.

ROBERTO: I'm serious. We got to find them.

BILL: Well, that's our job.

ROBERTO: But maybe we should let them go. We are just playing cat and mouse. If they see us in the forest, they go to the desert where there's no shade or water. If they see us on the road, they tie themselves under cars and drive by. They get killed hiding from us. If we weren't here, Bill, travesty wouldn't fall upon them.

BILL: That's their problem.

ROBERTO: Don't you feel anything?

BILL: There's a law about walking on someone's land without permission.

ROBERTO: And that's a rule that has been broken before.

BILL: Yeah. Like yesterday.

ROBERTO: Like 1492.

BILL: 1492? Columbus?

ROBERTO: And now, the same rule applies to . . . the new newcomers.

BILL: You're cracked. Problems have come —

ROBERTO: There's always a need to blame problems on the people with no voice.

BILL: They do things, Robert.

ROBERTO: When I see the face of a man with calluses on his hands, I know he's here to work.

BILL: It's getting out of control. There are Haitians who want to come in, too, but they can't. They have no skills.

ROBERTO: How do you know? Did you read that in the paper, or did you just guess that?

BILL: You are in need of sleep, real bad. I suggest you get it. Besides, this is our country and we have to take care of it, or it won't be any good for anyone.

ROBERTO: That has been said before. Take care of it, or it won't be good anymore. You know who said that? The Indians.

BILL: *(Trying to be politically correct.) Native Americans.*

ROBERTO: The Indians felt a need to protect the land. They were afraid that it wouldn't be good anymore if the white man traversed it. They've already proved careless by shooting all the buffalo.

BILL: Yeah, so what.

ROBERTO: And it happened. The land became worthless. Less hunting. The beauty became permanently scarred, the —

BILL: *(Overlapping on "scarred.")* I'm not going to listen to this shit, Robert.

ROBERTO: *Roberto.*

BILL: Since when?

ROBERTO: Don't call me Robert anymore. It's Roberto, my birth name.

BILL: Shit.

ROBERTO: And things have to change.

BILL: Lose your job why don't you.

ROBERTO: I propose accommodation. Here and now. Why not cut to the chase. Spare the ones who are doing what they have to in order to survive. Hang the greedy out to dry.

BILL: Who are the greedy?

ROBERTO: The ones who put up the wall. After the Indians were nearly annihilated.

BILL: Native Americans!

ROBERTO: Don't you see, the roles are reversed now. White men are the first illegals. They were doing the same thing for the same reasons. Just trying to fight hunger and improve their lives. Was it their fault they had to take the chance of going across a land that wasn't theirs? These majestic people had no concept of selling Mother Nature. You only borrowed, but some white men wanted to take. So the Indians fought to protect their borders. *They had a border patrol.* They sent the white people back! But they kept coming. You are proof of that. And when they wouldn't stop coming, they resorted to the last possible thing. War. I pity those white families, for they were only looking for a better life. What's wrong with that? What else was there to do? So they fought the Indians, probably screaming, "I HAVE NOTHING TO LOSE!" And they won. Don't you see, Bill? History is repeating itself. Now brown people are screaming the same thing, "I have nothing to lose." And, in a way, they already won. Desperate people can win. But at a price. They'll risk everything for the sake of a better life. For their families. For their future. And we are preventing them to the point of killing them.

BILL: COW DUNG.

ROBERTO: Bill, this land always gives improvements to newcomers.

BILL: That's it. *(Starts to exit.)*

ROBERTO: Come back when it's all soaked in. We'll talk about what to do.

BILL: You know, you're fucked!

ROBERTO: Maybe I am. But so are you.

BILL: Why are you talking like this?

ROBERTO: I have Aztec Indian blood. It's still North American Indian.

BILL: Native American.

(Bill exits. A meow of a cat. The Aztec Skull Dancer enters and faces Roberto.)

ROBERTO: There you are. My nightmare. Now you are bothering me in the day.

(The Skull Dancer gives Roberto a dead canary.)

ROBERTO: *(Continues.)* My grandfather loved canaries. He had cages lined up against his courtyard. I remember one bird that looked ill. I thought abuelito should see him. So my five-year-old legs took me and the cage up the stairs. Then the bird started to eat. His tail feathers poked out of the cage. I saw a cat staring at the bird from the top of the stairs. When I got there, he lunged at the bird's tail feathers and slammed it against the cage. He killed it. He killed it just like that . . . I opened the cage, and then . . . gave the bird to the cat. He devoured it as I was petting him.

(The Skull Dancer takes the dead bird and rips the head off. Then lights dim out on him.)

ROBERTO: *(Continues.)* Why do I help the predator?

(Fade out.)

SCENE FIVE

Fade in on Abuelita smiling and caressing a picture frame. Then fade out.

MANUEL: Beer. I need a beer, Pepe. Is Corona still your favorite?
PEPE: I don't drink anymore.
MANUEL: That's disgusting!
PEPE: Ulcers, compadre. The doctor said that one more beer will kill me.
MANUEL: That's not true. Beer is good for you. It's the drink of the Aztec gods. *(Luis turns over.)*
NOEL: Wake up that man over there. Why does he sleep so much? How many hours have gone by?
HERNAN: Three.
MANUEL: Wake him.
FRANCISCO: He's not bothering anyone.
MANUEL: But we haven't seen him up. *(Eyes Huero's blue jeans full of holes.)* What's wrong with your pants?
HUERO: I'm dressed like an American!
MANUEL: Too many holes.
HUERO: Americans like holes.
MANUEL: How many of you think he's dressed like an American?
NOEL: It depends . . . on the style, the comfort and the poise. He can dress like that, and if he is content, and feels comfortable, he does look like an American.
MANUEL: *(Sarcastic.)* How profound.
HERNAN: He's right.
HUERO: I've been dressed like this all my life. So maybe I'm Americano at heart and going to the right place.
HERNAN: You know, you remind me of someone.
PEPE: He reminds me of my son.
MANUEL: Number nine or number twelve?
PEPE: Number five.
HERNAN: He was dazzled by the stories of fortune in the United States.
MANUEL: Ah, fortune.
PEPE: What fortune?
MANUEL: The fortune you missed out on because you are stupid.
PEPE: I'm not stupid. You're stupid.
HERNAN: Can I tell the story? Okay, this friend was so impressed with the stories of fortune, that he climbed the fence.

HUERO: Which fence?

HERNAN: The fence which divides both countries.

HUERO: Oh, I knew that.

HERNAN: Then he would run as fast as he could to the river.

HUERO: Aye, a real wetback.

HERNAN: He would take off his pants and hold it above his head and —

HUERO: Oh, a partial wetback.

HERNAN: Please . . . Well, he did this for years.

HUERO: We can relate to that story, but how boring.

HERNAN: Here is where it's different. One day he was caught. La migra looked up his record, and right there in the computer, right there in the screen, they found out he was an American citizen! He just assumed he was like us, crossing back and forth when needed.

HUERO: Ah, come on! Why didn't his mother tell him?

HERNAN: She was dead.

HUERO: His father, then?

HERNAN: He was a stepfather. How would he know?

HUERO: Ah, what an unbelievable story.

HERNAN: It happened! It might be a story about you, if you didn't know your beginnings.

HUERO: Never! Despite this coloring of mine, I know that I'm a Mexicano. I don't need to check the computer.

(Huero takes off his shirt and pulls out the label.)

HUERO: *(Continues.)* It's right here: *Hecho en Mexico.* So that's proof I'm made in Mexico.

(They laugh.)

NOEL: *(Looks around and holds his groin area.)* What do you do if you need to go to the rest room? I mean, in here.

MANUEL: Oh, my friend. It's very simple.

(Manuel takes an empty soda bottle and pretends to urinate in it.)

MANUEL: *(Continues.)* And remember, one size fits all. In your case, you'd be swimming in it.

NOEL: I would not.

HUERO: I need a bigger bottle.

HERNAN: I need a barrel.

PEPE: No barrels.

(Noel takes the coke bottle and walks to the corner when Blackout.)

SCENE SIX

Luis rises from his sleep in a ghostlike manner. He sees the men in the boxcar.

LUIS: Look at these men. Optimistic, aren't they? Maybe not this one. *(Motions to Francisco.)* Aren't you glad you are not one of them? Yes, I know you've read the papers and the excesses has become a blur to you now. You say, "We all have problems." Sure. And if you have even bigger problems than these men, my sentiments are with you. And do accept my apology for bringing the matter up. Then just look briefly, and redirect your attention to your more important issues. It's your right. *(Motions to Noel.)* This one here. See him? Hasn't even lived. Pity.

(Huero and Hernan play dice as Noel watches and then joins in.)

LUIS: You've seen them clear your table. You've heard them laughing in the kitchens. You've seen them wait in the corners for work. Even selling oranges in parking lots. They want to be like you. If you think real hard, you'll notice that this situation is bad for you, too. And like everything, you won't notice until it's too late. There will be complaints, panel discussions, research, but it will all be too late . . . Much sadness makes the world go 'round.

(Luis walks to Francisco. Francisco militantly faces out.)

LUIS: State your sadness.

FRANCISCO: No.

LUIS: State your name, then.

FRANCISCO: Frankie.

LUIS: *Frankie* in the United States?

FRANCISCO: It's the name I chose.

LUIS: Explain your sorrow.

FRANCISCO: No.

LUIS: Francisco, no one but your subconscious will hear it.

FRANCISCO: I know that.

LUIS: Then?

FRANCISCO: I don't want to be reminded. What good does it do? If I think about it, I become bitter. If I think of how I hurt, I'll hurt more. It only becomes a waste of time.

LUIS: Then I'm sorry.

FRANCISCO: What good can come of it? If it is a confession you want, that is impossible. No more confessions. When I was born I was forced to confess.

My mother walked in labor from Mexico to the United States to give me a better life. For the effort, she died in her own blood. *For this* I had to confess to *her mother.* She never forgave me for killing her daughter. I was just a newborn. And all for what? An old woman found me next to my dead mother. She took me to my mother's family *back across the border.* Why couldn't she have left this shivering baby in the cold until I was picked up by the American authorities and given citizenship? That's what my mother died for.

LUIS: Then you wouldn't have suffered?

FRANCISCO: I would have suffered, but not so much.

HERNAN: This is lame! Why would you prefer to be raised in the United States? Human life isn't appreciated. At the border, when a hungry family is crossing the highway, people run over them on purpose, to prevent them from arriving!

LUIS: Do you want to speak?

HERNAN: We all know about this.

LUIS: Then why have you come forward?

HERNAN: Out of necessity.

LUIS: This is a dream, Hernan. Go on.

HERNAN: Why should I?

LUIS: To relieve the tension.

HERNAN: But it never leaves me.

PEPE: Nor me.

FRANCISCO: Luis, you're up to your old tricks again. Look what you are doing to all of us.

LUIS: If there is but one of you who wants to relieve anguish, then speak now.

HERNAN: I can understand the Americans not wanting us to come. But my own people behave the same way. Why do they resent us in sharing what they already have?

FRANCISCO: They're not your own people. They are wearing an American suit.

HERNAN: And one is my own cousin. He doesn't speak Spanish, but he does communicate his hate to me. While I visited my uncle and aunt, he took me to a field near the border. His friends were dressed like Rambo. They rounded crossers and verbally tortured them. They threatened them with "la migra." An old man had tears in his eyes as they pushed him to the ground. He feared the border patrol, but what a hell to be treated like an animal by an American teenager . . . That's it. I can't speak anymore. *(Hernan goes to the corner of the boxcar. The Skull Dancer appears.)*

LUIS: What more must I do to appease you?

(The Skull Dancer takes off his mask. His face is completely black. He places the mask on Luis. Luis wears it for a moment, then flings the mask off. It breaks into pieces — same crash sound as in the prologue. Luis lies down and closes his eyes. Dim to blackout.)

SCENE SEVEN

Temperature ninety degrees. Manuel is pretending to drink a beer. He takes a sip, savors it, and then wipes his mouth.

NOEL: Excuse me.
MANUEL: Yes?
NOEL: May I ask you something?
MANUEL: Yes.
NOEL: What are you doing?
MANUEL: Can't you see? I'm drinking beer.
NOEL: There's no beer in your hand.
MANUEL: Oh my God! Who took my beer? Well, that's life, isn't it. Pepe, you buy me a beer later.
PEPE: Get a job.
MANUEL: I will. Are you going to work in the fields?
PEPE: Maybe.
MANUEL: Ah, maybe me too.
PEPE: If I remember correctly, the women worked harder in the fields than you.
MANUEL: *You remember only certain things.* I'll work making mattresses. Making someone else comfortable is a pleasure for me.
NOEL: What other jobs are available?
MANUEL: Many. You find two or three to make enough money. When Pepe was stronger, he worked in the fields. Then in the evenings he would work in the restaurant cleaning tables.
PEPE: What do you want me to do? I had eight kids to feed.
MANUEL: You should have stopped porking her.
PEPE: *Shut up.*
MANUEL: Let's dance. Get up and dance with me you old man.
HUERO: I'll dance with you, but you better not call me a queer.
MANUEL: Huerito, you're a joker like me. I'll give you one advice that has been a blessing to me. Get a woman who will laugh at your jokes. Because no

matter how bad they are, she'll make you feel good. But don't get a wife like Pepe.

PEPE: My family is important to me. It's all I have that matters. I wouldn't be here if they didn't matter.

MANUEL: It's unfortunate that we leave the only thing that does matter. If we bring our children here, they turn into *Chicanos*. Hijo, they are worse than gringos.

(Manuel continues teasing Pepe. Hernan walks away and sits in a corner.)

HUERO: What's the matter with you?

HERNAN: I think it's the heat.

HUERO: It's not that bad.

HERNAN: Why has the train been going so slow? Look at how wet my hair is from the sweat.

HUERO: At least your hair isn't purple and sticking up. That's how my hair was last year. I was trying to look American, but then, no one wanted to give me a job. And I'm a man who does anything to get a job. I have to. I need to send money to my mother and sisters. She said I can stop when I get married and have to provide for my own.

HERNAN: When are you planning to get married?

HUERO: I'll give you the answer when I find myself a woman.

MANUEL: Big breast are the best, Huerinche.

HUERO: And small ones, too. Or any for that matter.

(The Skull Dancer appears. The occupants only sense the Skull Dancer. Suddenly the mood gets very dark.)

HUERO: *(Continues.)* What's the matter?

HERNAN: You know, I've crossed three times, but after the first, I quit for a long while.

HUERO: Where did you cross?

HERNAN: I crossed at the Texas border.

HUERO: Me, too.

HERNAN: And I got the shit beat out of me there.

HUERO: Oh, not me.

HERNAN: And that is why I stopped. I was very confused after that. They were people like me who did it.

HUERO: ¿Waddas?

HERNAN: Sons or grandsons of waddas. Latinos. Hispanos, Chicanos, or whatever they call themselves. People who were born here. Manuel is right. When you have children in the United States, something happens to them.

HUERO: But why beat you up?

FRANCISCO: Maybe they were just warning you, or just getting you used to what you should expect in the United States.
MANUEL: You all are too negative. *(To Noel.)* Innocent one. Stop listening to these men. They are filling you with lies. I always return to my family with pockets lined with money. I then buy them clothes, shoes, toys, whatever. I feel like a real man, until the money runs out. Of course, this wasn't my life in the old days. I was a butcher in my own shop. My wife would visit me every afternoon with a basket of bread and fruit. *(Pause.)* She was so beautiful.
PEPE: She's ugly now?
MANUEL: I wish she was. Then, I wouldn't miss her so much. I thought by now she'd have no teeth and hair coming out of her ears like her mother, but she still looks the same. Waist this size . . . You know, I wish I didn't have to leave.
PEPE: I, too, had to leave a beautiful family.
MANUEL: Your family is ugly, Pepe.

(All laugh.)

PEPE: *(To Huero.)* Here's a dollar. Kick his ass.
HUERO: You two together, are very funny.
PEPE: Us two together, have sad stories to hide.
HERNAN: And me, by myself, can't stop thinking about all this.
HUERO: Just stop.
HERNAN: I wish I could, but I can't. I don't know why I can't.

(The Skull Dancer appears momentarily behind Hernan. Hernan turns around quickly, but he's gone. Blackout.)

SCENE EIGHT

Canaries singing. Abuelita is making tortillas.

ROBERTO: *(Child-like.)* ¿Abuelita?
ABUELITA: ¿Si? *(Sees that Roberto wants nothing and smiles.)* ¿Tienes hambre Beto?
ROBERTO: *(Teasing.)* ¿Que?
ABUELITA: Are you hungry, mijo?
ROBERTO: Si.
ABUELITA: *(Pause.)* You are lucky.
ROBERTO: I'm not lucky.
ABUELITA: You're an American.

(Lights dim on her and we hear an eerie echo of "Eres Americano, eres Americano." Roberto is left with a tortilla. He eats it. Fade into Francisco. Francisco is staring into the face of the Skull Dancer. Luis is behind him.)

FRANCISCO: The poisons burn your eyes, and your hands. One time I asked why some of us were getting sick. One woman was temporarily paralyzed. They *put poisons on the fields from the air.* The plane flies over at night, spraying a mist of death. The sweet smell is supposed to kill bugs. I told the mothers not to work when they were pregnant. They told *them* what I was saying. The boss chased me through the fields. The next thing I knew, I woke up in a bus with other illegals. I was deported.

(The Skull Dancer provokes Francisco. He then lunges at him and Luis restrains him.)

FRANCISCO: *(Continues.)* Why do you want me to un-bury these things? I'm very careful now. I watch and listen, but now I don't react. I don't complain. You see, I want to eat.

(Skull Dancer turns away. Luis and Francisco lie down to sleep. Fade into Noel.)

NOEL: My university had Americans that never spoke of this. They praised and faulted the United States. It's this honesty I admire.

HERNAN: You're hiding in a boxcar. Doesn't that tell you something?

NOEL: That it's difficult to get in the proper way. This was recommended.

PEPE: Noel. When you get across, you'll be just like us.

MANUEL: But he's not a Mexican. Cubans, and Puerto Ricans have it much better. He's from El Salvador. Maybe he'll be treated better.

HUERO: I think we all get treated the same. Doesn't matter what nationality you are. They lump us together and say "DIRTY MEXICAN" or "LAZY MEXICAN . . ." Well, it does have a nice ring to it.

NOEL: I met these exchange students. They told me to drop by if ever I'm in the United States.

MANUEL: See! He's going to be treated better already. He knows some rich Americans.

HERNAN: I can imagine where they live. A big house.

HUERO: A big car.

PEPE: A big paycheck.

NOEL: *(Sensing their desire.)* Come with me. All of you.

PEPE: And they see wetbacks in the front yard? They'll call the police.

HERNAN: It's not a good idea, Noel.

HUERO: Why not?

HERNAN: If we are by chance treated well, we'd get used to it.

HUERO: Oh, yeah. And that's not good for us.

NOEL: Why is that bad?

HUERO: Because we may never feel it again. That, my friend, will make it hurt more.

(Cross Fade to the Skull Dancer watching Francisco. Francisco wakes up and faces the Skull Dancer.)

FRANCISCO: How much longer must we endure this?

(The Skull Dancer looks at his watch. Blackout.)

SCENE NINE

Temperature ninety-six degrees. Huero is standing in an eerie spotlight. Hernan is behind him. Roberto is on the other side with Bill behind him. The Skull Dancer is wearing a sombrero and poncho, and sitting on the floor watching the action.

HUERO: I want to buy a beautiful house for my mother. Instead of *she* being a servant, she'll have her own servant. She'll have her nails and hair done, at least every six months. And men will respect my sisters . . . We live in a house made of cardboard and whatever I can find. Sometimes, they steal the sheet of tin we use as a roof. I find the clothes I wear in the dump. My mother would be so happy and proud in a real house. Even a tiny house would do . . . Then, then, I'll buy myself a car.

HERNAN: What kind of car?

HUERO: One with a motor. *(Long movement. To Roberto.)* Well, What are you waiting for?

ROBERTO: What do you mean?

HUERO: Are you going to find us and take us away?

ROBERTO: I have already taken many of you.

HUERO: Are you coming for us now?

BILL: Robert, you're not getting soft, are you?

(Huero and Hernan fade away.)

BILL: Arrest them Robert.

ROBERTO: Roberto. My name is Roberto Muñoz.

(Lights dim on Bill. Lights on Roberto.)

ROBERTO: Who's out there? Hello. Show yourself. I know you're out there.

(Roberto strains to see. Then turns quickly.)

ROBERTO: Goddamn it, Bill. If you're playing tricks on me.

(Roberto hears another sound.)
ROBERTO: Fuck you, Bill.
(Another sound. The Skull Dancer is making the sounds.)
ROBERTO: That's enough. I order you to stop it. Who's out there? Hello? Hey! Show yourself! Immigration! Hey! I said *show yourself!*
(The Skull Dancer stands up.)
ROBERTO: It's me. It's me. Why am I wearing those clothes? What's wrong with my face? *(Pause.)* ¿Quien eres? Who are you? Control, control. I've got to control myself. It's the job. It's the work. This is a dream.
(Shadows of people passing Roberto. These could be the men in the boxcar walking in place in slow motion in a dim light.)
ROBERTO: *(Continues.)* Stop! Where are you going? All of you STOP! There's too many. Tio. Tia. Hey, uncle John. Abuelita. Hey, you guys. Where are you going? Para donde van? Wait a minute. You can't cross. I'm sorry, but you just can't . . . Don't look at me like that. You got to understand. I know you're hungry. I know you need a job, tio Juan. *I'm not lucky.* I'm not that well off. Go back. Go back. You have to because . . . I don't know why . . . I don't know why.
(The Aztec Skull Dancer walks up to Roberto and circles around him. Roberto breaks down and falls to the floor. The "undocumented workers," or shadows, surround Roberto. Roberto screams out in agony when he sees his grandmother, Abuelita, is among them. Blackout.)

SCENE TEN

Six hours later. The boxcar occupants have removed much of their clothing.

MANUEL: Pepe . . . Pepe. *(Pepe doesn't answer.)* Pepe . . . Pepe.
PEPE: *(Shakes himself awake.)* ¿Que hombre? What?
MANUEL: Go to sleep. *(Laughs.)*
PEPE: *(Annoyed.)* Stop that. You keep doing that.
MANUEL: You keep falling for it, sonso.
(They both close their eyes. There is silence as all nap. Luis wakes up. Noel sees him.)
NOEL: You are awake now.
LUIS: Yes.
NOEL: Why did you sleep so long?
LUIS: Why should I be awake?

NOEL: Who are you?

LUIS: A broken man. And you?

NOEL: Barely a man.

LUIS: What a pity. Are you afraid?

NOEL: A little.

(The sound of train wheels. Then the train jerks to one side. The rest wake up. Then it jerks to the other side. Silence.)

HUERO: Something's happened. We've been inching along for hours and now this?

HERNAN: Open the door.

FRANCISCO: It's locked, tarugo!

HERNAN: Try, anyway.

MANUEL: No. If "la migra" is out there, that's it.

HERNAN: Open the door!

HUERO: It won't open.

HERNAN: Try something else.

NOEL: Do something.

LUIS: *(With no tone of fear.)* Why? There's no escape. Haven't you seen the signs?

HUERO: Why do you talk like this?

HERNAN: What do you know?

LUIS: I know nothing.

HUERO: Why are we stopped here?

LUIS: Isn't it obvious?

HUERO: We were supposed to stop earlier and be let out. After the hills.

NOEL: Is that what he said? Then what's happening? Why have we stopped?

LUIS: We've stopped because the wheels are not turning.

HERNAN: That's not what he meant!

FRANCISCO: Leave him alone.

HERNAN: Why have you done this to us?

LUIS: I've done nothing. Except lie here in my sweat hoping to see God. But all I see is a saint in Aztec clothing.

HUERO: If you hadn't brought him here, we'd be off already.

HERNAN: Don't blame me!

(Huero pushes Hernan.)

HUERO: You brought a curse to us.

FRANCISCO: Stop it you two.

HUERO: He's the devil!

FRANCISCO: No, he isn't.

LUIS: Yes, I am.

HUERO: He admits it.
FRANCISCO: He's a man like us.
LUIS: I'm worse than that.
PEPE: It's very hot in here. Sit down.
HUERO: I want to know why he cursed us.
FRANCISCO: He didn't curse you.
LUIS: *(Interrupting.)* Francisco, let them. My life is worth nothing. Let them tear me apart if that will make them feel better.
HERNAN: Why did you come to the train depot so I can find you?
LUIS: Just that this time, my legs brought me there. Sometimes they take me to good places, other times not so good. Today it brought me here with you.
HERNAN: He's crazy.
FRANCISCO: Leave him alone. He was a man of God, for Christ's sake!
HUERO: What?
PEPE: *(Amazed.)* Aye Dios mio. A priest?
LUIS: Not anymore. And for that I am now being punished.
PEPE: *(Amazed.)* You've fallen?
LUIS: Yes.
HERNAN: I don't want to be punished with him. This is supposed to be his hell then, not ours.
HUERO: Let's kill him to save ourselves!
FRANCISCO: You are the ones who are crazy! Stop getting hysterical!
HERNAN: I can hardly breath. We're hallucinating. I'm remembering horrible things in my life. When this happens, it means you're going to die. I don't want to die! I don't want to die!
HUERO: He brought a curse!
HERNAN: It's my fault, so I'll kill him.
PEPE: *NO!*
HERNAN: *So we* can live, Pepe!
PEPE: *(To Hernan.)* You did us a favor, my boy. A very big favor. You brought us someone to give us our last rites.
(All the characters look at each other in horror. Lights dim out slowly to darkness. Aztec music — or Native American music — and country music is heard at the same time. Blackout.)

END OF ACT I

ACT II
SCENE ONE

Darkness. Roberto is aiming a flashlight down a deep hole. Bill is behind him drinking a Diet Pepsi. Both are sweating.

BILL: Could be cyanide down in that big hole. In the mining days, they used to take a bird down with 'em. The bird would just sit there, acting all pretty, chirping away. They'd take a look at the bird from time to time. See, birds are sensitive. They have little lungs, and well, if cyanide was seeping through, the bird would croak first. Then, they'd get the hell out of there . . . You know, this tastes like shit when it's warm. No wonder the mice get cancer . . . Can we quit, Robert? Gotta do something for the kid. Birthday party. I promised my wife I'd get the party shit for her . . . You know how my wife gets when I don't do stuff for her . . . Well, look at the time. If I don't get going, I'll have to blame it on you and she's not goin' to invite you to dinner again. *(Pause.)* Don't give me that look of *how she likes you better than me.* You're not married to her. You don't know what it's like to be with her day after day. Was okay at the beginning, but now the nagging. Stop being friendly with her. She expects me to treat her like that. It's beyond my nature to be sweet. *(Impatient pause.)* If I leave now, I'll catch *People's Court.* I like that show. Shows the American justice system in action . . . Robert . . . Roberto. *(No answer.)* Shit. Ever since you found those wetbacks —
(Roberto stiffens.)

BILL: All right. *Undocumented workers.* Trying to give dignity in a term? *(Pause.)* Ever since you found 'em we've been busting our ass.
(Roberto picks up some dirt and starts rubbing his face with it.)

BILL: Dried out and leathery. Fifth time this year. There are too many. It bothers you, huh? I know how you're feeling. I've felt that way, too. I get all emotional, too. Dads, sons, and grandfathers trying to get work. Even the women and children. It makes your heart sink when you see them like that. You know, when it's too late. But that's our job. Catch them like that or catch them alive. I prefer ALIVE, Roberto. I really do. Hell, I have a family. I know what it's like to have to put food on the table.
(Roberto picks up some grass and twigs and starts pushing it through his hair.)

BILL: It does bother me. I feel their hopelessness when I have to take them to the van.

(Roberto looks at him for a moment.)

BILL: It's true. I feel bad. Okay, I have to admit sometimes I don't care 'cause look what's happening to this country. I'm worried about it. You know I have kids, and I want 'em to live in a good place. I don't mind the good ones coming in, but the bad ones I have a problem with. They make it harder on everyone. They are putting graffiti everywhere and, well, I don't like it when they can't talk in simple English. If they want to stay, they have to learn it.

(Roberto opens his shirt and rubs the cow dung on himself.)

BILL: The ladies, are pretty, but they have to go back, too. if they are going to go on welfare, I have to put my foot down. I know you've told me that most don't do that. That they work the jobs that nobody wants, and don't care if they get paid a few dollars an hour, but come on Robert. One that does it is enough. It's a drain on the economy. There's already too many fat lazy Americans sucking the system dry. Can't have any outsiders doing the same.

(Roberto takes some more dirt and cakes it onto the dung that's stuck on his body.)

BILL: It's a crime when they push their children through the fence to run across. The schools are getting filled up with too many foreigners. What's to become of our children's education? They'll get short-changed. They do Robert, they do. Not enough for everyone, anymore. Some of them do okay in keeping their house nice, but tell me why some make their homes look like trash heaps? I know you said they get paid so badly they can barely cover food and rent, but come on Robert. That doesn't hold water.

(Roberto takes a whip and starts hitting himself with it.)

BILL: Robert. Are you listening? Rober-TOE. *(Pause.)* What? They look too much like your relatives, or something.

(Roberto freezes.)

BILL: Wish I knew what was bothering you. You depress me. My time clock's on overtime, Robert. Roberto. *(Pause.)* I'm going into town, anyway. Do you want me to bring you anything? How about a taco?

(Roberto looks at him.)

BILL: *(Realizing he insulted Roberto.)* I didn't mean it that way. Geesh. Too damn sensitive, like my wife. Well, I'm going into town. What do you want, Robert? What do you want?

(Cross fade quickly to boxcar.)

SCENE TWO

Temperature one hundred and nine degrees.

NOEL: What time is it?
HERNAN: There's sweat inside my watch.
   (Pepe is breathing loudly.)
NOEL: Where is el coyote?
LUIS: There is no movement. The soul is still. The thorns are prickling my feet. I've never noticed my feet until now. They are funny pieces of flesh. The toes extend outward, except this one. This one leans in. The toes are separate so you may walk with ease. The toes separate as it touches the ground, then spread more to finish the step. Then they press together until the next step.
NOEL: We can't just sit and wait. Huero. Stack up the crates and look for something up there.
HUERO: Like what?
NOEL: A door.
HERNAN: Wishful thinking.
HUERO: Why is he telling me what to do?
NOEL: Do it!
HUERO: *(While stacking up the crates.)* I already looked for an opening. We all did. There is nothing.
NOEL: Look again.
HUERO: All right.
   (Huero examines the ceiling. Then he holds out his arm as if he was holding on to a torch.)
HUERO: *(Continues.)* Look, I'm the statue of liberty.
NOEL: Stop it! Be serious.
HUERO: You sound like my mother. We have to liven things up, Noel. What's left?
NOEL: Get down and let me look.
HUERO: What if I say no?
   (They start shoving each other. Manuel stops them.)
MANUEL: Relax. El coyote will come. I know he will. The coyote has never failed me. He gets me across each time, with few problems. And each time I make money and go home to my wife and children.
FRANCISCO: A su India.
MANUEL: Si, mi India. My beautiful Indian wife with the soft eyes and hair.

Long eyelashes to match her silky straight hair. She's from the mountains. One of the few places the Spaniards missed. She is pure Indian, and I love her very much. She speaks very quietly, but she laughs loudly. She even says some ancient words of her ancestors. I ask her if she is speaking Nahuatl, the language of the Aztecs, but she smiles shyly. Her words are not from the Aztecs. They are of another language. Even the best anthropologists cannot truly decipher the entire language completely. It's her practical joke to me. She is good to me and I am good to her except when I leave.

FRANCISCO: How did you marry a true India if they are forbidden from mixing?

MANUEL: Her family saw how happy we both were together. They'd come from the mountains to sell goods on Sunday. I worked in a shop next to the mercado. After witnessing our great affection for one another, they finally told her to go with me. But it would mean that she can never go back. It was a tearful, yet happy event. Her family was supposed to kill her for going off with me. *This is customary when the indigenous falls in love with an intruder. They are trying to save what's left of their race.* Instead, they told everyone she fell from a high cliff. They even conducted a funeral at the ledge where they said she fell. We watched from across the valley. There was a procession, then the funeral. We imagined it was our wedding. We wept, and laughed at the same time. They left after throwing flowers over the cliff. We then kissed and walked to our future.

(*Long silence.*)

MANUEL: Well, let's sit quietly to conserve the air.

PEPE: Compadre. I feel terrible.

MANUEL: You'll be fine.

HERNAN: It's been eight hours.

PEPE: Eight were in the barrels. Should I have gone to find him?

NOEL: I don't know.

PEPE: He's in the desert. He's there.

MANUEL: You're wrong. He got out.

PEPE: He's dying in a can. Suffocating.

MANUEL: He's fine. You are fine. We all will be fine if we wait quietly. That's the trick. To wait quietly. Come on, don't be babies. What happened to the jobs? Eh? I thought you all wanted jobs.

HUERO: Of course, we do.

MANUEL: Then relax. Hernan, so much work in the United States.

HERNAN: That's why I go there.

MANUEL: Just sit down, and wait. Yes?

PEPE: Maybe at this time, we should confess our sins.

MANUEL: No. If we do that, we'll be knocking on the door of death. I forbid you all from talking to the devil.

PEPE: I think we should reflect on our lives. So you can leave with a certain amount of peace. The questions you've carried all your life gets answered the moment before you die.

MANUEL: Reflect yourself.

FRANCISCO: We're going to suffer the same fate as those Salvadorians.

NOEL: The Salvadorians?

MANUEL: *(Pissed.)* Let one stay innocent.

FRANCISCO: They walked in a line, holding everything they owned. The journey was long. They kept going until they found themselves nowhere.

MANUEL: No!

FRANCISCO: Then, we try again. *(Motions to Huero to assist.)*

HUERO: We are locked in from the outside.

MANUEL: We wait a little longer.

FRANCISCO: We cannot sit here doing nothing. If I cannot pray for death, then let me fight for life.

HUERO: Maybe the coyote was held up somewhere. What was the plan?

MANUEL: The plan was to hide us in here. Then when we passed the hills he meets us and unlocks the door.

NOEL: Then where is he?

MANUEL: I don't know.

NOEL: It's driving me crazy to be here.

PEPE: *(Delirious and looking at Noel.)* I used to have a face like him.

MANUEL: No, you didn't.

PEPE: Yes, I did. The face of innocence. It was at the very first time I came across. Oh, how lonely I was. I cried for my mother. I cried for my father. I cried for all my brothers. And I cried for Mexico, because of the state it was in. I came looking for the utopia. That's what they told me was here. Then, I saw my first Americans. They didn't live in big houses. They didn't drive big cars. They were paying for food with tickets. It scared me to see them at the mission waiting for food. I couldn't get into the line. I just couldn't. I didn't come for that. I didn't care if I was starving, I just couldn't get into the line. I came because of the good stories. The good jobs. But no one told me the other side of the story. I saw these Americans wandering around poor and hungry. Carrying all their possessions in a push cart. And I thought, *son Americanos.* If they're like this, then, what's going to happen to us?

FRANCISCO: Nothing, absolutely nothing.

NOEL: No! You say things I would never believe —

FRANCISCO: Who's going to tell you the truth?

NOEL: I heard —

PEPE: We heard, too.

NOEL: I was hoping —

FRANCISCO: That things would be different for you? Maybe.

NOEL: What will I really see?

FRANCISCO: You'll see what you want to see. That's being American.

HUERO: That's why you came. To become an "American" like your school friends.

NOEL: No. I didn't come for that. I didn't come for that.

(Bill, Abuelita, the Skull Dancer and Roberto are in different lights in the background.)

HERNAN: *(Overlapping on "you.")* Then why did you come?

BILL: *(Overlapping on "you.")* Then why did you come?

ABUELITA: *(Overlapping on "you.")* Then why did you come?

ROBERTO: *(Overlapping on "you.")* Then why did you come?

(Lights on Noel and the Skull Dancer.)

NOEL: I was in grave danger. You know the conditions in El Salvador. The problems, the war. The many innocent people that are killed. My father was a newspaper man. When he knew something, he wrote about it. He wrote it even with the threats. He had evidence of the military's involvement in the disappearances, and the violations of human rights, and he wrote it. He wrote it all. He had to tell the people. He had to let the world know. Then, a bomb in the editor's office ended his life. And that was it. I tried to find out who took my father away from me. I searched all his possessions, for some information. That was when I started being followed. My mother decided I had to leave before they took my life, as well. You see, she felt I was too young to get involved in the politics of the country. I am only sixteen, but I am big for my age. Don't you agree?

(The Skull Dancer nods his head yes.)

NOEL: *(Continues.)* Then are you going to spare me? I am only sixteen.

(Blackout.)

SCENE THREE

In the blackout, Roberto enters from the audience with a flashlight. He then turns the flashlight to his face. His face is painted to resemble a skull.

ROBERTO: *(Not himself.)* I found you. I found you hiding. Where do you think you're going? You're going nowhere, buddy. You know you're going nowhere. I don't even have to tell you. You already know . . . Don't hide in there. Don't change your clothes, your voice, or that look in your eyes. I know who you are. You are a goddamn Mexican. That's right. One of those stinking beaners that try so hard to fit in. To get part of the American pie. Well, there's none for you. No matter how hard you try. Someone is going to get you. Someone is going to find out who you are, and remind you, "You're *nothin.*" DO YOU HEAR ME, BOY!? FIGHT FOR YOUR COUNTRY. GET TO THE JUNGLES AND FIGHT LIKE A MAN. YOU'RE AN AMERICAN! NOT A CHICANO, OR A GODDAMN MEXICAN. And don't call yourself a LATINO! You're not a Roman, either. You're an American. That's what your parents wanted . . . That's what your grandfather wanted. *(Roberto turns around and searches behind him. Losing it.)* I know what you're doing to me. I know what you're doing to me. *(Roberto turns the flashlight toward the audience, then turns it off. Sound: Coyote howl.)*

SCENE FOUR

Temperature one hundred and twenty-three degrees. Twelve hours later. Huero and Hernan play a quiet game of dice. Pepe is near them with his eyes closed.

HERNAN: Te gane.
(Huero has no more money to play. He then reaches over to the sleeping Pepe's pocket. As he gestures that he is only going to borrow some cash, Pepe grabs his hand.)
PEPE: If I was younger, I would kick the shit out of you. Here! Take it and know you took an old man's lunch.
HUERO: I didn't take an old man's lunch. He gave it to me.
PEPE: You took an old man's lunch to gamble. Admit it.
HUERO: Admit it? If I do, can I keep the money as a gift?
PEPE: Crafty son of a bitch.

HUERO: I'm playing. I'll win it all back and I'll pay you with interest.

PEPE: Aren't you sick of gambling?

HUERO: We're doing it to pass the time, viejo. Play with us, then.

PEPE: If you lose it, you pay me back when you get your dish-washing job.

HUERO: I've done that.

PEPE: I bet you have.

HUERO: It's not that bad. It's like heaven. The dish soap are like clouds. The waitresses that drift by are angels. I'm in heaven with water all over me. The front of my shirt gets completely wet. I become a wet-front . . . Noel, we need more players. Let Hernan and me take your money.

PEPE: Just take it out of their pocket.

NOEL: I rather not play.

HUERO: Suit yourself.

NOEL: *(Long pause.)* You do nothing but watch us. It's making some of us nervous. Sleep again, Padre.

LUIS: I dream too much when I do. I start to see things I don't want to see. Then I tell myself what will happen *will happen*.

NOEL: Is being fatalistic a trait of the priesthood?

LUIS: Yes. It's the best thing I learned.

NOEL: Even your own humor doesn't amuse you. What made you leave the church?

LUIS: My advice is to sit, and wait for whatever.

NOEL: I am sitting. And I am waiting. And I'm beginning to see what will happen. Yet, I still have questions in my mind and believe it or not, I still have hope. So I sit here with my hope, and I go back in my mind and remember the things you all have talked about. These men have implied that I have been idealistic, and naïve. But being here and watching all of you, I feel I've grown. But what of it now? Will I be able to exercise what I've learned? We've tried several times to get out and each time the fear grips us more, and the temperature rises. Then I sit here and think of all my sins and I am saddened that I don't have enough to occupy my time. So I think of what you all have said, and I have questions.

LUIS: What questions do you have?

NOEL: First, what happened to those people?

LUIS: The Salvadorians?

NOEL: Yes. They're from my country, I should know.

LUIS: You are much too young to know about it

NOEL: Haven't you heard what I said? I've aged in here. This box is taking away my youth. I left El Salvador to keep my youth, but it's gone already. Too

late, isn't it. For a sixteen-year-old, I've lived in grave danger without realizing it.
FRANCISCO: So do we.
NOEL: I was almost killed.
FRANCISCO: When I was born, I was almost killed.
NOEL: They were after me in San Salvador where I lived.
FRANCISCO: Who's after you?
NOEL: The government.
FRANCISCO: What did you do? Get bad grades?
NOEL: *NO!*
FRANCISCO: Well, relax. They won't find you now. You're stuck in a boxcar.
(Noel goes to the door again and hits the door.)
PEPE: I'm very thirsty.
MANUEL: You've been thirsty before.
PEPE: Not like this.
MANUEL: It won't be long now. The cerveza is coming real soon. We'll be dancing in Chicago before you know it.
PEPE: That's good. *(Dry heaving cough, then stares at Manuel.)*
MANUEL: Maybe he fell after locking the car. It started rather suddenly, remember? Maybe he got into an accident and couldn't reach us.
HUERO: *(Annoyed with Luis' staring.)* Stop looking at me! In my town, you are scum for falling away from Christ.
LUIS: I'm still a believer.
HUERO: Not in my family.
LUIS: Where is your sister?
HUERO: Sister? . . . Which one? The pretty one, or the not-so-pretty one?
LUIS: She looks like you, doesn't she?
HUERO: Ah, then it is the pretty one.
LUIS: She has two moles on her cheek, very close together. She's very beautiful.
HUERO: How did you know?
LUIS: When did you see her last?
HUERO: She's in San Fernando. A town in California.
LUIS: She is?
HUERO: *Yes, she is.*
LUIS: When did you last see her?
HUERO: Why are you asking me these questions?
LUIS: She is with some very bad people.

HUERO: She's in San Fernando! You didn't even know me until we got here. How can you say you saw her?

LUIS: I'm just passing the time telling you what I believe. As you play with dice, I go into my mind, and recall faces. One face in particular had the resemblance of you. The instant I saw you, I knew it. And that was when my blood curdled once again. I am going to tell you where and when, and you can decide what you want to believe.

HUERO: Then go on.

LUIS: Not only is she extremely lovely, they can use her American looks. To save time the officials wave people across the border glancing briefly at their identification cards. They only stop the darker ones . . . I think they have her against her will. But hunger keeps you against your will. If she was allowed to cross on credit, then they are making her pay the debt by working for them. She has blue eyes. Yours are green. A little while ago, you looked like you were going to cry. That's when I was able to see the resemblance even more.

HUERO: I wasn't going to cry! Everyone has a sister! Leave me alone!

HERNAN: Where is she, then?

HUERO: I don't know. She stopped writing. I want to find her. A man came to our door and told us she's safe, but didn't tell us where she is. He said it would open her to deportation.

HERNAN: Who came to you?

HUERO: A stranger.

LUIS: A stranger that was the devil himself.

HUERO: *Callete.*

LUIS: She has the same eyes, lips, and —

(Huero grabs Luis and tosses him about. The others are too tired and hot to react this time.)

HUERO: WHERE DID YOU SEE HER? TELL ME!

LUIS: A beautiful child. So quiet. So lifeless in your sister's arms. It was a very dark child. Almost blue. La huera was crying. I came up to her. She was already trembling with fear. She turned so fast that the baby fell. The bundle rolled open and I stooped over to pick it up. I looked, full of wonder, expecting the baby to cry. The baby didn't cry. It didn't bleed. It didn't move. La huera motioned me to return it to her. She pleaded with her eyes for me to remain silent. We were being watched. She then walked away. I stood there, ready to die. I knew that the huera was dying, too.

HUERO: You're wrong! You hallucinate!

LUIS: She was forced to be a mule.

(Huero slaps Luis.)

HUERO: *NO!* No, she would never smuggle drugs. And never like that! Hernan, he's crazy, right? Why is he saying this to me? Tell me where you saw her? . . . See! You never saw her!

FRANCISCO: Sometimes the very desperate fall victim to taking drugs across. The drug lords can convince them easily for they are watching their families starve. They know it's wrong and may end up in prison, but they have to take the chance . . . The money is too good and the job so simple. Strap the drugs to your body and go one mile. But in this case, carry it in a bundle. This is a cruel world.

(Huero goes and hides his head. A sick stillness in the boxcar.)

NOEL: I don't understand.

HERNAN: You don't want to understand.

NOEL: What does this all mean? If I am going to die, I want to know all that I can in my last few hours. Tell me about the blue baby. Tell me about the Salvadorians. Only then will I be happy.

HERNAN: You want to know misery in order to be happy?

NOEL: Apparently, that's all everyone knows here.

HERNAN: There is joy. Don't mistake us Mexicans for only talking about misery. It helps cleanse our souls to talk about it, then eventually, with some effort, we forget it. That is what we must do before a small remnant of joy comes.

NOEL: You're all trapped in misery.

HERNAN: Maybe we are. And looking around in here, I see that you are totally right.

NOEL: Then cleanse my soul and tell me what I need to know. Tell me everything you can think of. Take me to the corner and talk to me until I can no longer hear. Tell me about what Luis saw. I want to know.

HERNAN: Don't put that burden on me.

NOEL: I want to know.

HERNAN: *(Hesitates.)* I heard that babies. I *just heard it once, Noel.*

NOEL: *Tell me.*

HERNAN: I heard that babies were stolen from their mothers and made into mules. They cut the babies open and gut them like fish. Then wrap cocaine in bags and stuff it inside their bellies. Hueras would bring them across the border. They have to hurry because the babies turn blue. I heard it once. Just once. It can't be true.

NOEL: No.

(Silence. Everyone looks at each other. Francisco starts carving at the floor with a belt buckle.)

LUIS: I was a priest in Francisco's village. That's where I began my work. I didn't last long. I was missing one important ingredient of my priesthood education. I didn't understand them. I was too Spanish and ignorant to know the indigenous people. My family has less Indian. My heritage is more Spanish. More European . . . They enjoyed their ancestral ideas. The Spanish priests before me had better luck. They resorted to paintings of a fiery hell to scare them into believing. I didn't want to do that. I just wanted to love them. Funny how faith and the stomach are connected. Hunger devours the faithful, and believing stops. When I caught a parishioner kneeling before a collection box, crossing himself before he took the lord's money, I knew we were finished.

(Cross fade.)

SCENE FIVE

Roberto stares at the Skull Dancer. He then directs each line to him. In a choreographed response, the Skull Dancer reacts to the lines.

ROBERTO: I've picked you up at the factories. I've picked you up in the fields. You're hiding from me because you want to keep your job. Sometimes you embarrass me. Let them walk all over you! Stand up! Stupid waiter. Stupid cook. Goddamn custodian. Maid! Then I admire you because you are so fucken humble. The dedication to an endless job and the limited dollar. *(Sarcastic.)* God bless America . . . Yeah, right.

(The Skull Dancer approaches with a torch and swings it around. He then stares at Roberto.)

ROBERTO: *(Continues.)* Go ahead, spit on my face, man. Well! What do you expect?! Stop coming!!!

(Roberto puts a red bandana around his head and stands like a cholo, [Low Rider, a sub-culture of the Chicano movement of the 60s]. He and the Skull Dancer move forward in unison. The two have the same affectation for the next lines.)

ROBERTO: *(Chicano-like. Almost schizoid.)* Stop finding ways to hide from me, fulano. Stop giving the damn coyote your money so he can entice you with the enticement of the American employer. I found you underneath a car. You were tied under the motor. Nice skin graft. Once you were stuck in a freezer of a damn camper. Don't you know you are hot-blooded? Como eres, ese. Shit life. You know what I mean? Where are you today, eh, Mickey? Where are you, flaco? It's going to be a hundred-and-fuck. Tell me where you're at, Chapulin! You, from the jungles of Yucatan! Don't you know there's a desert between you and the jobs?! Horale. Hey, Goofy. Come and give me five, ese. Tar por qual. Todo menso.

(Grandmother crosses. Roberto sees her.)

ROBERTO: Abuelita? Abuelita! *(Roberto breaks down. He takes off the bandana.)* Aye, abuela mia.

ABUELITA: Que te pasa hijo?

ROBERTO: I'm losing it.

ABUELITA: No, mijo. Are you hungry, mijo?

ROBERTO: I'm scared.

ABUELITA: Scared of what?

ROBERTO: Of what I am doing.

ABUELITA: What are you doing, Roberto?

ROBERTO: Losing your respect.

ABUELITA: But you are "mi nieto." My wonderful grandson. You love me. You would never lose respect for me, nor I of you.

ROBERTO: If you only knew what I was doing.

ABUELITA: What are you doing?

ROBERTO: I've been killing you.

(The Border Patrol Officer with no face points a gun to her head.)

ROBERTO: RUN FROM ME, ABUELITA!

ABUELITA: I can't run from you. If I do, I'll be like the hungry farmer.

ROBERTO: Run!

ABUELITA: He was so hungry, Roberto.

ROBERTO: For God's sake, Abuelita, run from me!

ABUELITA: *(To the faceless Border Patrol Officer.)* If a grandmother cannot tell stories, then what good is she? Allow me one story, devil.

(The faceless Border Patrol Officer puts down his gun.)

ABUELITA: The drought was terrible this time. This farmer's crops died. All he could do was gather herbs and sell them to the local pharmacist. Sometimes a curandero would buy it. Not at a very good price, but it was good to sell it to him. For someday he may make a potion for you with the very herbs you gave him. That would guarantee a cure. Other times the farmer would cut *tunas* from the cactus miles away and sell them in the street corners. The only competition were the desert turtles. Their jaws were stained red from the sweet meals of the cactus fruit.

ROBERTO: I have to kill you.

ABUELITA: He would then bring the *tunas* to town in a basket and stand on a street corner. He would stack the red, purple, and yellow tunas in descending color. He made beautiful towers from them. Tourist would come and take pictures. Everyone was saying how rich these people were. For even the children had cameras around their necks. They said they lived like kings and queens in their country. The farmer decided to go to this place of the kings. He said that before sun up, he was going to see the king. At dawn he went to the airport. He found the section behind the airplane wheels. He hid there. The plane went up, but as the wheels folded behind, he was crushed. The pilot had to readjust the wheels. The farmer then fell out. He was later found in the cactus patch, near many tunas. The turtles nibbling his body.

(Abuelita looks at Roberto, sadly. Long silence.)

ROBERTO: Don't look at me like that. Don't look at me that way! Don't you understand? IT'S MY JOB! DON'T YOU UNDERSTAND?

(The Skull Dancer runs in front of Abuelita as the faceless Border Patrol Officer begins to shoot. Blackout seconds before gunshot. Gun blaze seen in the darkness. Then a dim light showing the Skull Dancer's reaction at being shot. Blue blood drips from the wound. It then turns white, then red. He then looks at Roberto. Slow Blackout.)

SCENE SIX

Temperature one hundred and forty-two degrees. Incredible heat. Manuel drips the few remaining drops of water into his mouth. He throws the bottle down.

MANUEL: Que me lleva la trampa.

(Pepe coughs heavily. Luis goes to him and starts to pray. Manuel shoves Luis.)

MANUEL: No prayers until I say so. The instructions are to wait.

FRANCISCO: Look what your "coyote" has done to us.

MANUEL: How do you expect to get here without his help? Maybe his other idea would've been better! Strapping us on to the birds that fly north. That would have worked. Right, Pepe? *(No answer.)* You are to laugh and say, "There is no bird big enough for you." Say it Pepe. SAY IT Pepe.

LUIS: There is no bird big enough for you.

MANUEL: Good. Now everyone, gather around. Let me tell you about the time

I was in New York City. I worked as a window washer in one of the tallest buildings. I was very afraid of heights and —
(Pepe coughs heavily and hoarsely.)

MANUEL: *(Continues.)* Stop that. Stop that, I say!
(Pepe tries to stop himself.)

MANUEL: *(Continues.)* I did everything and hated it, but I had to work. I worked for my family. A man works for his family. A MAN MUST WORK FOR HIS FAMILY, ANYWHERE.
(Manuel kicks Huero.)

MANUEL: *(Continues.)* Get up. I said get up.
(Huero gets up weakly.)

MANUEL: *(Continues.)* There, now lets sing a song to entertain these men. They're in need of some amusement.
(Huero is about to fall in exhaustion.)

MANUEL: *(Continues.)* I didn't say dance, I said sing.
(Huero falls to his knees. Manuel holds Huero's right shoulder to keep him from falling over.)

MANUEL: *(Continues.)* I know a song made famous by Pedro Infante in the early 40s. Have you heard of him? It goes like this.
(There is a moment of strength as he begins to sing the following. The rest of the men have empty looks. On his knees, Huero swerves to the rhythm of the song. [Song available on Linda Ronstadt's Album "Canciones De Mi Padre."])

MANUEL: *(Sings.)*
Han nacido en mi rancho dos arbolitos,
(Translation.) Two little trees have been born on my ranch.
Dos arbolitos que parecen gemelos,
Two little trees that look like twins
Y desde me casita los veo solitos
And from my house I see them all alone.
Bajo el amparo santo y la luz del cielo.
Under the holy protection and light from the heavens
Nunca estan separados uno del otro
They are never separated, one from the other
Porque asi quiso Dios que los dos nacieran,
Because that is how God wanted for the two of them to be born,
Y con sus mismas ramas se hacen caricias
Como si fueran novios que se quisieran.
And with their own branches they caress each other
Ask if they were sweethearts who loved each other

Arbolito, arbolito, bajo tu sombra
Little tree, little tree, under your shade
Voy a esperar que el dia cansado muera,
I'm going to wait until the end of this tiring day
Y cuando estoy solito mirando al cielo
And when I'm all alone looking to the sky
Pido pa'que me mande una compañera
I'm going to ask Heaven to send me a companion
Arbolito, arbolito, me siento solo
Little tree, little tree, I feel alone
Quiero que me acompañes hasta que muera.
I want you to accompany me until I die.
(Huero drops to the ground. Manuel then walks away humming. The Skull Dancer approaches wearing a sombrero. He has a hole in his chest.)

MANUEL: *(To the Skull Dancer.)* Didn't you hear the song? I asked the tree to accompany me until I died. I didn't ask for you to accompany me. Do you have a cigarette?
(The Skull Dancer offers a cigarette to Manuel and lights it for him. He then lights a cigarette for himself. They sit there calmly, smoking, occasionally looking around.)

MANUEL: *(Continues.)* I suppose it's almost time. Is that why you are here? I thought so. Did you like my song? Well, I did my best. I always did my best. *(Long pause. Manuel gets determined.)* You know something? I'm going to fight you. So you better go away before I kick your ass.
(The Skull Dancer exits.)

MANUEL: *(Continues.)* MI ARBOLITOS ARE WAITING FOR ME! Get up all of you! If you lie there, you are asking for death to come to your door! You with the university education, I have an education. I do. I do. I even belonged to a fraternity: SIGNA-FY-NOTHING. See Noel, we are university students. We are the ones with the education and our education tells us to relax and wait with our eyes open. Keep them open to avoid the dancing devil of death.
(He steps on the dice.)

MANUEL: *(Continues.)* Get rid of those dice!

FRANCISCO: We've taken a big chance and lost.

MANUEL: We haven't lost yet!

FRANCISCO: I only detest that we gambled with our lives.

NOEL: *(Feeling the hysteria.)* I should have crossed on foot!

FRANCISCO: I used to cross on foot. I walked to any town that was willing to hire me. I'd do anything for whatever they paid me. I know that there are many who take those same paths. I've seen them. The path has widened. I'll stop to talk if they are carrying their own water. If not, I pass them by quickly.

NOEL: Why would you pass them?

FRANCISCO: I don't want them to see in my eyes, their death.

MANUEL: You see, they should've had coyotes! To tell them the right way!

FRANCISCO: THEY HAD A COYOTE.

MANUEL: Look, now you're scaring the boy! The truth is, it takes time!

FRANCISCO: We don't have time!

MANUEL: Why are you scaring him?!

FRANCISCO: Look at his face! He's just a boy!

MANUEL: I used to have face like that!

PEPE: No you didn't. Manuel, he's making more sense. Francisco, what do you want us to do?

FRANCISCO: We use the rest of our energy, whatever is left, to scratch our way out. Or we'll end up like those Salvadorians.

MANUEL: We should sit and remain quiet. He will open that door. Trust me!

FRANCISCO: He said it was one mile of a walk through the desert to the farms. It turned out to be sixty! They only had water for two miles.

MANUEL: What are you talking about? We have enough water.

(The men shake their heads "no.")

FRANCISCO: Thanks to the border patrol who pick up bodies before the buzzards get to them. Oh, how they suffered. They drank their urine to survive. Later, they took their own lives by cutting their throats with the stem of a belt buckle. Out of the thirty, there were only two that survived. They were the ones who slit their own throats improperly.

MANUEL: We didn't have to walk through the desert. We rode.

FRANCISCO: We're not riding now! Except we have a ready-made coffin.

(Pepe rises in a delirium. He looks out and sees the Skull Dancer in the last row of the audience.)

PEPE: I saw their faces when el coyote was convincing them that the plan would work. He had to leave several behind because there were not enough barrels. How sad they looked when they were given back their money and told to wait. Wait and wait and wait. His arms are wedged tight against him. Who would hear him? Who would stop if they noticed an old barrel on the side of the road? His body is waiting. Waiting along an interstate to nowhere. Someone has to help him.

FRANCISCO: First, we help ourselves.

(*Pepe reaches into his bag and gives Francisco a small knife. Francisco uses the knife to pry edges. He stops and looks at them, then bashes his fist against the wall. Receiving the signal the others start banging the walls with their shoes and bags, screaming for help. It is out of control. The heat in the boxcar is even more unbearable with their racket.*)

MANUEL: (*During the racket.*) STOP, STOP. YOU ARE WASTING THE AIR. BE QUIET, LISTEN TO ME. WE PAID OUR MONEY. WE WILL MAKE IT. IF THE BORDER PATROL FINDS US, THEN WHAT? THINK OF YOUR SISTER, HUERO. NOEL, THEY'LL GET YOU BY THE BALLS. PLEASE PEPE, WE'LL FIND HIM AND TELL HIS FAMILY TOGETHER. LET ME SHOW YOU WHAT A GOOD DANCER I AM. LISTEN TO ME!!!! (*Ad-lib.*)

(*There is yelling and groaning. Banging and frustration. In time, they fall onto the floor exhausted.*)

HUERO: I can't anymore. I can't. I need some water. (*Sobs.*) I need some water. Please, does anyone have a little water. Please.

HERNAN: We all need water.

MANUEL: Cerveza mejor.

(*Noel pulls out a bottle with a small amount of water in it. He quickly realizes his mistake.*)

NOEL: It's not enough! It's mine!

HERNAN: That's all. That's not even enough for one man!

HUERO: (*Grabs for it.*) Give it to me.

NOEL: It's mine! It's mine!

HERNAN: We can't divide that!

NOEL: Francisco! It's mine!

MANUEL: El coyote viene. He'll bring plenty of water.

HUERO: I want it!

HERNAN: I'll pay you for it.

NOEL: It's mine. I brought it!

FRANCISCO: Another rule when you cross, Noel. You give up your valuables, or get killed for it. Your decision.

(*Noel drops the bottle. Hernan and Huero pounce on it and fight viciously for it. Francisco steps in during the animalistic behavior and takes the bottle away.*)

FRANCISCO: (*Continues.*) You like to gamble? Then we let the winner take it. Where are your dice? Throw for it. We love a game of chance, don't we? We love to take chances with our lives. Let's see who's going to win. The lowest number gets what's left of the water. Manuel, you go first.

MANUEL: No gracias.
HERNAN: I'll go first!
FRANCISCO: NO! MANUEL!
MANUEL: I'm not a gambler!
FRANCISCO: Yes, you are! ¡Tira!
MANUEL: *(Reluctantly throws the dice.)* Ocho.
HUERO: *(Takes the dice and throws.)* Cuatro.
NOEL: *(Looks at everyone and throws.)* Tres.
LUIS: Let me throw for Pepe. *(Luis picks up the dice. He looks at Pepe, says a quick prayer and throws it. The dice is high. He looks at Pepe.)* Doce, para mi. *(Luis throws the dice. This time without prayer.)* Siete, para Pepe.
FRANCISCO: *(Throws dice quickly.)* Nueve.
HERNAN: *(Throws dice.)* Dos. I won.
(Hernan takes the bottle and puts it to his lips. Pepe starts coughing. Luis takes the water away.)
PEPE: WHAT ARE YOU DOING?!
LUIS: How quickly we forget the old and sick!
PEPE: Give it to the children.
HERNAN: BUT I WON.
LUIS: Give it to him.
HERNAN: I'll kill you!
(Hernan grabs at Luis and they fight for the water. All the men jump into the fight. Pepe gets up to attempt to stop them.)
MANUEL: STOP IT! STOP IT! LISTEN TO ME. YA! YA. CABRONES! PINCHE HUEVONES STOP! *(Ad-lib.)*
(Manuel also tries to stop them. Luis has the water again then it's ripped from his hands by Hernan.)
(Luis grabs the knife from the floor and tries to plunge it into Hernan. In the mass of men and commotion, he accidently stabs Pepe. All freeze and watch Pepe fall slowly to the ground. Manuel goes to Pepe and cradles him.)
MANUEL: *(Softly.)* Pepe. Pepe.
PEPE: *(Opens his eyes slightly.)* ¿Que hombre?
MANUEL: Go to sleep.
PEPE: I am . . . But what about the girls?. . . The dancing?
MANUEL: You can dance with the one with the big breasts.
PEPE: You dance with her. I want to see her slap you, again.
MANUEL: *(Smiling through his tears.)* The pollacks will beat me up!
PEPE: I love those pollacks. *(He tries to laugh.)* I love them very much.
(Pepe slowly expires. Manuel looks at his hands covered with Pepe's blood.)

MANUEL: Luis. Luis, pray for him. Then, pray for me, too. Padre. The last rites are needed. At least one of us has had his misery ended.
NOEL: No! He'll come for us! He has to! He said he will! He'll open the door.
(Noel hits Francisco across the face.)
FRANCISCO: Andale. Mas! Mas!
(Noel strikes him repeatedly then falls to the ground.)
NOEL: *(Long moment.)* Why didn't you strike back?
FRANCISCO: Because every time I do, nothing changes.
(Coyote howl in the distance.)
MANUEL: Listen everyone. I know that the door will open soon. He'll come for us. Our guardian angel. He'll come for us. He will. Listen to me. All you have to do is trust me.
(Cradling Pepe in his arms. Lights start to dim.)
MANUEL: Trust me, this time. Trust me when I say someone will come for us. Trust me. Trust me. Trust me. TRUST ME. Trust me. Trust me. Trust me. Trust me. Trust me, trust me, trust me. TRUST ME!!!!!!!!!!!!
(Lights changes to an array of darks.)

SCENE SEVEN

Temperature one hundred and sixty degrees. Series of light changes. Then Light on Manuel with Pepe in his arms. The rest of the men are in the same positions as in Act One, Scene Three.

MANUEL: Aye, Pepe. Pepe, you idiot. Let me tell you a story about a man I knew. You'll like this one. He was a desperate man. Not like us. We never were that desperate. He didn't have enough money for a coyote so he had this idea. He found a dead cow. There were buzzards circling all over it. Some of them were jumping on it, excited over the rotten meat. When the buzzards were almost finished, he took a knife like yours, and cut the hoofs off . . . You know what he did with the hoofs? He tied them to his feet! Then he started to walk across the desert. All the way to the border. He knew the border patrol watched for human footprints. *(Laughing and crying.)* He was caught. He was caught. The border patrol noticed how the cow didn't stop at the patches of grass. They followed the prints. They then found my friend exhausted on a rock. Ese pinche gato. The cat got him. *(Manuel slumps over Pepe.)*
ABUELITA: *(Off.)* Beto. Beto. Venga aca.

(Light fades to a black. Sound: Birds in a distant jungle. The sound of a knife pounding on the boxcar floor. When the pounding stops, a jeep is heard in the distance approaching. The boxcar door slides open. Bright lights rush in as Roberto stands at the door. The lights stream from his body almost angelically. Roberto and Bill stare inside. Bill runs off to vomit. In Roberto's face you see that his nightmare has happened. The Skull Dancer appears in a three-piece suit. He points a gun at Roberto. A trembling hand reaches up from the mass of men, then falls. The Aztec Skull Dancer lifts one finger to show that there is only one survivor. Outraged, Roberto throws the Skull Dancer to the ground. They wrestle until the Skull Dancer is on top holding the gun to Roberto's face. They stare at each other for a long while. Final blackout. Temperature one hundred and eighty degrees.)

END OF PLAY

A Bicycle Country

Nilo Cruz

BIOGRAPHY

Nilo Cruz has written several plays including *A Park in Our House, Night Train to Bolina, Dancing on Her Knees, Hortensia, The Museum of Dreams, Lorca in a Green Dress, The Beauty of the Father,* and *Anna in the Tropics*. His work has been developed and performed at the McCarter Theatre, the New York Public Theatre, New York Theatre Workshop, South Coast Repertory, Florida Stage, The Alliance, and the Magic Theatre in San Francisco. Nilo is a writer in residence at New Theatre, Miami through an NEA\TCG grant for playwrights. An alumnus of New Dramatists, he has held residencies at the Royal Court Theatre in London and the Public Theatre/NYSF. He has taught playwriting at the University of Iowa, Brown University, and New York University, Gallatin School.

ORIGINAL PRODUCTION

This play was commissioned by the Public Theatre and received a workshop at Portland Stage, Maine, Mark Taper Forum, and the Oregon Shakespeare Festival.

CHARACTERS

JULIO, a man in his forties.
INES, a woman in her thirties.
PEPE, a man in his thirties.

TIME AND PLACE

Before the U.S. intervention on Cubans fleeing to the United States on rafts. The set is a square platform with a column in the middle. To the right of the column there is an old trunk and two wooden chairs. The wooden platform becomes a raft in the second act. Objects needed in the play are taken out of the trunk or the characters bring them in from the offstage area. A white cloth or screen, on the upstage area frames the stage. A large round orange spot light is reflected on the white drop for the day scenes and a large round white light for the night scenes. The white screen can also change in colors according to the mood of the scenes. For the last scene the white screen or cloth should open or drop, to reveal a green landscape.

A BICYCLE COUNTRY

ACT I: TIERRA
SCENE ONE

Music plays. Projected on the screen: TIERRA
Julio is standing up against a wooden board. The board leans against a column. His body is strapped to the board with a rope. Ines stands close to him. She writes a few of Julio's instructions on a small paper. Pepe sits at the table.

JULIO: I don't have an alarm clock. My eyes open at seven o'clock. That's the time I wake up. The first thing you give me are the pills. They are right here by the night table —.

PEPE: He takes one of the pink ones, two of the yellow. Right, Julio? After he takes the pills you give him —

JULIO: After I take the pills she gives me the bedpan.

PEPE: Yes . . . It's under the bed.

JULIO: I take two to five minutes on it. Sometimes more.

PEPE: *(Trying to ease the situation.)* That's a good time for you to occupy yourself doing something else. You can smoke a cigarette —

JULIO: No. She goes to the kitchen to heat up the water for my bath.

PEPE: Yeah, you go to the kitchen —

JULIO: At seven-ten I should be ready. She takes the bedpan and cleans me. When she finishes cleaning me, she gets rid of what's inside the pan. Then she goes to the kitchen to get the bucket of water for my bath, and she comes back to me. — That's around seven-fourteen . . .

PEPE: Seven nothing, Julio! . . . *(To Julio.)* I'll instruct you as you go along. Don't worry. I'll teach you.

JULIO: I want to be dressed by seven thirty, and that is our goal.

PEPE: Yeah, no shoes till he's ready to stand.

JULIO: *(Looks down at his feet.)* I have to get used to the standing position. It's good for my circulation. We do this twice a day, when I get up in the morning and an hour before I go to sleep What time is it now?

INES: It's almost nine. At what time do you go to sleep?

JULIO: Sometimes nine . . . Sometimes eleven. It depends . . .

INES: What do I have to do to help you?

JULIO: Well, there are things that have to be done before I go to sleep. It's part of the nightly routine. Please, unstrap me. I'm ready to go to bed.

(Ines unstraps him. She places her right shoulder under his arm to help him sit in a wheelchair.)

JULIO: I'll sit here for a bit to catch my breath. You can go to the kitchen and heat up some milk. I drink a glass of warm milk before I go to bed.

INES: You won't fall?

JULIO: I can hold myself up.

INES: *(To Pepe.)* Would you help me in the kitchen? Show me where everything is kept.

PEPE: Sure.

(Ines and Pepe move to another part of the stage.)

INES: Pepe, I want to talk to you.

PEPE: What's the matter?

INES: You didn't tell me . . . You didn't tell me everything had to be so . . . I don't know . . . So, paranh, pin, punh . . . So by the clock.

(Julio wheels himself close to them to hear the conversation.)

PEPE: I told you he likes things done a certain way . . .

INES: He's like a commander. I don't know if I can work under these conditions. I don't know if I can. I worked in a hospital, but I don't know if . . .

PEPE: He's a good man. You have to get —.

JULIO: *(In a loud voice.)* Pepe . . .

PEPE: He's calling me. *(In a loud voice.)* Coming. . .

(Walks toward Julio.)

JULIO: Is she all right?

PEPE: Yes . . . I mean . . . No. I think you're scaring her away.

JULIO: *(In a loud voice.)* Ines.

INES: *(Enters the space.)* Yes.

JULIO: *(To Pepe.)* Why don't you explain to her that it takes time getting me dressed?

PEPE: I've helped him — .

JULIO: *(Interrupting him.)* Why don't you explain to her, that if she follows my instructions we can make more use of time?

PEPE: He says — .

INES: I heard.

JULIO: Explain to her that if she follows my method — .

PEPE: You see, it takes time getting him up from — .

INES: I understand.

PEPE: *(To Ines.)* It's different when you can't do things on your own.

INES: How much is he going to pay me?

PEPE: Julio.

JULIO: Half of what I'll receive every month.
PEPE: He's going to get money for being on relief. He hasn't gotten it yet.
INES: So, how does he expect me to start working, when he doesn't have any money?
PEPE: Julio.
JULIO: Pepe, come here. Come close.
   (Julio whispers something in his ear. Pepe nods. Julio unclasps a gold chain from around his neck. He takes the chain and gives it to Ines.)
INES: What's this for?
JULIO: Your first salary. That's your pay.
INES: I'm not taking his chain.
JULIO: Why not? You can sell it or trade it for something.
PEPE: You see, he's paying you already. You can start working.
INES: No, give it back to him. He can pay me when he gets his money. Tell me what else needs to be done.
PEPE: He listens to the radio before he goes to sleep. And you have to give him one of the yellow pills.
INES: You'll have to excuse me I want to change my shoes. These shoes bother me.
JULIO: You should make yourself at home. You can take off your shoes if you like.
INES: No, thank you. I don't like to walk barefoot.
   (Lights fade to black.)

SCENE TWO

Date projected on screen: A Month Later, Julio is sitting on his wheelchair exercising. He lifts his arms up and down. Ines helps him with his right arm.

JULIO: That was twenty.
INES: Again.
JULIO: That was twenty-one.
INES: Again!
JULIO: Twenty-two
INES: More!
JULIO: Twenty-three.
INES: Two more.
JULIO: I can't.

INES: You want to get better!
JULIO: I can't anymore!
INES: One more time.
JULIO: Twenty-four.
INES: Come on . . . You're strong.
JULIO: That's twenty-five . . .
INES: One more. Try again.
JULIO: That's it! No more!
INES: You can't rest now.
JULIO: You're killing me!
INES: You'll go to waste if you don't exercise.
JULIO: I can't do all the repetitions.
INES: To say "I can't" is to say "I won't do it."
JULIO: It's too much.
INES: You want me to blow some air on your face? Are you fatigued?
JULIO: We're done for today.
INES: No. You have to do more.
JULIO: You're out of your mind. What do you think I am, an athlete?! I'm sick!
INES: You're better than you think you are.
JULIO: You're not inside my body! I hurt.
INES: I'm just here to help you. If you don't want to do anything for yourself, then stay the way you are. I'm going outside, it's hot in here.
(Starts to exit.)
JULIO: No. Wait!
INES: What?
JULIO: What are we going to do next?
INES: Walk.
JULIO: *(Moves away.)* No walking. I told you I'm not walking.
INES: You walked yesterday after the exercises.
JULIO: I can't today.
INES: Then I'm going outside to smoke!
JULIO: Ey, don't get angry!
INES: I just want your cooperation.
JULIO: I don't like pain. My whole body aches.
INES: It's going to hurt. What do you expect? You don't use your muscles. They're flaccid.
JULIO: I need nutrition. I need to get stronger. It takes time for the body to heal.
INES: Of course, I know that.

JULIO: So, it's not going to happen over night!
  (Pepe rides his bicycle. He rings the bell.)
INES: That's Pepe with the mail.
  (Pepe parks the bicycle.)
  Come in, Pepe.
PEPE: Good morning!
INES: Good morning.
JULIO: 'Morning.
PEPE: *(To Julio.)* You don't look good. *(To Ines.)* And you don't have a good face either. *(Puts his bag down.)* What's wrong?
INES: What do you think happens in this house every day!
  (Turns to Julio.)
JULIO: What do you mean? I don't always complain!
INES: You complain every day, Julio.
JULIO: I'm not an athlete. She makes me exercise as if I was training for a tournament.
INES: He's exaggerating.
JULIO: Explain to her . . . Tell her how I was a month ago. How I had tubes coming out of my mouth and IV's in both arms.
PEPE: So now you're better. What's wrong with exercising?
JULIO: *(Moves away in the wheelchair.)* Ah, the hell with you! You're just like her.
INES: He's mad because I added five repetitions to his exercises.
JULIO: She says it like it's nothing.
PEPE: Why don't you try helping her out? Pretend you're training for a sport. Baseball. It's not any different. If you have to run five laps, you run the five laps. You condition your mind to do it.
JULIO: When I played sports I wasn't sick.
PEPE: Here, mail for you.
  (Goes through a bundle of mail.)
  You got a postcard from Venice. And you also got a letter from the Interior Ministry. . .
INES: Don't give it to him now. I'll take it. He has to finish his exercises.
JULIO: Give me my mail! Let me see my postcard.
INES: Here. The rest stays with me. If it's bad news you'll get in a rotten mood, and you won't do anything else. *(Gives him the postcard.)*
  You still have to walk.
JULIO: What did she say?

PEPE: Come on, be a good sport. You have to cooperate. Be more hopeful, my friend.

JULIO: That's all I need hope. What can I hope for?

PEPE: That's unlike you. You've turned into a lazy animal.

INES: Yes he has. He's turned into a hippopotamus that wants to stay in the water and do nothing for himself. Don't look at me that way. I read a magazine article about the hippopotamus.

(Julio gives her a dirty look.)

The hippos don't want to evolve. The penguin is an evolving animal. Penguins want to move forward. They're up on their feet and walking about. The seals, too. Those are evolving animals. But hippos want to stay in the water and do nothing for themselves. Just like Julio.

JULIO: You like to bother me, don't you? You like to bother me.

INES: No. I'm just not going to move from here until you walk.

PEPE: And neither am I.

(There is a pause. Julio looks at them in disbelief.)

INES: What are you doing on Sunday, Pepe? Do you want to go to the Botanical Gardens?

(Julio wheels himself to another part of the room.)

PEPE: What's at the botanical garden?

INES: There's a flowering tree from India I want to see. I was reading about it in the newspaper. This tree lives for two hundred years. It grows and grows for all these years, then it blooms once in its lifetime and dies away. It gives so many blooms that the weight of the flowers makes the tree bend down and fall to the ground.

PEPE: That sounds like a nice thing to do on Sunday, go see a tree.

JULIO: She also said, she wanted to talk to the tree, and sleep under it before it falls down. I have lunatic in my house.

INES: So what's wrong with visiting a falling tree, Julio! I'm going outside to get the laundry, when I come back you'll take a walk.

(Ines starts to exit.)

JULIO: Give me the rest of my mail . . . Give me my mail

(Ines is gone now.)

She's not giving me my mail . . . She's mad, crazy . . .

PEPE: *(Walks in the direction she has left. He contemplates her from a distance.)* She's beautiful. Passionate. I love her. I remember the first day I saw her. She was trying to catch a canary that had gotten out of the cage. I just stood there and watched her make her way slowly to the bird, her hands full of seeds. After two minutes the bird couldn't resist her anymore and flew into her hands. Couldn't resist her, I tell you. I'd like to have a woman like her in my life.

JULIO: No you wouldn't. She's like a sergeant.

PEPE: Well, that's what you need. Somebody to get you back in shape.

JULIO: You're talking as if — .

PEPE: Treat her well. You don't want to lose her. We found the right person to take care of you. She's hard-working, kind, and determined. I'd marry her if I were in your shoes.

JULIO: What are you talking about? I'm a mess. Who's going to want to look at me in this condition?

PEPE: You never know. She's a good woman. I don't like to see you alone. I'd like to see you get married again. You deserve someone like Ines. She's a giving person. Nowadays a person calculates what they can afford to give. The world is changing, my friend. It's not how it used to be.

JULIO: Are you sure you're not the one who likes her?

PEPE: Me? Of course not! I can stay alone. I like my freedom. I like being alone.

JULIO: Have you tried getting back with Lolin?

PEPE: Lolin is gone, Julio. She's gone. She must be in America, for all I know. Got away on a raft. Didn't even say good-bye.

JULIO: Why not?

PEPE: Who knows with women! She wouldn't talk to me after we had that big fight.

JULIO: She probably thought you would turn her in for leaving the country.

PEPE: *(With contained anger.)* Would I do that! Would I do something like that! *(Pause.)* Give me a cigarette, will you? You and I have rotten luck with women.

(Julio gives him a cigarette.)

JULIO: When did she leave the country?

PEPE: I don't know, probably two or three weeks ago. I didn't know she had left. Somebody told me.

JULIO: You're not taking this well, are you?

PEPE: No, I'm not. It's pointless. Why don't we talk about you?

JULIO: I have nothing to say. I feel rotten, like always.

PEPE: We should've left this place long ago. Look at the two of us, alone again. It's getting tough out there. You don't know how bad it is, because you never leave the house. But I can tell you, we're slowly going back to the Iron Age. We're in the Bicycle Age out there. We've gone back to the wheel. A whole country riding bicycles. You only have to look outside the window and see for yourself. Everywhere signs, slogans, "Save energy. Save energy." What energy is there to be saved, when there is no energy! No oil. Hardly any buses running. I think this is the worse it's gotten in years.

I mean last night the only thing I had to eat was an egg. I sat down to have dinner. I saw the miserable egg, in the middle of my plate looking at me, like an eyeball. The thing gave me the creeps. I mean it looked like it was hungrier than me. Just didn't have dinner at all, ran out of the house, got on my bicycle and went for some fresh air. I could feel my adrenaline going through my veins and up to my mouth. I think that's what filled my stomach last night, my own fuckin' anguish frothing on my tongue. Do you know what I'm trying to do now? Did I tell you? I'm trying to learn Italian.

JULIO: Italian? Why do you want to learn Italian for?

PEPE: Sure. Why not? Learn a few words. . . . I want to hook up with an Italian tourist. Imagine if I find an Italian woman. That would be my ticket out of this country. I'll get married, she'll send for me. . .

JULIO: Ah, give me a break. Do you really believe it's that easy?

PEPE: Why not? Even if I don't get to marry her, it's one way out of this mess.

JULIO: So who's teaching you Italian?

PEPE: Who's teaching me Italian, hunh?! Someone lent me this Italian sewing book.

(Takes out a small book from his pocket.)

JULIO: A sewing book. And what are you going to learn with an Italian sewing book?

PEPE: Oh, you should've seen me carrying on a conversation. I went to a bar and found an Italian woman and I said . . . Listen to this. . .

(He flips through the book and finds a section. He enunciates every word with natural speed and mastery.)

Questa giacca é strappata, desidero che mi sia rammendata. Tell me if that doesn't sound good!

JULIO: What does it mean?

PEPE: Can you sew a button on this coat for me?

JULIO: You told her that!

PEPE: Doesn't it sound good? Listen to this . . . *"Desidero che mi si prendano le misure per un abito."* That means I want to be measured.

JULIO: You're out of your mind.

PEPE: Ey . . . She thought it was amusing. I got her talking. I needed a punch line.

JULIO: Did she punch you back on the face?

PEPE: No. We had a good conversation. Then, she went to the bathroom, and I had three drinks waiting for her to come back.

JULIO: Did she come back?

PEPE: No. I spent all my money on drinks. Today I'm poor and shitting blood. I have an ulcer. I can't drink.

(Ines enters with a bundle of clothes wrapped in a white tablecloth. She places it on top of the table. She continues talking as she makes a couple of knots with the four corners of the tablecloth.)

INES: Did you hear me from out there? I was calling you to come out onto the patio. There was a whole flock of birds flying over the house. Hundreds of them. You can tell the season is changing. You can tell by the birds, they come here for the winter, then start making their way back North.

Are you almost ready, Julio? Have you had a chance to rest?

JULIO: I've already told you, it's enough for today.

INES: Did he tell you what the doctor said?

(There's silence.)

PEPE: What's the matter, Julio?

INES: Julio, he's talking to you. Was he always like this?

PEPE: No. I don't know what's gotten into him. He was always well disposed.

JULIO: I have to have surgery. *(To Ines.)* Does that make you happy?

PEPE: What kind of surgery?

INES: I told him he should do it. It's the only way he's going to get cured.

JULIO: When I leave this place, I can have surgery. When I get my travel permit.

INES: When you get a travel permit! When you get a travel permit! You're going to have to wait a long time for a travel permit. You better find somebody with a boat and leave this place. If you wait too long, you're going to go pim, poom, right there and have another stroke!

JULIO: *(To Pepe.)* Pim, poom . . . Everything is pim, poom to her! Everything happens in a matter of seconds.

INES: He could have another stroke, if he doesn't have surgery. That's what the doctor said.

JULIO: In her mind she has gotten a raft and sailed up north from this room.

PEPE: And why not, Julio?

INES: That's right. He knows he can't be waiting around. Do you know how long it takes to get a travel permit?

JULIO: And where am I going to get a boat?

A BICYCLE COUNTRY 123

INES: *(To Pepe.)* Can't you get somebody to build a raft? I told him I'll go with him. What's important is to go, leave this place.

PEPE: It's not impossible. We can get a raft.

JULIO: Then you two can get inside the raft because I'm not going anywhere. What if something happens, enh?

PEPE: Why do you always have to think of the worst!

JULIO: Because you only have to look at me sitting in this wheelchair! I can't do much for myself, goddamit! I'm an invalid! *(There is a pause.)* — Come on, let's go. Let's go . . . I'll take a walk.

INES: *(Tenderly.)* Good. That's a good sport. Pepe, as soon as I stand him up, you take the wheelchair and stand there where you are. Julio, you're going to walk to him.

JULIO: That's too far. Take two steps forward.

INES: You stay where you are. Let's see, put your arms around me, as if we're going to dance.

PEPE: You want me to play music?

JULIO: Shut up will you! Don't be a clown.

(Julio stands up to walk. Pepe turns on the radio. A rumba plays.)

PEPE: Why not? You need something to liven you up.

INES: Don't drag your feet. Lift up your feet.

(Dialogue overlaps. Pepe goes for the wheelchair and gets back to his place.)

JULIO: I'm trying. Turn that shit off!

  INES: Lift up your leg.

  PEPE: That's it, Julio. . .

JULIO: Turn that shit off! It doesn't let me concentrate!

  PEPE: Bravo Julio! Bravo! You're doing it!

  INES: Push forward!

  PEPE: Go Julio! Go! Walk! To the finish line . . .

JULIO: Tell him to shut up!

  INES: Shut up! Can't you see he's concentrating.

JULIO: just tell him to put the chair behind me.

  INES: No. You walk all the way to him.

  PEPE: Go Julio! Go!

JULIO: Turn the chair around big mouth!

  INES: Don't do it, Pepe.

JULIO: Tell him to bring the chair.

  INES: Let him finish turning around.

PEPE: That's it . . . That's it Julio. There you go.

(Ines lowers him down.)

Bravo Julio . . .Bravo . . .
(Pepe goes to turn off the radio.)
INES: Are you all right?
(There is a pause. Julio catches his breath.)
JULIO: You want me to throw myself to the sea, and look at me! How can I put myself in a little raft, on a truck tire, when I can't walk well enough? Can't you see I'm drowning! I'm sinking in my own body. I'm sitting here on solid ground and I'm drowning.
(Julio wheels himself out of the room. There is a pause. Ines looks at Pepe. He gives her the rest of the mail.)
PEPE: Here, give him the rest of his mail.
(He takes his bag.)
I'll come by later.
(He starts to exit.)
INES: Pepe, what is this thing that he has that won't let him move forward?
(Lights change.)

SCENE THREE

Date projected on the screen: Five Months Later. Ines gets a sheet. She drapes it around Julio. She gives him a photo album. She gets a pair of scissors and starts cutting his hair.

INES: How long ago was that? You look young in that picture.
JULIO: I was seventeen.
INES: And this guy standing by the seawall?
JULIO: Guess?
INES: Pepe. But it doesn't look like him.
JULIO: He was probably twelve. Look at him in shorts. He used to love the sea.
INES: And that doesn't look like you either. You look handsome with that mustache. You should grow one.
JULIO: Let me look in the mirror. Let me see what you're doing.
INES: No. Not until I'm finished. I still have to cut your sideburns.
Who are those people wearing sunglasses, in that picture?
JULIO: That's me and Ana Maria. She was feeding the pigeons in the park.
INES: Let me see. You still love this woman, don't you?
JULIO: That was the past.
INES: I know when she's on your mind. I've seen your eyes water. I know you

A BICYCLE COUNTRY 125

well enough. I've worked in this house for more than five months now. The only thing left is to pin myself to your skin. Sometimes I feel like I am your body, and you are my brain.

JULIO: I don't want to talk about her.

INES: Then cut her out of your mind, like I cut your hair. She's not coming back and thinking about her won't do any good. It's just like those pills you take, when you get depressed — she doesn't go away with pills. She left you. She could've taken care of you.

JULIO: Ines please . . .

INES: I just see you sad-eyed sometimes . . .

JULIO: Now come on, that's none of your business.

INES: You are my business. You're my work. That's why I come to this house every morning.

JULIO: But we're not married.

INES: Ha! That I know.

JULIO: Good. Is that all you have to say?

INES: Yes.

JULIO: Then that's enough! Please, just get on with the haircut!

(She continues to cut his hair. There is silence.)

(Pepe rings his bicycle bell.)

JULIO: That must be Pepe with the mail. He'll cough now. He always does.

(Pepe coughs. Julio laughs. Ines chuckles.)

PEPE: Good morning!

JULIO AND INES: Morning . . .

PEPE: What are you two laughing about?

JULIO: I was telling Ines that I know when you're here by the cough.

(Pepe is taking off his bag now.)

PEPE: Well, at least this ship won't get lost in the fog.

— It looks good Julio. You do a good job. Can I be next?

JULIO: This is not a barbershop.

PEPE: She's good at it. I need a haircut.

INES: Today is Julio's birthday.

PEPE: I know, happy birthday! Here. *(Throws him a pack of cigarettes.)* I got you a pack of French cigarettes for your birthday.

INES: I'm giving him my present later this afternoon. It's a surprise.

JULIO: Thank you, Pepe.

PEPE: How old are you?

(Ines undrapes Julio.)

JULIO: Ancient. Old. Let me look at myself in the mirror. Pass me the mirror.

INES: You stand up and get it.
JULIO: I guess no one is cordial anymore.
INES: That's right. We're mean and awful people.
   (Julio gets up to get the mirror.)
   See how well he's doing. See how good he looks.
PEPE: *(Applauds.)* Bravo, Julio . . . Bravo.
JULIO: I'm getting there.
INES: I told him we should go to the seawall and get some fresh air. I told him we should have a party.
JULIO: That's for kids who like birthday parties. I'm too old to be celebrating my birthday. *(He takes a small lamp out of a trunk.)* I want you to sell this lamp, Pepe. I need money. I want to pay Ines.
INES: That's a beautiful lamp. You don't have to sell it to pay me.
PEPE: Aren't you getting paid at the end of the month?
JULIO: No more payments. They want me back at work. They say I'm capable of working at the office. How much do you think we can get for it?
   (He lights the lamp. The light reveals a painting on the lamp shade.)
PEPE: I don't know. It's an old lamp. I can never estimate the price of old things.
INES: Don't sell it, Julio. Things get passed on in our families and we take them for granted. But these objects have a life. They become part of the family. They've lived with us.
JULIO: Like this lamp, Pepe, she's my cousin.
INES: I'm not saying anything else! It's your house, those are your objects . . . You do what you want! He knows he doesn't have to pay me. I can get by until he gets back to work.
   (Julio gives him an old silver pot)
JULIO: Here. Take this too. How much can we get for this?
INES: That's silver. Don't sell that.
JULIO: I don't use it. How much?
PEPE: You won't get much money for it . . . I could exchange it for food, a couple of chickens.
INES: Get a tire. Exchange everything for a tire. Let's build a raft and get out of this place.
   (There is a pause. Julio stares at Ines. She was so direct in her response, it's as if her mind had spoken before she could come up with the words.)
   It's not going to get any better here. Every day more and more slogans. The permanent war, "Contribute . . . Resistance . . . Do it for your country" . . . Every day the same story, no room for questioning. They take away your food and they tell you keep on going . . . You can go on . . .

Call this moving, call it going on. The spirit of the system . . . They take away the fuel, no more buses . . . Now a bicycle, just ride it. Call it a bicycle to take you the sea, fresh air . . . That's it. You have adopted the right spirit toward things . . . Only one dress to wear, call it one dress for a year. A year for a dress . . . A dress without a year. I'm tired of fooling myself.

— If you don't want to leave this place, I do! I do! You can give me a raft for payment.

(Silence. She doesn't know what else to say and Julio doesn't know what to respond.)

INES: I'm going outside for some fresh air.

(Pepe tries to make light of the whole situation. He drapes himself with the sheet. He sits on the chair. Ines starts to leave.)

PEPE: Aren't you going to give me a haircut? Does this mean she's not going to give me a haircut? What happened, Julio? Where is she going? *(In a loud voice.)* Eh, I'm ready for the haircut. *(To Julio.)* Is she coming back? *(In a loud voice.)* Ines . . . Ines . . .

(He goes out of the house, draped in the barber's cloth. Ines takes Pepe's bicycle.)

PEPE: Hey . . . come back . . . come back . . . *(Pepe enters the house.)* She took my bicycle.

(Music plays. Lights fade to black.)

SCENE FOUR

Date projected on the screen: Later in the Evening. The men are waiting for her outside of the house. Ines rides the bicycle. She rings the bell several times, expressing joy and excitement. She comes into the house with a package.

INES: I'm back. I'm back . . .
PEPE: I was getting worried. Next time tell me where you're going.
INES: I didn't take long. Come inside. Close your eyes, Julio
JULIO: What for? What's this all about?
INES: Just close your eyes. I have a surprise for you. Come on . . . come on . . . Close your eyes.

(Julio closes his eyes. She leads him into the house. She places a box on his lap.)

Open your eyes.

(Julio opens the box. It's a radio.) Yours doesn't work well and this one is portable. Now you can listen to the news all day.
(Kisses him on the forehead.)
JULIO: Why did you do this? You don't have to give me a present.
INES: Happy birthday! Let's have a drink.
(Takes out a bottle of rum. Goes for three glasses.)
Find a good station on the radio. We'll have to toast. Say something Pepe.
PEPE: To . . . To Julio del Valle. To many . . . many more. That didn't sound good. I want to say something brilliant.
INES: To his health! And next year in another land.
PEPE: Yes, why not? All of us somewhere else. Somewhere else . . . Good appetite! Isn't that what the French say?
INES: Something like that.
PEPE: Then grand, big, good appetite. Appetite to eat a whole cow to you, Julio.
(Toast.)
JULIO: Salud . . .
INES AND PEPE: Salud . . .
INES: We'll have to dance.
JULIO: No, no, no, no . . .
INES: Come on and dance with me.
(Ines pulls his arm to dance.)
JULIO: Dance with him.
INES: You have to dance.
JULIO: I can't dance. I don't know how to dance.
INES: Oh come on!
JULIO: No . . . no dancing . . .
INES: You're lying. You can dance.
JULIO: You're crazy. I don't want to dance.
INES: Well, I won't force you. I'll leave you alone because it's your birthday. *(Pause.)* I went real far to get this rum. I know this is the one you like. I wanted this day to be special.
JULIO: *(Pours more rum in her glass.)* You want more, Pepe?
PEPE: Sure. "To your health! We would all like something better. Life is like that. We all want something better." See, I'm getting better at this.
(They drink.)
INES: Play music, Pepe. We'll dance. Oh, I can feel the rum rising to my face.
(Pepe switches on the radio. An old bolero plays. "Veinte Años")
INES: Leave that song on! I love old music. I used to collect music like this one. Oh! I collected all kinds of things . . . Oh! So many things gone.

Got rid of everything . . . All of it gone . . . *(Dances by herself.)* Gave everything away . . . I thought I was going to leave this place. But it never happened. *(The alcohol makes her giddy. But she's in control. She laughs.)* I was stupid. Gone mad in the head. And all for a German tourist. With him I went to all the nightclubs. I wore sunglasses and pretended to be a foreigner. All the waiters thought I was from Brazil, Italy, Portugal, until the German would get stuck ordering something, and I would have to open my mouth. *(She laughs at herself.)* He was gone at the end of summer . . . August . . . September . . . Gone away . . . *(She becomes bitter.)* Like all foreigners, they leave when the seaweed comes to the shores. The scum of the sea. He left dressed the same way I met him, starched white shirt . . . I stayed a mess, a shipwreck . . . *(Determined.)* — Oh, I'd like to live in a place where the land extends and I can walk for miles, where I can run and never reach the end. Here, there's always the sea. The jail of water. Stagnant. Just the sea. — Oh, this rum is going up to my head, Pepe. *(Ines stops dancing and goes to the table.)* Are you happy, Julio? Are you happy on your birthday?

JULIO: I'm as happy as can be.

INES: That's the most important thing, for you to be happy. Drink with me! Drink Pepe! Drink some more!

(She pours more rum on their cups.)

JULIO: No, that's too much.

PEPE: Drink up . . . Drink up . . .

INES: That's it drink . . . Oh, I want to dance again. Let's dance.

PEPE: No. No dancing. No more dancing . . . *(Switches off the radio.)*

JULIO: Let's just sit. Let's just sit and talk.

(The rum is loosening her spirit now. But she's not drunk.)

INES: Can you drink a lot, Pepe? Can you drink a lot without getting drunk?

JULIO: Oh, he can drink like a fish. I've seen him drunk more than a couple of times.

(Both men laugh.)

INES: I can't drink. *(Lifts up her glass.)* It all goes to my head, it opens my mouth and I talk too much. That's why I never drink. We talk too much, period. We are too loud and loose with our tongues.

JULIO: And what's wrong with that? What's wrong with talking.

INES: We should measure our words, like the English.

PEPE: If I do that, then I wouldn't speak my mind. If you measure your words, then you don't really say what you feel inside.

INES: *(Sits down.)* I think the Germans are like the English. They can talk to you about their deepest sorrows and still keep their calm. The German man, he was always talking about politics. He was always arguing whether we had gotten stuck because of the Americans or the Russians, whether we would survive all alone in the middle of the sea.

JULIO: Probably saw the worst year we had. The first year the Russians abandoned us . . . We were all like ants, running here and there. Wondering what would happen next.

INES: — Oh, I don't like talking about politics. To me wars seem useless and unreasonable. Destruction. God destroys, but his destruction is always justified. He destroys in perfect order. He's an artist at it. After his hurricanes and earthquakes, there's always a blue morning with clouds. And if there's rain, it's because he hasn't finished cleaning up after himself. But we haven't learned to master that art. Man is sloppy and messy and he can never master that art.
(There are tears in her eyes. She seems to be lost in memory. Her own destruction swells up to her throat and she can't contain it.)
Oh, why couldn't I leave this place! What's the use of staying in one place for so long?
(She has lowered her head to her arms. Julio reaches out to her. Pepe remains quiet and still, looking at the two of them. Lights fade to black.)

SCENE FIVE

Date projected on the screen: Ten Days After Julio's Birthday, October 11, 1993. Sound of rain and thunder. Ines sits to the center of the table. The stage is semi-lit. There are folded sheets and pillowcases on top of the table. She is mending a pillowcase. Julio stands next to her.

JULIO: Pepe came by late last night and I gave him a few things to sell. I gave him a vase and some old jewelry I had.
INES: You're selling everything, Julio. The house is starting to look sad.
JULIO: That's all right.
INES: You're not going to sell these, are you? I'm mending them.
JULIO: No. I did give him some more old frames and silverware. I told him to get what we need to go out to sea.
INES: Does this mean . . . Oh Julio!
JULIO: Yes, I'm ready to do it. I'm ready to plunge myself into the sea. What do I have to lose?

INES: Oh, Julio! *(Embraces him.)* So? So?

JULIO: He's going to find somebody to build a raft.

INES: When is it going to be ready? When are we leaving?

JULIO: Calm down. We still have to find more things.

INES: Is Pepe coming?

JULIO: Yes he is.

INES: *(Hugs him.)* Oh, Julio . . . *(There's an awkward moment when their bodies touch.)*

JULIO: Is there food?

INES: Yes. There's soup left from last night.

JULIO: Shouldn't we turn on the lights? You're going to hurt your eyes.

INES: It's not that bad, I can see. The rain brings a light of its own and I like sewing in this light. The rain makes me do things I don't normally do. It makes me sit down like an old woman and do this. Look at this pillowcase . . . The string got pulled out, and you can't make out the initials. The D looks like a C backwards.

JULIO: All that linen is falling apart. They've been in the family for so long.

INES: I know it's old. But it's still beautiful. Who knows how many generations! How many heads have slept on this pillowcase.

    I was just imagining all the women in your family, who slept on this pillowcase. I like your last name. I've always liked last names that begin with the letter D: del Campo, del Valle, de las Casas, de los Angeles. It makes one's name seem more regal. It makes you feel as if you belong to something, of this, of that. It just flows like history. I want to lay my head on this pillowcase. Close to you. *(Looks at him. They embrace.)* I love you, Julio. *(Embraces him.)* I want us to forget who we are. Start a new life away from here. Let's forget who we are.

(She kisses him on the forehead. She takes the pillowcase and gently tries to cover his face.)

JULIO: What are you doing?

INES: A game. Just a game to start a new life. Just let me do it. Look at me. *(She takes another pillowcase and places it over her head.)* When we lift up the cloth we'll start a new life.

(Music plays. Julio lets his face be covered by the pillowcase. Now she's covering her own face with the pillowcase. He touches her face through the cloth. He brings her close to him. They kiss through the pillowcase. The sound of the sea fills the stage. Lights fade.)

END OF ACT I

ACT II: AGUA
SCENE ONE

Projected on the screen: Agua: The Sea. Blue lights. The sounds of wind and sea fill the stage. On a raft in the middle of the Caribbean Sea, Ines and Pepe are rowing. Julio is standing, facing upstage with a compass in his hand.

PEPE: A good-for-nothing, I tell you. A miserable-wretched-mind-blind-deplorable beast. You can ask Julio what it took to get food, a piece of meat out of that moron.

JULIO: Yeah, she was an imbecile.

PEPE: It took bidding didn't it?

JULIO: Persuasion, eh! The imbecile wouldn't take anything.

INES: This rowing is getting to me, Pepe.

PEPE: Don't think about it. I said to the mountain woman, "What does it take to do an exchange? You give me a few pounds of jerked beef and I give you this radio. Good condition. The radio plays music like an orchestra. Long antenna. Picks up northern stations at night . . . Western stations, eastern stations, as far as Vienna." I even told her that I had danced to Viennese waltzes at night, and all from the radio. And what did the moron say, Julio?

JULIO: "No. No love. No music."

INES: What did she mean by that?

JULIO: I said to her, "Love yes, much love. You sitting on a horse riding through the prairies, playing the radio."

PEPE: Yes, then he told her, "Jerked beef for us, radio for you . . . Radio for love."

JULIO: Ines and the moron started to laugh, and she said, " Hee . . . hee . . . Love . . . No love . . .Hee . . . hee . . . A scratch . . . A scratch in my heart. . . My big sister stole my love."

PEPE: I felt sad when she said that . . .

JULIO: Let me finish, Pepe . . . She said, "Maybe radio for crying." But then she said, "No . . . No . . . If I cry, Mama will holler at me." That's when she told us to go to Adolfina, that she had fat chickens and lots of jerked beef. Then I saw the mountain woman looking at Pepe's bicycle and I pulled him aside and told him, "I bet you anything that if you give her the bicycle, she'll give us the 10 pounds of jerked beef." And wasn't I right?

PEPE: Yes, you were.

JULIO: I said to him, "Even if we have to walk ten miles, we're not going anywhere without getting the jerked beef."

INES: Is this it?

JULIO: Yes. We figured it's the only thing that wouldn't spoil.

PEPE: Do you think we're on the northeastern current? Roberto said that when we reach the straits of Florida, the currents flows eastward. Are we still moving toward the northeast?

JULIO: *(Looks at compass.)* If this compass is any good, it looks like we're moving north. What does it look like to you?

PEPE: Yes we're moving northeast.

INES: Are you sure we're not moving toward the northwest? Which way is east?

PEPE: *(Points to the left, then the right. Then makes up a new direction.)* This way. No, this way. This way. This thing can't make up its mind. It doesn't like pointing north now.

INES: I don't see the current moving us to the east or to the west. I just see waves. How can you tell the current is moving eastwards? How can you see in this darkness?

JULIO: The compass, Ines. The compass.

INES: I've been rowing for more than five hours and it feels like we haven't moved a bit. That thing doesn't work. Look at what happened to Columbus, he wanted to go to India and ended up in the Bahamas and Puerto Rico.

PEPE: We can't even see the city lights. Of course we're moving.

INES: *(Stands up and looks at the seascape.)* I can. I can still see the shimmering lights.

JULIO: Where?

INES: Back that way.

PEPE: That must be the reflection of the moon on the water.

INES: It feels as if we're inside the mouth of a wolf.

JULIO: A whale.

PEPE: *(Rowing.)* Let's get to it, Ines: One, two . . . One, two . . .
(Continues to count between the lines.)

JULIO: Take a break.

PEPE: *(Rowing.)* We have to pass the picket line! We have to pass the picket line!

INES: How do we know when we pass the picket line?

PEPE: There'll be ships, American coast guards. Balloons . . .

INES: Will they be able to see us in the dark?

PEPE: There'll be thousands of ships, people waving at us. Come on, one, two . . . one, two . . . one, two . . . one, two . . .
INES: Take a break. I can't rest if I see you rowing. I start feeling guilty.
JULIO: Take a break!
PEPE: *(Stops rowing and lies back.)* Give me a cigarette, Julio.
INES: *(After a pause.)* I don't know about you but I'm afraid. I get this bad feeling in my heart. Ay, I start to think that we'll end up drowned!
PEPE AND JULIO: Ines!
INES: *(Covers her ears.)* No . . . I didn't say that. Tell me you didn't hear me say that. *(Uncovers her ears.)* But I had to say it.
JULIO: That's why we have to keep our minds away from those thoughts. We have to think about other things. When I was in the military, one time we got lost for days stranded in the wild, under the scorching sun. We just couldn't find our way back to camp. And I used to tell myself, "We're getting there . . . We're getting there." I'd repeat it over and over again in my mind. I would picture the city, the streets, the buildings and that's what kept me going.
INES: What we need is a nightcap, something to put us to sleep. I just never thought that water could be so frightening.
JULIO: It is frightening.
INES: All this darkness.
PEPE: I've never seen so many stars.
INES: And look at their reflection on the waves. You can't even tell if the stars belong to the night or the sea. It makes me want to fish them out of the water. Give me something to drink, Julio.
JULIO: We have to save the water.
INES: I've been rowing for five hours I need some water.
PEPE: He's just trying to save the water. If we run out of water, we're in bad shape. Remember what Robertico said, no matter what happens we can't drink saltwater.
JULIO: You guys are going to have to turn around. I have to take a leak.
INES: Yes, I've been wondering how I'm going to pee, because you guys can just pull out your thing. I'm afraid of sticking out my butt and getting bitten by a shark. I've seen a few circling us.
PEPE: So have I. I just didn't want to say anything. They've been following us for some time.
JULIO: So aren't you going to turn around?
(Pepe and Ines turn around. There is a pause.)
INES: Well?

JULIO: Give me a second, will you!
INES: Did you finish? *(After a pause.)*
JULIO: I can't do it.
INES: How come?
JULIO: I can't pee when there are people around me. It takes me longer.
INES: You better get used to us.
PEPE: Listen to the water, it will make you want to pee.
INES: Pssssssssssssssssssssssssssssssssssssssssss ....
JULIO: What are you doing?
INES: That's what my mother used to do when my brother couldn't pee.
JULIO: Forget it. I'll pee later.
INES: You better get used to us.
JULIO: I will. I'll pee later.
INES: Why don't you play some music from the little radio? If we get an American station we'll know we're moving north.
PEPE: *(Switches on the radio.)* No American stations.
INES: See, who knows where we're heading, we can't even get a northern station! You're not a seaman and neither is he and I don't know anything about the sea, except it's a good place to cry.
JULIO: Give me a cigarette, Pepe. It's going to be a long night.
INES: Give me one, too. Being in the middle of nowhere makes us nervous. Not enough room to walk. Not enough space to run. I know I won't be able to sleep tonight.
JULIO: Me neither.
PEPE: That makes three of us. I have a hard time sleeping on land.
INES: You can't find a damn station?
JULIO: No.
INES: I want to hear an American song to make me feel we're getting closer. Billie Holiday, so I can a have good cry and calm myself. Don't get mad at me, Julio. I feel like crying. *(A Cuban bolero plays "Lagrimas negras." She moves to the rhythm.)* Leave that station on . . . Paranh . . . pan . . . pan . . . pan . . . panh . . .
JULIO: Don't sing. Control yourself. You're making the raft move.
INES: Let me sing . . . I feel like singing . . .

Tu me quieres dejar
Yo no quiero sufrir . . .
Contigo me voy mi santa
Aunque me cueste morir . . .
Sing with me, Pepe. Sing Julio

PEPE AND INES: *Yo no quiero . . .*
Yo no quiero llorar . . .
Contigo me voy mi Santa
Aunque me cueste morir de amor
(Ines gets a spoon and makes music with a metal cup. Pepe uses the wood on the raft as a drum. Julio joins to sing.)

Tu me quieres dejar
Yo no quiero sufrir
Contigo me voy mi santa
Aunque me cueste morir

Yo no quiero sufrir
Yo no quiero llorar
Contigo me voy mi santa
aunque me cueste morir de amor
(The sound of the ocean swells as the lights dim. The sound of the waves drowns all music. Silence. Darkness. Lights change.)

SCENE TWO

Projected on the screen: Second Day Out at Sea. Ines coughs. Julio holds a bottle of water.

JULIO: Drink some water.
INES: This thirst is getting to me. My mouth fills up with a bitter foam.
JULIO: Have some more water
(She takes another drink.)
INES: That's enough. I was having a bad dream. I was thirsty as a dry lake and my left breast overflowing with water. But I couldn't drink, because I couldn't bring my mouth close enough to my chest. But you came close to me and suck the water from my breast and gave me some water to drink. And I couldn't stop drinking from your mouth from my breast, because the thirst was insatiable. I drank and drank water. The more I drank the more water flowed out my breast. And I couldn't stop and neither could you. If you stopped giving me water, the flow would stop. And it felt I had enough to quench a desert. Just thinking about it gives me a strange sensation, as if I had water in there

(Brings her hand to her breast.)
JULIO: Come here . . . *(She moves close to him.)* Closer . . . Closer . . . *(She squats over his legs. He starts unbuttoning her dress.)*
INES: What are you doing?
JULIO: Shshshh . . . I want to see your breasts.
INES: Here Julio, in the middle of the sea with Pepe next to us!
JULIO: Yes. . .
(Pulls her close to him. He starts kissing her breasts and her neck.)
INES: No. You're insane.
JULIO: Why? Come here. I need to drink from you.
INES: But it was a dream.
JULIO: *(He is unzipping his fly.)* Dreams become real.
INES: No. Stop it.
JULIO: Why not? I want to taste you.
INES: We'll wake him up.
JULIO: Stay like this on top of me. We don't have to move the sea is already moving. Stay like that, like that.
INES: No, Julio.
JULIO: *(Kisses her.)* Yes, stay there.
INES: We'll wake him up. *(She starts giving in.)*
JULIO: No, this could be the last time.
INES: Don't say that!
JULIO: Yes. What if we never make it, my love?
INES: We'll make it.
JULIO: Stay like this as if it were the last time.
INES: We'll make it. Don't say we won't make it.
JULIO: If we don't make it, we can say we did it one last time. I was inside you one last time. One last time.
INES: Why are you so stubborn!
JULIO: Because you make me stubborn. Your skin, your face, having you so close to me, knowing that at any moment life could end for me.
INES: No, not for you. Nothing will happen to you while I'm here. Even if death comes near us I would let it take me first.
JULIO: *(As if reaching an orgasm.)* Oh, Ines . . . Ines . . . Ines . . .
INES: Ay, Julio!
(He lies back.)
JULIO: You see there was water inside you, like rain.
(She embraces him. They lie back on the raft. The sound of the sea fills the stage. Lights change.)

SCENE THREE

Projected on the Screen: Third Day Out at Sea. Julio and Ines are asleep. Pepe speaks to the sea. He's on top of the sail, looking out at the distance. He is hallucinating.

PEPE: If your voice is coming from there, say something! *(Pause.)* If your voice is coming from there, say something! *(Pause.)* Push me! Push me, like you said you would. *(Sound of children laughing. A distant angelic aria. Then the continual sound of the rippling waves.)* Don't think you can play with my mind? You can't trick me. You're not going to make me lose my head. I'm not sentimental. I'm not. I'm like a fish. Scales. Sharp bones. You never see a fish cry. Why cry when fish live in the water. If I cry, I'll cry in the shower, enh! So no one can see my tears. Tears to the water. Water to the sea. *(Sound of roaring sea. The sound of a child calling someone in the distance. Then it all subsides.)* I've heard what the ocean does to people. I've heard. Like the desert. A fever. You see things. A mirage. You play tricks on the eyes. Whatever became of that day, eh? Whatever became of that day when I was a child, and my father brought the whole family together and said, We're moving to the coast, and I'm going to show you the sea. And we sold all the chickens to buy the bus fare. We sold the cows and the pigs to rent a house close to the seashore. Look . . . Look . . . You can't trick me! I can close my eyes . . . I can close my eyes and see you like that first day, when the driver said, "We're in Havana. We're by the seawall." And I climbed down from the bus, with my eyes closed, and my father said, "Open your eyes, Pepe. Open your eyes. This is the sea. This is the sea." And when I saw you, you were blue and big as the falling sky. Calm and full as bowl of blue soup . . . You were all I imagined you to be.

Look . . . Look . . . Look at me running to you. *(Starts running in place.)* Look at me running to drink you! Look! Look! You can't trick me! *(Sound of children laughing.)* You can't trick me! You're not a lie! You're not a lie! You're not a lie! You're not a lie! Look at me swimming! Look at me swimming! Look at me walking on your water, like Jesus. Julio! Ines! I'm walking on top of the sea like Jesus! *(Sound of a woman laughing in the distance. Julio and Ines wake up.)*

JULIO: One can't even . . .

(Pepe continues running in place.)

PEPE: I'm walking . . .

INES: Pepe, what's gotten into you!
PEPE: I'm walking . . . I'm walking on top of the sea like Jesus.
INES: Stop that Pepe! He's hallucinating Julio! Grab him! Stop it! Stop! You're going to turn over the raft.
(Ines tries to make him stop. She tries to pull him down.)
(Sound of children laughing in the distance.)
PEPE: I'm walking! I'm getting there!
INES: Stop it!
JULIO: Stop it, Pepe! Stop it! STOP!
(Silence.)
(Pepe is transfixed.)
PEPE: I'm thirsty.
INES: I am too. Are you all right?
PEPE: My mind I . . . I thought
INES: Yes, Pepe
PEPE: I saw things . . . The sea I thought . . . I thought . . . My mind . . . It left me . . .
(Sound of loud thunder. Lights change.)

END OF ACT II

ACT III: FUEGO — FIRE IN THE SEA
SCENE ONE

Projected on the screen: Fourth Day Out at Sea. Sunset. Orange lights. Each character in his own world. Spotlight on Julio looking at the sea. He holds a metal cup and is peeing into the cup. The sound of bongo drums.

JULIO: Nothing but water and no water to drink. . . I'm in the fuckin' middle of nowhere . . . I must think of cities and streets, fountains of sweet water . . . I'm starting to smell like codfish . . . sardines . . . No, mustn't try to think of those things . . . *(Closes his eyes.)* It's raining inside me and the rain flows downwards from the mountains, to the valleys . . . And the water is so pure that women wash their hair and let their children bathe . . . *(Julio takes a swig of urine.)*
(Spotlight on Pepe looking up at the sky.)

PEPE: If I close my eyes . . . If I empty my mind and calm myself maybe sleep will come. Maybe sleep will come . . . I'm in the middle of nowhere . . .
(Spotlight on Ines. She is looking at the sea.)

INES: No, mustn't have bad thoughts. I always wanted to leave. Always wanted to go . . . Now I have it front of me, the sea . . . The sea . . . I finally got to go . . .

JULIO: If I close my eyes . . .
    PEPE: If I calm myself . . .
        INES: If I think of nothing . . .

JULIO: If I think of land, sweet water
    PEPE: I have to tell myself . . .

JULIO: Land . . .
    PEPE: . . . that is all a dream. . .
        INES: Maybe sleep will come. . .

JULIO: Maybe sleep will come . . .
    INES: It will come.
    PEPE: I have to tell myself . . .
        INES: I have to tell myself . . .

JULIO: I have to tell myself. . .
    INES: The sea is my hammock, my hammock . . .

JULIO: *(Abruptly.)* We're in the fuckin' middle of nowhere! How the hell did we get into all this rice and mangoes? *(The drums stop. Full lights.)*

INES: *(Hallucinating.)* Somebody is waving at me.

JULIO: Who?

INES: There . . .
PEPE: Wave back . . . *(In a loud voice.)* Hello!
INES: Hello . . .
JULIO: There's nobody there . . . It's the sea . . . Just the sea . . .
INES: It's not the sea . . . Somebody is waving at me . . .
JULIO: Nothing but water. It's our minds . . .
PEPE: Our minds? . . . Your mind . . . Not my mind . . . I like my mind . . .
INES: *(In a loud voice.)* — Hello out there! *(Waving. Opens an umbrella. She squints as she looks into the distance.)* Hello out there . . . Hello . . .
JULIO: *(After a pause.)* See . . . No answer . . .
INES: What's the matter, you're jealous? Hello, out there!
PEPE: It's not a man it's a woman . . .
JULIO: There's nobody out there, get that straight. Let's go to sleep, it's getting dark. When morning comes . . . When the sun rises . . . It will all be blue again . . .
PEPE: And we'll see rooftops at last . . .
INES: Windows . . .
JULIO: Windows she says! We're in the middle of nowhere.
INES: A sewing machine . . . When the wind blows gently I hear a sewing machine . . .
JULIO: She keeps seeing gondolas and sewing machines . . .
PEPE: Are you sure is not a train? I keep hearing a train.
JULIO: She said a sewing machine, and now you — .
PEPE: Then somebody is out there sewing . . .
JULIO: *(Looks at Pepe in disbelief.)* Oh, God.
INES: Yes, sewing, sewing, Julio . . .
JULIO: Sewing what?
PEPE: Handkerchiefs . . . White handkerchiefs to wave at us. Somebody is out there waiting for us . . .
JULIO: *(Gives up on the whole thing.)* I'm going to sleep.
INES: I'm still going to keep an eye on my suitcase.
JULIO: What suitcase?
INES: A man took it to the end of the platform . . .
JULIO: What platform? What's the matter with you! It's the sea . . . I keep telling you . . . Put this in your head . . .
PEPE: *(Trying to explain to her.)* Yes and every time . . . What he's saying is that every time . . . Every time we see something . . .
JULIO: Yes, tell her . . .
PEPE: What he's saying is that every time . . . Every time we see something . . .

JULIO: *(Applauds waiting to hear something brilliant.)* That's it . . . Finally . . .

PEPE: *(Puffing himself.)* Every time . . . Every time we're getting somewhere, it's just like another time without getting anywhere. Right, Julio?. . .

JULIO: Bravo . . .

PEPE: *(He turns away and looks at the sky.)* Then one more night to add to the list, till the next night . . . Then the moon again . . . *(Looking at the moon now.)* Same old glare . . . *(Points up.)* One more night with the moon . . . And there she is again wearing white gloves, green slippers, reeking of perfume, smoking her cigarette . . . And I have to tell her, "Why do you do this to me! . . . Why are you dressing up for me! Why are you trying to fool me . . . Let me go, enh. Let me go. Just let me be . . ." And I have to say, *(In a loud voice. Confused now.)* Is there anyone out there who knows what's happening!!!!

JULIO: What is he saying now?

INES: *(Closes her umbrella.)* I don't know what he's saying.

JULIO: What are you saying? What are you saying? Who are you talking to?

(There is a pause. Pepe is still looking at the sky waiting for an answer.)

INES: He's talking to the moon.

JULIO: He's talking to the moon . . . *(To Pepe.)* You better pull yourself together.

PEPE: *(In a vacuum.)* Something has happened, Julio . . . You hear? *(Pause.)*

JULIO: Nothing has happened . . . Nothing . . .

PEPE: Yes something has happened and the world has gone away. There's nobody to talk to . . . Nobody to ask.

INES: Ask the man who is waving at me. Julio doesn't like him, but he's still waving at me.

JULIO: There isn't any man and there isn't any moon . . .

PEPE: Then we're fucked.

JULIO: You both are scaring the shit out of me . . . We're in the middle of nowhere and you're talking nonsense . . .

INES: *(Gently.)* When the sun rises, it will be over Julio. I keep seeing a bridge in my dreams. A white bridge, curved like a fallen halo in the middle of the sea.

PEPE: *(Laughs with joy.)* When the sun rises I'll wash and shave my face like before . . .

INES: *(Full of joy.)* And I'll walk into my balcony and water my geraniums. . . How about you, Julio?

(Julio finds relief and starts to laugh.)

JULIO: Me . . . Oh I wish I could have a cigarette . . .

PEPE: *(With an imaginary cigarette.)* Yes, smoke in your mouth, like before.

Look at me, smoke in the air taking us back to your house, your table. Opening the windows to let in seven o'clock . . .

INES: Ah yes, seven o'clock! That's the time I like to get up. The smell of seven o'clock . . . The oleanders by my window . . .

PEPE: Coffee . . .

INES: Moist leaves . . .

JULIO: *(Entering their world.)* Mist . . . Bread. . .

PEPE: Barbershops . . .

INES: Clocks ringing . . .

JULIO: Beds being made . . . And light making its way under doorways . . .

INES: *(Suddenly seeing an imaginary airport.)* You must tell those men to be careful with my suitcase, Julio . . . *(To an imaginary person.)* — Be careful. That blue suitcase has never gone anywhere. It's liable to get lost. Doesn't know of farewells and train windows, people waving good-bye . . . *(To the Men.)* Ay, you don't know how much I wanted a picture sitting on top of my suitcase!

PEPE: I'm thirsty, Julio . . . Give me some water . . .

JULIO: We don't have any water.

PEPE: You drank it?

JULIO: Me? *(Lost for words.)* We . . . You know well . . . We didn't have anymore. . .

PEPE: But there was . . . I saw it . . . We had . . . I saw it with my eyes . . . Where's the bottle?

INES: What bottle?

(Pepe starts searching for the bottle. He starts making a mess.)

PEPE: It was full. . . Where is it? Where is it? Where did you hide it?

JULIO: I didn't take any water . . .

INES: Where did you see it?

PEPE: I saw it . . . It was full.

INES: I didn't drink it.

PEPE: Someone drank it.

JULIO: I didn't drink it.

PEPE: Then who did? Who was it? Give it to me. . . You're hiding it . . .

JULIO: I'm not hiding anything. . .

PEPE: Give it to me . . . *(Grabs him by the shirt.)* You took it. He has it! He has it! Give it to me . . .

(Pepe notices he has lost control. He lets go of Julio. He looks down at the waves. Silence.)

PEPE: *(Softly.)* I'm sorry . . . I'm . . . Something has happened, and I don't know what it is . . . I don't know who I am, what to do, what I've done. . . . What's happening, Julio? What's happening? What's happening to me?

JULIO: Calm down.

INES: *(Softly.)* You are Pepe, that's who you are . . . And . . . And I am Ines . . . You are Pepe, and I love you like I love Julio. *(Touches his face.)* How can you forget who you are? How can you forget?

JULIO: Let's go to sleep. Tomorrow we'll be a little bit closer.

PEPE: Oh, God . . . Now . . . I . . . I . . . Now . . . Now . . . Julio, she . . . she . . . Did you hear what she said?

JULIO: Let's go to sleep . . .

INES: But I love . . . *(Reaches out to him.)*

JULIO: Leave him alone.

PEPE: *(Looking at her.)* Why?

JULIO: Leave him alone.

PEPE: Didn't you hear what she said?

JULIO: Let's go to sleep We are weak. We are weak and tired, and we don't know what we're doing. We don't know what we're saying.

PEPE: *(Full of joy he shakes Julio.)* But she says she loves me, Julio. Didn't you hear? *(Moves toward her. Pause.)* How can I go to sleep? Why go to sleep, when I feel like shouting!

(Pepe laughs. He touches her face. She smiles and kisses his hand. Julio turns in the other direction. Ines lies back on the raft. Pepe admires her beauty. Sound of a large wave. Lights fade to black.)

SCENE TWO

Nighttime. Fog. Projected on the screen: Fifth Day Out at Sea
The men are asleep. Ines is awake looking into the distance. She is hallucinating. Sound of a large ship approaching.

INES: Julio, Pepe . . . Are you awake? *(Pause.)* I'm going to get ready, you hear. They're out there. They've come for us. You two can stay here sleeping, I'll come back for you . . . Where's my shawl? *(She starts looking for her shawl.)* What did I do with my shawl? I bought it years ago. I'm going to wear it when we get there. I'm going to run through the seaport with my shawl. Julio, Pepe, can you just see me! You both have to carry me in your arms and lift me up in the air. Best to put some powder on. I probably look like a scarecrow. Don't want those people on the ship to see all

these long nights on my face . . . *(She takes out her compact and starts powdering her face hurriedly. Sound of a large ship approaching.)* Eyes red . . . Lips dry . . . Lucky for this . . . Couldn't leave it behind, same compact Mamá used for years . . . just in case I had to see her face in the mirror . . . Oh, if she could peek from the sky and see that I'm finally getting somewhere! She used to say, Ines, has butterflies in her head. Well, you could tell her now. I'm going to some big land, Mamá. They've come for us! . . . And when you have to go you have to go . . . Even if I had to leave like a thief, without my traveling shoes, my old blue dress which I hung in my wardrobe years ago, and my alligator bag . . . You both have to hold tight to me when I come back for you. Don't want you falling behind. *(Continues powdering her face.)* Morning comes and it's all the same here. The two of you should've been awake a moment ago, an Angel came from heaven and said he was going find us a lightbulb to light this part of the sea. You have to light it when he gives it to you. It would make things better, you hear me. That way I can look for your light in the distance. *(Closes her compact. She has powdered her face so much she looks like a clown. She takes out the umbrella. She turns upstage and opens it. A blue glow emanates from the umbrella. She sticks her foot in the water. The stage lights slowly start to dim.)* I'm just going to make my way to that ship — to that man waving at me. Good-bye, Julio. Good-bye, Pepe . . . You just keep your eye on my umbrella, you hear me? Water is warm, Julio, like a glass of warm milk . . . You liked to drink warm milk at night. They say it soothes the mind, like summer rain. Oh, I can feel the warmth rising to my face. *(The sound of a ship approaching will echo throughout the following section.)* That's a good omen. It's warm like a winter coat, as if a fallen star had bathed in it . . . Look at all this blue water, Julio . . . Nothing like the sea . . . Nothing like the sea . . . *(Her voice echoes. Sound of fog horns.)* All these different blues . . . Prussian blue, Pompeii blue . . . Aquamarine . . . Aniline . . . Indigo . . .
(All we see is the glow of the blue umbrella moving through the stage and the light from the kerosene lamp on the raft.) Calamine blue . . . Capri blue . . . Egyptian blue . . . You just keep your eye on my umbrella, you hear me? *(Julio wakes up.)*

JULIO: Ines . . . *(Pause.)* Ines. . . Pepe wake up. Where is Ines? *(Lifts up the kerosene lamp.)* Where did she go? *(Pause.)* Ines. Ines. . .Where did she go? Where is she?

(The sound of a large ship fills the space. Lights change.)

END OF ACT III

ACT IV: AIRE
SCENE ONE

Projected on the screen: Aire. Daytime. Both men are still in a hallucinatory state and are looking out into the distance.

PEPE: Nowhere to be found. She's . . .

JULIO: No. Don't say she's gone. She's not gone. She's not gone. Look to your right. She's bound to appear. *(Picks up the compass and throws it.)* Oh, this shit!

PEPE: Julio, you've lost your mind. She's gone . . .

JULIO: No. Don't say she's gone. When it's quiet like this . . . When it's quiet I can hear her.

PEPE: Me too.

JULIO: Then don't say she's gone.

PEPE: No, I hear her, too. But I think it's a ghost . . . Then you start screaming at me, and we lose her. We see her then we lose her.

JULIO: I won't yell at you anymore. When it's quiet like this . . . Do you hear now?

PEPE: No.

JULIO: When it's quiet . . . I can hear her so clear.

PEPE: Then it's real. Then she's really with us . . .

JULIO: You think so, too?

PEPE: Sure.

JULIO: Then it's her.

PEPE: It's a ghost, Julio

JULIO: No.

PEPE: Then we have to tell ourselves that we're not seeing things that it's really her.

JULIO: Yes . . . Yes . . .

(Ines enters the stage singing. She holds her umbrella and makes her way to the raft and sits by Julio.)

INES: *Que te importa que te ame*
Si tu no me quieres ya?
El amor que ya ha pasado
no se debe recordar.
Fui la ilusión de tu vida un dia lejano ya. . .

JULIO: Ines . . .

INES: Shshhhhh . . . You see the blue calamine waves over on that side. . . That takes us to a sleepy island where I like to go for tea in the afternoons.

JULIO: *(Looks at Pepe then at her.)* It's her . . . It's you . . . I told him . . .

INES: Shshhh . . . Not too loud . . . A woman told me that if I stay here for too long, someone is liable to recognize me . . .

JULIO: No. Stay. We won't say anything . . . We won't tell.

PEPE: No we won't tell.

INES: She said, you go on. You just go on . . .

JULIO: She said that! That's good . . . We . . . We're glad . . .

PEPE: We thought . . . We thought you had gone . . .

JULIO: Don't say it, Pepe . . . She's here now . . .

INES: Well I said, I need to get out of this limbo . . . What about Julio and Pepe!

JULIO: You said that?

INES: The woman told me I could sit here and wait for the ship with you . . . *(Laughs.)* I said to her it's easier for others to do this . . . It's easier for a real person, for a man to do these things, because he can hide his face under a hat . . . I'm not supposed to be here. Someone could recognize me. She said she would get me a red scarf . . . *(Becomes excited.)* Can you believe it, me sitting here with you wearing a red scarf? And I said, could I possibly be dreaming this? I mean, if I'm not . . . If I'm not . . .

JULIO: *(Looks at Pepe.)* No, it's real. It's *real* like my skin and bones . . . You . . . You . . . You're here . . .

PEPE: Sure, it's real . . .

JULIO: As long as you don't go anywhere . . . And you stay here with us . . .

INES: Of course, my love . . . Someone said there's a bus that comes around this time . . . We don't want to miss it . . .

JULIO: *(Going along with her.)* No, we don't want to miss it.

PEPE: But tell them not to send us any ugly phantoms, like last time . . . The ones that took you away . . .

JULIO: Pepe, that's enough!

PEPE: They did. They came here in a black bicycle . . . They came here and drank all our water and . . . and . . .

JULIO: It's all right. This morning I was making my bed before I got up, because I had already gotten up in my mind and made the bed . . . And I made the bed because we had things to do. We had to look for you, my love . . .

PEPE: Where's the northeast current? That's what we're looking for . . .

INES: You must follow the north star, if you want to find the northeast current.

But who can trust stars, I've noticed they're like dizzy sailors, who faint and fall into the sea.

JULIO: Then how do find our way through this mess?

INES: By the blue trains of the sea . . . The constant trains crossing the sea . . .

(Sound of a distant train.)

JULIO: I never heard of a train crossing the sea. You mean . . . You mean the currents?

INES: There are trains of water sailing everywhere . . . *(Sound of a train getting closer.)* Can you hear them? I must go! I must go! The trains . . . The trains . . . *(Gets up to go.)* I'll try to come back! I'll come back!

(The sound gets louder.)

JULIO: Wait Wait . . . Don't go . . . You can't go . . .

(All sounds subside.)

INES: Soon . . . Very soon . . . Any minute now trees and flowers will surround you again. I know so . . . I must go now.

PEPE: The water . . . The water . . . It's getting shallow around here, Julio . . .

INES: *(Starts looking for her shawl.)* Oh Julio, where's my shawl? What did I do with my shawl I'm going to get to wear it when we get there . . . I'm going to run through the seaport with my shawl . . .

(Julio starts helping her look for the shawl. Julio finds a cloth bag.)

JULIO: Could it be here? What's in here?

(Julio hands her the bag.)

INES: *(Opens it and pulls out the pillowcases.)* I brought those. Didn't want to leave them behind. Take one for you and one for you, Pepe . . .

PEPE: What is this for?

INES: I invented this game . . . Put it over your head, Julio . . . Show Pepe, how to do it . . .

(Julio takes the pillowcase and puts it over his head. Pepe lets his head be covered by the pillowcase. She looks at the two of them, then looks into the distance.)

INES: Soon it will be over. Look at our night almost coming to an end, just like everything else. That's what I'll miss Julio, seeing the morning get dress before my eyes — how she pulls her clothes from the sea. Well, what can I do? I move on. That's one thing I learned from the sea . . .

JULIO: Ines . . .

INES: Yes . . . I move on, Julio . . . When you lift up the pillowcase, you'll begin a new life . . .

(Music plays . . . She opens her umbrella and starts to walk away and

disappear. Both men stay with their faces covered. The white scrim opens up to reveal a green landscape. The men uncover their faces. A flash of white light illuminates the stage. Then blackout.)

END OF PLAY

The Negro of Peter the Great

Carlyle Brown

Based on the unfinished novella by Alexander Sergeyevich Pushkin

The Negro of Peter the Great was commissioned by the Alabama Shakespeare Festival, Montgomery, Alabama; Kent Thompson, Artistic Director.

BIOGRAPHY

Carlyle Brown, an alumnus of New Dramatists and a Playwright-in-Residence at Alabama Shakespeare Festival, is the author of *The Negro of Peter the Great,* which the Southern Writers' Project produced as a world premiere in the 2000–2001 season at Alabama Shakespeare Festival. He was a founder of The Laughing Mirror Theatre in New York, an experimental ensemble company devoted to the research and development of African-American theatrical forms. He also has taught expository writing at New York University, African-American literature at the University of Minnesota, and playwriting at Ohio State University and Antioch College. His plays include *Yellow Moon Rising, Little Tommy Parker Celebrated Colored Minstrel Show* (which won six Audelco Award nominations), *The African Company Presents Richard III* (which received two Audelco Awards), *Sea Never Dry, Buffalo Hair, The Pool Room, A Big Blue Nail, Arabian Nights,* and most recently, *The Beggars' Strike* at the Children's Theatre Company in Minneapolis. Mr. Brown has held playwriting fellowships sponsored by the Jerome Foundation, the McKnight Foundation, the Minnesota State Arts Board, the National Endowment for the Arts, the New York Foundation for the Arts, and Theatre Communications Group.

CAST OF CHARACTERS

IBRAHIM PETROVICH HANNIBAL
KORSAKOV
THE FRENCH OFFICER
THE SECOND
COUNTESS LEONORA
MARQUIS MERVILLE
COUNT L.
MADAME DUBOIS
THE CZAR, PETER THE GREAT
LIZA
NATALYA GAVRILOVNA RZHEVSKY
PRINCE ALEXANDER MENSHIKOV
GAVRIL AFANASYEVITCH RZHEVSKY
TATYANA AFANASYEVNA RZHEVSKY
GUSTAV ADAMYCH
THE SERVANT/IVAN
VALERYAN
A SERVANT MAID

THE NEGRO OF PETER THE GREAT

ACT I

Dawn on a dueling ground in the woods of France. A French Officer and his Second are at one end of the dueling ground, Korsakov and Ibrahim are at the other. Ibrahim holds his hat in hand, brimming over with fresh cherries. A cloth is wrapped around his head to cover a scar from a wound.

KORSAKOV: Ibrahim, I beg you, put off this madness. Don't fight. Don't do it.

IBRAHIM: I will have that man's discretion or I will have his life.

KORSAKOV: What gossip can any man make that's worth taking his life? Or maybe losing your own?

IBRAHIM: You know, Korsakov, that this is more than just a matter of my own honor.

KORSAKOV: Ibrahim, you poor fool. What do you need with that kind of honor. You're too good for that. Why do you persist in dueling? It's endless, Ibrahim.

IBRAHIM: What is it brother? Have you never done this before?

KORSAKOV: No, this is my first time.

IBRAHIM: The first time is the hardest. Listen Korsakov. You hear the birds singing? And smell how heavy the dew is. The sun will be up soon. Can you feel your heart beating? Feel the blood rushing through your veins? My mouth is dry, my stomach upset, my hands are shaking. I have no where else to go now, but oblivion. Yet somehow, I feel confident, cheerful, energetic, unafraid. I stopped to pick these cherries from the trees. I have a taste in my mouth for cherries. Would you like some cherries, Korsakov?

KORSAKOV: No, Ibrahim, I have no stomach for cherries. I have no stomach for this. This is madness. How can you risk your life, or maybe kill a complete stranger over a woman, you can never have. A married woman and a nobleman's wife, no less.

IBRAHIM: Because it gives me pleasure just to be in the same room with her. To look at her, to hear her voice. Why should there be any sense in it?

KORSAKOV: He only slanders her because she spends her idle hours with you.

This has nothing to do with her. It's your reputation he's after. He only wishes to make a name for himself.

IBRAHIM: Then we shall carve it out for him in blood.

FRENCH OFFICER: Well are we ready? Can we begin now? You were already late. We thought perhaps you had lost your pistols, and were still at home sharpening your spear.

(The French Officer and the Second laugh.)

IBRAHIM: Sorry. I was picking cherries off the trees and lost track of the time.

SECOND: Before we begin I must ask you gentlemen to reconsider. Is there any possibility of reconciliation between you.

IBRAHIM: No. None.

FRENCH OFFICER: On that we agree.

KORSAKOV: Gentlemen, I warn you. This man is the protege of Peter the Great, the Czar of Russia.

FRENCH OFFICER: Then the Czar will have to find some other black, sooty toy to amuse himself. A monkey, or a gorilla perhaps.

IBRAHIM: These cherries are so red and ripe now. So delicious. Would you like one?

FRENCH OFFICER: No thank you. I would rather put a pistol ball in your heart.

SECOND: It seems there can be no peace between you. Therefore let me read you the terms of the duel. "The terms of the duel between the parties . . ."

IBRAHIM: Mention no names. It is the indiscretion and misuse of names which brings us here. I don't care who he is. Describe him as nobody. You may indicate me as anybody. But there will be no names.

SECOND: The terms of the duel between parties who must be nameless. The terms and the rules. They are simple. You will go to your places and stand your ground. On the first command you will cock and ready your weapons. On the second command you will aim your weapons. When I drop this handkerchief, and it touches the ground, consider that the command to fire your weapons Once the two parties have fired, if there is no result, we will begin again, and again, until the affair of the duel has been satisfied. Are there any questions? Gentlemen, take your ground please. Ready! Aim!

(Second drops a white handkerchief. Ibrahim and the French Officer aiming at one another prepare to fire. Blackout. Spotlight on the handkerchief. Lights up on the home of Countess Leonora in Paris. Ibrahim picks up the handkerchief. Enter Countess Leonora.)

LEONORA: Ibrahim, my love, my heart.

IBRAHIM: Where is everyone?

LEONORA: They're all inside, listening to him go on and on about one thing or the other. Oh, how I've missed you.

IBRAHIM: Leonora, we have to talk.

LEONORA: I don't want to talk, I don't want to think, I just want to feel you.

IBRAHIM: Listen to me Leonora. I met a young French cavalry officer in the field this morning.

LEONORA: Not another duel? You're not hurt are you?

IBRAHIM: And it wasn't just for my sake that I took up his glove.

LEONORA: Tell me you're not hurt.

IBRAHIM: He insulted you.

LEONORA: Ibrahim, how could you? I begged you, never to defend me. A scandal will dishonor me more than any insult. Or what if something should happen to you? I don't want you risking your life for my sake.

IBRAHIM: A soldier's world is not polite society. A pistol ball was the only way to assure his discretion.

LEONORA: Is he dead?

IBRAHIM: What does it matter? It only proves that I have to go.

LEONORA: Go? What do you mean you have to go? Go where?

IBRAHIM: I've received a letter from the Czar. He wants me to return to Russia.

LEONORA: But the Czar has sent you these letters before, and you didn't leave then.

IBRAHIM: Sooner or later your husband is bound to discover us. What if he should call me out?

LEONORA: He wouldn't dare. He knows your skill. It would be certain death.

IBRAHIM: Fate always has a hand to play in these things Leonora. But whatever it is, whatever his fears, whatever his feelings, he's a gentleman. He has no choice. He must protect his honor.

LEONORA: Then you must refuse him.

IBRAHIM: My honor is as precious to me as his. My honor is all I have. What else is there to stand between me and complete oblivion, but my honor? I have neither a title or lands. I receive an allowance like some fop. I'm the Czar's Negro. I can barely claim my own name. My uniform is threadbare. I'm wretched. And this society, this frivolous society persecutes, pitilessly persecutes everything it claims it will allow in theory. It's just a matter of time before that cold, pompous derision, the insinuations, the deceit, will catch up to us. And what will become of us then? Then you will become ashamed of me. Of us. Then your fascination with me will be finished.

LEONORA: Fascination? You can't really believe that I could ever feel that way? About you? I thought you knew me. It isn't fascination. I love you Ibrahim. You, for yourself.

IBRAHIM: Then how can you pretend that baby in there, that changeling is your son? You and the Count. While to stop a scandal, our boy lives some miserable life somewhere, with some peasant woman, who we don't even know who she is.

LEONORA: Please Ibrahim, don't make me talk about him. Don't make me remember our son. I don't want to think about him. I can't. And I can barely look at that child in there now as it is. And the Count is convinced it's the spitting image of him.

IBRAHIM: I saw him today.

LEONORA: You saw him? Who? Our son?

IBRAHIM: Yes. I went there just after the duel.

LEONORA: How is he Ibrahim?

IBRAHIM: He is as well as to be expected. He lives in a hovel in the worst part of Paris. I found him suckling at his new mother's breast. He's not as dark as he was when he was a born. He's a little fawn-colored now. His hair is curly and he has your eyes. I named him Abrashka.

LEONORA: Abrashka? What kind of name is Abrashka?

IBRAHIM: It's a Russian name.

LEONORA: Ibrahim, I was in despair. In utter misery. It all seemed so hopeless. We were going to be ruined. There was nothing else we could do. I know you think it was frivolous and capricious of me, Ibrahim, but a woman must secure her future in any way she can. But that has nothing to do with love.

IBRAHIM: There it is Leonora. Don't you see? You cannot leave your husband. You're safe. You have nothing to gain by being with me, and I have everything to lose.

LEONORA: We just have to be more careful, that's all. We just must be more discreet this time.

IBRAHIM: Leonora I have to go.

LEONORA: But why do you have to go? And what will I do when you're gone to half-savage Russia? What will I think about, or look forward to, or dream of, if not for you? Of all the things that stand between us, why must you always put yourself in our way? Why do you behave as if it were just you? As if you're the one who's always alone?

IBRAHIM: Because I am always alone. It's an aloneness both vivid and terrifying. It's all I've ever known. We must see that Abrashka has an allowance.
LEONORA: Yes Ibrahim. I will see to it. My maid knows where the woman lives. We will see that he is provided for. Oh, what will become of you my little Abrashka?
COUNT L.: *(Offstage.)* Leonora!
LEONORA: Coming!
COUNT L.: *(Offstage.)* Leonora!!
LEONORA: Yes, I'm coming! Ibrahim please, kiss me quickly.
(Enter the Marquis Merville.)
MERVILLE: Ibrahim. I didn't see you come in. Welcome. Countess, your husband has been calling for you.
LEONORA: Excuse me, Ibrahim.
(Exit Leonora.)
MERVILLE: Look at her. Isn't she lovely? Of course she's no longer in that first flower of her youth, but still, she's a beautiful woman. You know the story as well as I do. She came out of the convent and was married off to the Count when she was only seventeen. She's never learned to love him, and he makes no effort to teach her. Remember what I told you before, Ibrahim? That love without hopes or demands is more certain to capture a woman's heart than all the calculations of seduction. Well, was I right? Did you have her?
IBRAHIM: Careful what you say from here on, Marquis. I happen to be a very good shot.
MERVILLE: Yes, so I have heard. As it seems a young cavalry officer has discovered only this morning. The pistol ball shattered his wrist, so I'm told. To shoot a wavering hand at twenty paces, it's remarkable. And that's not the only reason that you're the attraction of Paris. Why I imagine you get more invitations to Parisian salons than Montesquieu or Fontenelle, or even that young upstart Voltaire. All the ladies of Paris wish to be the hostess to "Le Negre du Czar." Yet he is always here. Why?
IBRAHIM: I envy men who are in no way remarkable at all. I consider insignificance a blessing. That gentleman who presented me with his glove and who is now left-handed, he also took an offensive interest in the affairs of Le Negre du Czar.
MERVILLE: Forgive me, Captain Petrovich, but I am very proud to be a coward. I was only trying to say, that I think the Countess has enchanted you.
COUNT L.: *(Offstage.)* Ibrahim! Marquis! Come have a look at the baby.
MERVILLE: Oh yes, the baby. Let's have a look at our new baby boy.

(Ibrahim and Merville go inside. A Maid Servant holds the baby for all to see.)

COUNT L.: The whole of the ritual of fatherhood was bereft me. No running for the doctor, no pacing in the halls, no distress, none of *it*. The Countess is in the agonies of labor, and I'm off shooting ducks in the countryside.

MERVILLE: Well, I should at least hope you were there for the conception.

COUNT L.: Yes Marquis, I seemed to have benefited from only the best of it. Welcome Ibrahim. I didn't see you come in. I was just about to tell Korsakov and Madame DuBois how you stood in for me at the birth.

MERVILLE: Ibrahim, what a thoughtful fellow. Very accommodating. And extremely attentive to the Countess. But tell me, Count, how is it you were duck hunting while your wife is giving birth?

COUNT L.: It was Leonora's idea. She knows I become a complete wreck if the least little thing distresses her. The sight of blood? The thought of her in pain? I would have been altogether useless and in the way.

MERVILLE: Indeed, you may have.

MADAME DUBOIS: Isn't he beautiful, Korsakov? I'll wager you were like that once. You are a little like that now.

KORSAKOV: You are so wicked Madame DuBois.

MADAME DUBOIS: Oh, how you flatter me, Korsakov

MERVILLE: Congratulations, Count. You are a lucky man. A beautiful wife, a lovely new baby, wealth, influence. Your home and your honor intact. What more could you ask?

COUNT L.: Thank you, Marquis. Darling, come have a look at our son.

LEONORA: I see him quite enough, darling. Let our friends have a chance to look at him.

COUNT L.: Here, Nurse, let me have him. Jean Paul, come and see Ibrahim. Remember Ibrahim, Jean Paul.

IBRAHIM: He's a fine-looking boy.

COUNT L.: Jean Paul, Ibrahim is a bombardier. A captain in the artillery. He's a Russian soldier in the French army. He's a Negro, godson of the Czar.

LEONORA: Count, please.

COUNT L.: I'm sorry, Ibrahim. I didn't mean anything. Here hold him. Hold Jean Paul.

MERVILLE: Seems as if there is a new man born in Europe. Wouldn't you say Ibrahim? Tell us, which of the happy couple you think he resembles the most?

MADAME DUBOIS: Speaking of something new, Captain Petrovich, shame on you. Why didn't you tell us that your good friend Korsakov was such a marvelously talented person? I didn't know he was a handsome young poet.

KORSAKOV: Thank you, Madame DuBois, but I am not really a poet. I am an improvisator. An improviser.

MADAME DUBOIS: An improviser? An improviser. An improvisator. Oh, it sounds so stimulating.

KORSAKOV: Yes, you see my poems are all extemporaneous inspirations of the moment. The spoken words are like notes in music. Once they are gone in the air, we can never catch them again. I never write them down. All I require is your participation. My audience is my muse. Simply give me a theme. A hidden secret. A lost desire. Some wild, wanton thought lying deep in your mind. And I will improvise a poem of it. We will need pen and paper. Write down your themes, and we will then have Madame DuBois pick one out by lot.

(The Maid Servant dispenses quill and paper, and the guests write down their themes.)

MERVILLE: Ibrahim, you are very quiet tonight. You're not yourself, my old African friend. Countess Leonora, do you remember the first time I introduced you to Captain Petrovich?

LEONORA: Yes Marquis, I do. You were rude as usual. He introduced poor Ibrahim as Peter the Great's Negro. I told Ibrahim not to be shocked, he often introduces me as if I were the Count's property.

COUNT L.: Leonora, you are a treasure to me, and not my property.

MERVILLE: Louis XIV ate with his hands, we all could do with more manners. But still, when you met, there was a look in your eyes, the two of you.

LEONORA: Count, don't you see how awkward Ibrahim is. Jean Paul is only an infant.

COUNT L.: Yes, I suppose a baby is an awkward thing in a soldier's arms. Do you want to hold him, Leonora?

LEONORA: Yes, give him to me. I'll hold him.

COUNT L.: Give Jean Paul to the Countess, Ibrahim.

LEONORA: Thank you, Ibrahim.

IBRAHIM: Yes, Countess.

MADAME DUBOIS: Well, Korsakov, you have your themes. May I choose your improvisation now?

KORSAKOV: Yes, of course.

(Madame Dubois chooses a paper from an urn and gives it to Korsakov.)

KORSAKOV: The theme on this paper is, "Cleopatra and her lover." Would the writer please explain this thought to me. *(Pause.)* Will no one confess to the authorship of this theme?

MERVILLE: Well, if no one will confess, neither will I. But I will suggest what it might be. Cleopatra was like a queen bee to her lovers. Wasn't death the price of her love? Yet there were lovers who did not hesitate to pay the price, for the sake of their passion for her.

KORSAKOV: Yes, I see. Thank you, Marquis.

(Korsakov composes his thoughts and begins.)
Twilight
O' morning twilight
O' golden twilight
When comes the dawn
The dew is heavy, my heart is beating
My blood is rushing, all fast and warm
This day in the shade of a cherry tree
A young love dies with the death of me
This is the price for love I'll pay
My life like a trifle, I'll throw away
And give it to her, a small gift from me
A life that was for her to command
Even though she could never see
That she held a life in the palm of her hand
Better for me to leave this world
When love is young and wild and sweet
Then to see her grow a gray-haired girl
Who crushes dreams beneath her feet
And while the darkness crawls around me
This summer morning in the wood
I know that the dark is only dark
To be conquered by the good.

MADAME DUBOIS: Wonderful, Korsakov. Very good.

KORSAKOV: Thank you, Madame DuBois.

COUNT L.: Excellent. Astonishing.

MERVILLE: Bravo. Bravo, Korsakov. Bravo.

KORSAKOV: Thank you

COUNT L.: You are truly a man of inspiration, Korsakov. Poets labor for weeks to write such verse, and yet you, take another person's thoughts barely formed in their own thinking and make music of it. It's astonishing. Leonora? Ibrahim? How did you like it? You both seem so distracted this

evening. You've both barely said a word. How did you like Korsakov's improvisation?
LEONORA: Beautifully done, Korsakov.
KORSAKOV: Thank you, Countess.
IBRAHIM: It was very good, Korsakov. Thank you.
KORSAKOV: Thank you, Ibrahim.
COUNT L.: Truly you are not yourself tonight, Ibrahim. Is there something the matter?
IBRAHIM: I have sad news. At least the news is sad for me, in any case. I have orders from the Czar. I leave for Russia tonight.
LEONORA: Tonight?
IBRAHIM: Within the hour.
LEONORA: Jean Paul is waking up. Take him, nurse, before he starts to cry.
COUNT L.: This is sad news, Ibrahim.
MERVILLE: Tragic. Most unfortunate.
LEONORA: Tonight? In an hour? I had no idea you were leaving this soon.
(Through Ibrahim's speech, we are transported from Paris to St. Petersburg in Russia.)
IBRAHIM: Please. This is difficult enough. I can't stand good-byes. Usually I just go away. I was going to write. I hadn't the courage to tell you all until now. But I wanted to thank the Countess for her pure, spontaneous soul. Her passionate devotion and her boundless tenderness toward me, I shall never forget. When I first came to Paris, Korsakov and I only slept in carriages, going from one ball to the other. You see, I was born in Abyssinia, a land where the night air is too sweet to sleep in, and my brother Korsakov and I, we are Russians, and we Russians can dance forever. But it's difficult being a foreigner. You stand out. Everyone immediately thinks they know who you are. And once they see you, they will never accept anything else about you other than what they think they see. It was only in Countess Leonora's salon that I found friendship, and a place to be myself, and not Le Negre du Czar. I will not dishonor myself with tears. These memories must last me for a long time. Perhaps forever. Memories to carry me on the long journey ahead. Memories to carry me through memories. Through France, the Austrian Netherlands, the Holy Roman Empire, Saxony, Poland, and from Prussia, to the Russian frontier. And then on to St. Petersburg, a journey as long as it took to cross nearly all of Europe. It's just turning autumn now. The thick woods of birch trees along the River Neva are wearing their winter shadows, and in the orchards at Oranienbaum, the apples are falling to the ground. St Petersburg. In

the heart of my homeland, Holy Mother Russia, where they will welcome me like a prodigal son. Bring me the rest of my baggage footman.

THE SERVANT/IVAN: I don't know that I should, sir.

IBRAHIM: What?

THE SERVANT/IVAN: My instructions from the Czar were to bring you here. There was nothing said about your baggage.

(Enter Peter the Great.)

PETER: Aha, Ibrahim! Ibrahim Petrovich Hannibal. How is my godson? Look at you. It seems not long ago you were no bigger than a pig, and now look at you. A handsome young man from abroad. And a captain, no less. Paris was good to you? And the women? The women? And dueling? I hear you've been dueling again, Ibrahim Petrovich. You'll have to tell me all about it.

THE SERVANT/IVAN: Shall I bring in this man's baggage, your highness?

PETER: *(Beating the Servant/Ivan with his cane.)* Yes, you lout. This man is a gentleman. He's my godson. Is this how you treat him, as if he were a Turk?

THE SERVANT/IVAN: No, your majesty.

PETER: Are you hurt?

THE SERVANT/IVAN: No, your majesty.

PETER: *(Striking the Servant/Ivan again.)* What?

THE SERVANT/IVAN: Yes, your majesty. It hurts.

PETER: Well, let that be a lesson to you. Bring in Captain Petrovich's baggage. And be careful you don't strain yourself.

THE SERVANT/IVAN: Yes your majesty.

(The Servant/Ivan exits.)

PETER: That servant is a fool. But I love him . . . And your wound. Your wound in the war with Spain. I would covet such a wound. A good wound is a good honor. Wear it proudly. Do you still carry those pistols I gave you.

IBRAHIM: Yes, godfather. I practice every day.

PETER: Without practice the steady hand loses its cunning. Still a good shot, I'll wager. Where are they? In this bag? . . . Oh, they are beautiful, are they not, Ibrahim Petrovich? Still want them?

IBRAHIM: Yes, godfather, I do.

PETER: Are they loaded?

IBRAHIM: Of course, godfather; I was crossing the frontier.

(Enter the Servant/Ivan with bags.)

PETER: Good. Choose. It's tight in here, so we'll have to settle for ten little paces. Close range, that takes nerve. Give me your back. You there. Put down those bags and count off ten paces.

THE SERVANT/IVAN: But, your majesty . . .

PETER: Count!

THE SERVANT/IVAN: One . . .

PETER: Was the money I sent you sufficient?

THE SERVANT/IVAN: Two . . .

IBRAHIM: Yes, godfather. Most generous.

THE SERVANT/IVAN: Three . . .

PETER: The letter I sent you, Ibrahim . . .

THE SERVANT/IVAN: Four . . .

PETER: I did not intend to put the least pressure on you.

THE SERVANT/IVAN: Five . . .

IBRAHIM: I know, godfather.

THE SERVANT/IVAN: Six . . .

PETER: I would never forsake my protégé.

THE SERVANT/IVAN: Seven . . .

IBRAHIM: Or I you, godfather.

THE SERVANT/IVAN: Eight . . .

PETER: It is completely up to you whether you remain in Russia or not.

THE SERVANT/IVAN: Nine . . .

IBRAHIM: I have decided to come home, godfather.

THE SERVANT/IVAN: Ten!

PETER: Good.

THE SERVANT/IVAN: Turn!

(Peter turns and aims.)

PETER: I am extremely pleased with you, Ibrahim.

THE SERVANT/IVAN: Aim!

IBRAHIM: I would die before dishonoring you, godfather.

PETER: Welcome home, Ibrahim Petrovich.

(Enter Menshikov, Liza, and Natalya.)

PETER: Alexander! You are just in time. We were just about to shoot holes into each other. My trusted advisor Prince Alexander Menshikov, you know my godson, the little Negro page Ibrahim Petrovich. Now, he is a Captain returned from France. I wish you not to quarrel with him. Besides, he's the best shot in this room.

MENSHIKOV: Captain Petrovich.

IBRAHIM: Prince Menshikov.

PETER: Liza! Come! Bring your friend. Come you little fresh roses, come. Liza, do you remember the little Negro boy who used to steal apples for you, from my garden in Oranienbaum? Well, here he is.

IBRAHIM: You still seem very shy, and very full in your cheeks. Like an apple. Are you still fond of apples.

MENSHIKOV: Liza is my wife.

LIZA: Yes, I still like apples very much. And I still get little boys to go into the Czar's garden to fetch them for me. This is my friend, Natalya Gavrilovna. Natalya, this is an old friend, Ibrahim Petrovich Hannibal.

NATALYA: It is a pleasure to meet you, sir.

IBRAHIM: On the contrary, the pleasure is all mine. Had I but remembered that there was such beauty in Russia, I would have left Paris long ago.

PETER: Listen to him. Has my godson been to Paris or not. Are you ready, Ibrahim? Ready to drink and get yourself drunk? There is plenty of malmsey wine and vodka! I want to make a toast to Ibrahim. Aha, godson, welcome home to Holy Mother Russia.

LIZA: Tell us all about Paris, Ibrahim.

IBRAHIM: I wish I had a good report of Paris. As always the outward show of the Parisian gentlemen is serene and harmonious. Pious, yet witty. Courageous and disdainful of passionate excesses. But, in truth Parisians are as full of duplicity as they are vain. The Duke of Orleans lives only for amusements and pleasure. The orgies of the Palais-Royal were no secret in Paris. There is greed, dissipation, low moral standards, and squandered estates lost at the gaming tables.

LIZA: It sounds perfectly terrible. His majesty must take us all there at once. What else Ibrahim?

IBRAHIM: There are balls every night, and operas, and satirical vaudevilles everywhere.

NATALYA: And what do they wear?

IBRAHIM: Wear? Why, they have less things underneath their dresses than Russian women do and their necklines are very low.

NATALYA: (*Touching her breasts.*) Oh.

IBRAHIM: Even lower still.

NATALYA: Oh.

MENSHIKOV: And did you like Paris, Captain Petrovich?

IBRAHIM: Yes, I liked Paris very much.

MENSHIKOV: Then why did you leave?

IBRAHIM: To come home.

MENSHIKOV: To come home?

IBRAHIM: Yes, to come home. It marvels me, every time people ask me, "Where are you from?," and I say Russia. And they say,"Russia?" Even in Russia they ask me. But I am Russian. This is my homeland.

LIZA: I remember when we were children, the games we used to play, in exchange for your apples. They were always imaginary adventures in far-off lands. Strange, magical, mysterious places. Happiness is so easy when you're a child, and still sometimes we waste it. That was your homeland when you were a boy. A little boy's memory of home. That's where your home is Ibrahim, with that little boy.

IBRAHIM: Well, then home and that little boy are gone. Russia is my homeland now.

PETER: Well said, godson. The reason he left Paris, was because it was my order. Now, I want to make another toast. To the newly promoted Ibrahim Petrovich to the rank of Lieutenant-Captain in the Artillery Company of the Preobrazhensky Regiment. In which I myself am only a bombardier.

LIZA: Congratulations, Ibrahim.

IBRAHIM: Thank you, Liza.

NATALYA: All the best of luck to you, Lieutenant-Captain Petrovich.

IBRAHIM: You are most kind, Natalya Gavrilova. As kind as you are beautiful.

(Menshikov nods his head.)

IBRAHIM: Thank you Prince Menshikov.

PETER: Ladies, you must leave us now. I wish to speak to my godson in private. No, you stay Alexander. But, ladies you must go.

(Liza and Natalya bow and exit.)

PETER: So, what has really made you finally return to Russia, my godson? Certainly not my letters bidding you to come home.

IBRAHIM: Your last letter touched me deeply, godfather.

PETER: Yes, especially since you were spending your mornings thinning out the Parisian army.

IBRAHIM: Excuse me, your majesty?

PETER: I have heard from the Duke of Orleans. He says you have made a habit of shooting his officers.

IBRAHIM: Only in defense of my honor, godfather.

PETER: You sound like an aristocrat. What did they do? Call you names?

IBRAHIM: One in particular, said that I was a Black, sooty Russian, that the Czar uses to amuse himself.

PETER: What? And you killed him of course?

IBRAHIM: No, godfather, but he will have to learn to shoot a pistol and use his sword with his left hand now.

PETER: Good. He will suffer to tell others that Russia will not be dishonored.

THE NEGRO OF PETER THE GREAT 165

But come now Ibrahim, tell me straight brother. What was all of this dueling all about?

IBRAHIM: It's difficult for me to say, godfather. I simply seemed to be drawn into them. I have been called out either because I am a Russian, or because of the color of my skin. The pretexts were many, but they all amounted to the same thing.

PETER: Were these Frenchmen really offending you, or was it your pride?

IBRAHIM: There is something in what you say, sire. But I could hardly be the one to know, because it was always a matter of honor. They were unavoidable. I have never had the chance to choose. At least until now, when I have only just stopped.

PETER: And make certain that it has "stopped," brother. There will be no dueling in Russia. The penalty to the survivors is death.

IBRAHIM: You have my word, godfather; my dueling days are no more.

PETER: Good. We have great plans for you, Ibrahim. But first we must teach you about politics. After more than twenty years of war, we now have peace. All those years of defeat after defeat by the Swedes, they have finally taught us how to defeat them. Once we were the nobodies of Europe, now we are among the family of nations. Now when the monarchs of Europe consider the balance of powers, they must put Russia on the scale. The Baltic is open to us now. We have a window to the sea. Livonia and Estonia are ours. Poland is our cousin. France and Prussia are our new allies. And we have a treaty with the Turks. At least for the moment. The Turks are a formidable enemy, Ibrahim. A nation of men who all look like you. The ambassador who stole you from the Turkish palace is getting very old and feeble. You have some knowledge of the place, you would make an excellent ambassador yourself. But that is for the future. For now I want you to take over as the engineer for the fortifications at Kronstadt. We must be as powerful in peace as we were in war. And it will do good for our fat, lazy nobles to take their orders from an Arab. It will teach them a lesson. Show them how a subject earns his place.

IBRAHIM: Yes, sire. Thank you.

PETER: You will need a place to yourself. We will set you up were you lived in summers as a boy, in Mon Plaisir. Would you like that?

IBRAHIM: Yes, sire. Thank you.

PETER: Menshikov, you will excuse us for a moment.

(Exit Menshikov.)

PETER: You seem out of spirits and melancholy. You make chitchat like a Parisian. Tell me straight, what is the matter?

IBRAHIM: Nothing. Everything is perfectly fine, sire. I'm glad to be home. I look forward to my new duties. I could wish for nothing more.

PETER: You must never be too satisfied, Ibrahim. It will kill your ambition. Now out with it. What is it that's troubling you? Is it your lover in Paris? Countess Leonora? You miss her?

IBRAHIM: My lover, sire?

PETER: Come now, Ibrahim. I am the Czar. I have informers everywhere. It's the Czar's business to know everything. If she were just any French woman, you could bring her here with us. But for a subject of mine to break up the marriage of a favorite of the Regent of France is not good for Russia just now.

IBRAHIM: I had no such intentions, sire. The thought never occurred to me.

PETER: Good. Now, if this is why you are depressed, I think I know how to cheer you up. That young girl who was with Liza before, Natalya Gavrilovna, did you like her?

IBRAHIM: She was very charming, sire.

PETER: And beautiful.

IBRAHIM: And beautiful.

PETER: And modest, and poised.

IBRAHIM: And smart.

PETER: You go too far, brother. But, who knows, perhaps she is smart. How would you like to get to know her better?

IBRAHIM: That would be very nice, sire.

PETER: Then you shall have her. We will marry her to you.

IBRAHIM: Marriage? But, sire, the girl, she doesn't even know me. And her parents, how could they agree to a marriage with a complete stranger.

PETER: A girl must obey her parents, and they must obey me. I will take care of the parents. The girl, Natalya Gavrilovna, is the end of a long line of the great Lykov and Rzhevsky families. Marrying Natalya will give you a title and land.

IBRAHIM: But godfather, how could they accept someone like me, in such a family?

PETER: Why not? There's nothing amiss with you. They will be honored by whatever match I choose. What a curious thing to say. It's just as I thought. Paris has softened your brain. That is why I've brought this gentleman here to teach you something Ibrahim. I hope you haven't forgotten your old duties. Take up that slate and an abacus over there, and have a seat. Menshikov!

(Enter Menshikov.)

MENSHIKOV: Yes sire.

PETER: I am informed by the Governor of the Ukraine that there are as much as fifteen thousand serfs missing from our tax rolls. Are they all in the army?

MENSHIKOV: No, your majesty. There are no new recruits in the Ukraine. Not fifteen thousand.

PETER: Well, we must have either fifteen thousand recruits in the army, or seventy-four kopecks for each of the fifteen thousand serfs. How many kopecks is that, Ibrahim?

IBRAHIM: Over a million kopecks, sire.

PETER: A million kopecks? Menshikov?

MENSHIKOV: Your majesty.

PETER: You know everything that goes on in St. Petersburg. You have informers. Do you know who this thief is? This traitor who is robbing Russia? Perhaps he's the new owner of the old Mazeppa estate. There would be fifteen thousand serfs on the Mazeppa estate. If we find who is the new lord of Mazeppa's estate, we may have ourselves someone to hang. Do you know who he is? You don't have to tell me his name. Just tell me that you know who he is.

MENSHIKOV: All right, I confess. It was I. The serfs are mine. I took Mazeppa's estate in payment for his debts. All right taxes. I took his land, why not? I work for the state. When my country calls on me, I spare no expense.

PETER: Where are the serfs now?

MENSHIKOV: The serfs are all over. Some here in St. Petersburg, some are at my palace in Moscow, some in Riga, they're everywhere. And I haven't paid taxes on a single one. Not a soul. I confess. But, before you punish me, just remember what Yaguzhinsky said, when you threatened to hang him and all corrupt officials? "So you wish to be alone, sire, without any subjects but the serfs?" My Lord, everyone does it. Everyone. Why punish me?

PETER: Everyone? You must be careful I don't ask you who they are. You will remember that I did hang Yaguzhinsky. Here, take my staff Ibrahim. I want you to cane the Prince. And if you do not lay it on him hard, I will have the Prince cane you. Place your hands on the chair, Menshikov. Menshikov, you are a rascal. A thieving rascal. You may begin Ibrahim. *(Ibrahim begins to cane The Prince on his bottom.) I* have made you Most Serene Prince! Duke of Izhora! Count of Dubrovna, Gorki, and Potchep! Sovereign of Oranienbaum and Baturin! General, admiral, governor of St. Petersburg. You, a pastry cook! And you steal from *me! (Peter stops Ibrahim with a wave of his hand.)* Let that be a lesson to you. Ibrahim, mark Prince Menshikov down for a million kopecks.

MENSHIKOV: Forgive me, sire, but you will remember that I'm giving a small gathering at my palace, in a month or two, to celebrate the coming of our Russian winter. I should like to invite Lieutenant-Captain Petrovich. I would be most honored if he would attend.

PETER: Yes, brother, it would be good if you were there.

IBRAHIM: Yes, Prince Menshikov, I will come. Thank you.

PETER: Leave us for now, Alexander. I will see you later.

(Menshikov bows and exits.)

PETER: Now you have a formidable enemy. He was humiliated. And of course he will not take his spite out on me. His invitation was a declaration of war, you know.

IBRAHIM: Why did you do that, godfather?

PETER: Because in certain matters, I must do with you as I have to do with all the Russian people. Drag you into the modern world, kicking and screaming. There is great war within this peace we are having. And, as in war, you must secure allies, hold what ground you have, and look to the future. Besides, it is putting people at each other that gives a Czar his power. With Menshikov for your enemy, you will have to be a very careful soldier.

IBRAHIM: Sire, I am happy in your majesty's favor and patronage. I pray God that I may never outlive my Czar and benefactor. I wish for nothing more.

PETER: Listen to me, Ibrahim. You are a lonely man. Without kindred or friends. A stranger here to everyone but me. What if I should die tomorrow? What would become of you then? You must get settled while there is still time. Find support in new ties. Be allied to Russian nobility. That is why you must marry this girl.

IBRAHIM: Sire, I was just a young man when I went to France. I really am a stranger here. I need time to think. To get settled.

PETER: I will give you time to think, in the meantime I will get Liza to probe the girl. Very discreetly mind you. We will arrange a few meetings and the rest is up to you. You have been to Paris, you know what to do.

IBRAHIM: As you wish, sire.

PETER: I do wish it. Look, Ibrahim, godson, brother. There are men like Prince Menshikov, who was nothing more than a pastry cook and pie seller on the streets. These men rule worlds and did nothing more than be at the right place at the right time. This is that time for you.

IBRAHIM: Yes, sire. I see.

(Blackout.)

. . .

Lights up on the study at Mon Plaisir.

IVAN: This is the study. The fireplace works best here. It's the warmest room in Mon Plaisir.

IBRAHIM: Yes, I know. The Czar is my godfather. And as a boy, in summers, I lived here. And often slept in this very room. Why you can see the Gulf of Finland through those windows.

IVAN: You lived here with the Czar?

IBRAHIM: Is that strange to you?

IVAN: No. It is as you say, sir. But it has always been my understanding that Mon Plaisir was for the strict use of the Czar's family and only his closest friends.

IBRAHIM: I say he is my godfather man. Is this the new uniform?

IVAN: Yes it is.

IBRAHIM: "Yes it is, my lord."

IVAN: Yes it is . . . my lord.

IBRAHIM: Well, hold it out. Let me try it on.

IVAN: It doesn't seem to suit you somehow.

IBRAHIM: Truly? Listen, whenever you utter even a single word to me, you will follow it by the words "my lord." If this should become tedious for you, you may use "master" in its place, with a few "sirs" to give your speech some variety. Or Captain Petrovich. Your expressions will be about me and what I want, and how you are immediately about to accomplish that end. Is that clear?

IVAN: It doesn't seem to suit you somehow . . . my lord.

IBRAHIM: What is your name?

IVAN: My name is Ivan, my lord.

IBRAHIM: And where are you from, Ivan?

IVAN: From Moscow, master. My family belongs to the Moscow estate of Prince Menshikov.

IBRAHIM: Menshikov? And how came you to the Czar?

IVAN: He saw me one day. He thought I was bright, and he put me in his service.

IBRAHIM: And do you have any idea, why the Czar has sent you to me?

IVAN: No, my lord. The Czar is my master. I but obey his wish.

IBRAHIM: I will tell you why. The Czar wishes you to learn how to be more respectful to a Russian officer.

IVAN: May I speak freely, my lord?

IBRAHIM: Yes, go on.

IVAN: You will forgive me, my lord, but a uniform does not make the man. I am Russian. Which you are not. This is where I was born, and my family, and all their families before them. You cannot become a Russian, you must be Russian to be worthy of the name.

(Ibrahim goes to the pistol case and with powder, cap, and ball he loads the pistol.)

IBRAHIM: You are very proud, my friend. You are also, so very young. I have had many an early morning with proud boys like you. But being a peasant lackey, who has no doubt never worked in the fields, you cannot possibly know your geography. Russia goes east to the Chinese Empire, south to the Ottoman Empire, west to Europe, and north to the ends of world. What it is to be a Russian shrinks and grows with time, my friend. Time. A thing which I could take from you, within a flash. Do you understand me, sir? *(Aiming his pistol at Ivan.)*

THE SERVANT/IVAN: Yes, my lord.

(There is a pounding on a door.)

IVAN: Someone is at the door, my lord.

IBRAHIM: Then you must go answer it.

IVAN: Yes, my lord.

(Ivan exits. Ibrahim smolders in his anger. Enter Ivan.)

IVAN: Forgive me, my lord, but a gentleman is waiting to see you. He refuses to give me his name. He says that it's a surprise.

(Ibrahim again aims at Ivan as Korsakov enters.)

KORSAKOV: Ibrahim, my friend, you must have more servants than you need to shoot them just because they can't keep an old friend from the door.

IBRAHIM: Korsakov. What are you doing in St. Petersburg?

KORSAKOV: Paris wasn't as much fun after you left. Always the same old thing. Here, I have a gift for you.

IBRAHIM: What is this?

KORSAKOV: A book of my improvisations. Madame DuBois became my patron, among other things. She dragged me to every salon in Paris to do my improvisations. And do you know what? She wrote them all down. Every one. And then had them printed and sold in bookshops. And in the salons they demanded to hear my improvisations from this accursed book. I stopped being an improviser of fresh verse, and became a reader of yesterday's tired, over worn words

IBRAHIM: I wish I had this book with me these past few months. It would have been like having you here . . . You may go, Ivan.
(*Ivan exits.*)
KORSAKOV: So, what do you do, to keep yourself from dying of boredom in this barbarous St. Petersburg? Do they have an opera house, at least?
IBRAHIM: No, no opera house. Not even a salon. All we do here is work, sleep, and drink Vodka. Let's have a glass of vodka, Korsakov. A toast to your return to Russia.
KORSAKOV: Vodka. I can't believe it. To tell you the truth Ibrahim, the reason I returned was because, like you, I received a letter from the Czar. Not a personal letter, like yours, but an official letter signed by some clerk. It seems they are rounding up all of the noblemen's sons who were sent abroad for education. Remember, when they made us go, I didn't want to leave. Now, they want us back and I didn't want to return. I was never coming back here.
IBRAHIM: But, Korsakov, this is your home.
KORSAKOV: This isn't my home. It's just a place where I was born. I feel like a complete stranger here. I always have. And now after six years away, I've completely forgotten the customs of the place. I'm nothing but a foreigner here.
IBRAHIM: I know. I feel the same way.
KORSAKOV: You could get out. You could go.
IBRAHIM: Go where?
KORSAKOV: You could go back to where you were born. To Abyssinia. You must still have relatives there.
IBRAHIM: What would I do there? I know less of that place than I do this. I would be even more of a stranger, in an even stranger way.
KORSAKOV: We're trapped.
IBRAHIM: You must not look at it that way, Korsakov. The Czar has divested all distinction. In his court there are Germans, Poles, Dutch, English, me, a pastry cook. Today in Russia it doesn't matter whether we're noblemen or foreigners. Whether we're rich or we're poor. What matters is how we serve, what we do. Deeds are our birthright now.
KORSAKOV: I do not doubt what you say, Ibrahim. But for me the fact is, that if I did not return, my father's estate would have been taken from him. My father is very old. I am just a poet. I cannot support him. Without my pledge to the Czar, he would die in poverty. And therefore, for the sake of a life who has given me life, I am trapped in Russia. You must

help me, Ibrahim. If I am to be trapped here, don't let it be in the army. I would rather be a supercilious clerk in Siberia than a soldier in the army.

IBRAHIM: What do you want me to do, Korsakov?

KORSAKOV: Intercede for me. As a favorite of the Czar, get me a position where I don't have to compromise my principles as a devout coward.

IBRAHIM: Of course, Korsakov. I'll see what I can do. We'll start working on it tonight.

KORSAKOV: Tonight?

IBRAHIM: Yes, tonight there is a celebration at Prince Menshikov's palace. The Czar will be there. I'll introduce you, and simply tell him you're looking for a position. You're not a soldier. I'm sure he'll grant you something that's not in the army.

KORSAKOV: Oh, thank you, Ibrahim. Thank you.

IBRAHIM: Anything for you, Korsakov. So, how is Paris?

KORSAKOV: Our Paris friends send you their greetings, and they are sorry you are not with them. Otherwise it's always the same old thing in Paris. There is no news except, the Countess sends you this letter.

IBRAHIM: And how is the Countess?

KORSAKOV: Naturally, at first she was very much grieved by your departure and wanted you back at all cost. Then she gradually took comfort and found herself a new lover.

IBRAHIM: A lover?

KORSAKOV: Yes. Can you guess who he is?

IBRAHIM: Who?

KORSAKOV: The licentious Marquis Merville.

IBRAHIM: Merville? It isn't true. It's a lie. It hasn't been more than a few months since I've been gone.

KORSAKOV: Do you find it strange? Don't you know that it isn't human nature, especially not in a woman's nature, to be grieved for very long? Life goes on, Ibrahim.

IBRAHIM: It goes on endlessly, Korsakov.

KORSAKOV: You mustn't take it so hard, brother. One cannot rely on a woman's fidelity. Those who don't care or bother about it, are lucky.

IBRAHIM: You know, Korsakov, when the Turks attacked Abyssina and they stole me up, I watched my sister drown in the River Mareb, trying to swim after me. As a child, seven years old, before I was bought by the Czar's ambassador, when it was fashionable to have clever little Negro boys at court, for a year I was the plaything to all the bored sultanas in the

Sultan's harem. Yet I still don't know women. And now it seems that I am to be married.

KORSAKOV: Married?

IBRAHIM: Yes, to Russian nobility. A girl named Natalya Gavrilovna has been promised to me by the Czar. Promised? Did I say promised? More like given to me, like you would give away a pet cat. I don't even know her.

KORSAKOV: Then you really are trapped.

IBRAHIM: Have you a place to stay?

KORSAKOV: No, not yet.

IBRAHIM: Then, you must stay with me.

KORSAKOV: Thank you, Ibrahim. I would like that. Look, I see you have no thoughts to spare for me now. We'll talk later to our heart's content. If you'll just point me the way, I'll go and freshen up from my journey, and leave you to your letter.

IBRAHIM: Thank you, Korsakov. Ivan!

(Enter Ivan.)

IVAN: Yes, my lord.

IBRAHIM: Put this gentleman's baggage in the room next to mine.

IVAN: Yes, my lord.

KORSAKOV: I'll see you later, Ibrahim. Don't forget to call on me for the gathering at Prince Menshikov's.

IBRAHIM: I will call you, brother.

(Korsakov and Ivan exit. Ibrahim reads the letter as we hear the voice of Leonora.)

LEONORA: Dear Ibrahim, my dearest, my darling:

Since you've been gone, the days are so long and so lonely. I miss so much your arrogant, aristocratic airs. Your anger, so loose and wild and sincere. The touch of your skin, the texture of your hair. Your sighs and your kisses. Once you said that my peace was more precious to you than anything. But how can my peace be precious when you are gone from me. I know that you were angry that I tried to detain you, to keep you from leaving me, and that you are very disappointed in me and the choices I have had to make. But, I want you to know, that in losing you, I lose the last joy in my life. And so good-bye my precious, my peace, my only friend. Think of me sometimes, and write to me from time to time, even though there is little hope of our ever seeing each other again. With all my heart, your ever-loving Leonora.

(Ibrahim crushes the letter in his hand. Enter Ivan.)

IVAN: Excuse me, my lord

IBRAHIM: What is it?

IVAN: The Grand Duchess awaits your pleasure.

IBRAHIM: Grand Duchess? Liza. Of course, show her in.

(Enter Liza.)

LIZA: Ibrahim Petrovich Hannibal, shame on you. How could you be so cruel? And to an old friend. You have been gone away for years, and in all these months since your return you haven't come to call on me, not even once. And now, I am the one who must sacrifice her pride and come to see you. Why should you be so angry with me?

IBRAHIM: No, not in the least Liza. Never could I be angry with you.

LIZA: Do you remember when we were children? I did all I could do to get you to steal apples for me from the Czar's garden, until I had more apples in my room than were on the trees. I adored you then. I adore you now, and this is how you treat me.

IBRAHIM: I am sorry Liza. Please forgive me.

LIZA: Well, only if you satisfy my curiosity. It was interesting to hear the things you had to say that first night about your years abroad. What was it like for you there in Paris, Ibrahim?

IBRAHIM: Paris? Paris was not very interesting. Always the same old thing in Paris.

LIZA: It seems interesting to someone who's never been anywhere, but between St. Petersburg and Moscow. I envy you, Ibrahim. You've been around the world. Seen so many things and had experience.

IBRAHIM: Thank you, Liza, but much of *it* was not very alluring.

LIZA: You must lie to me, Ibrahim. Tell me that every moment was completely and utterly romantic. That the only reason you returned, was because your happiness was more than you could bear.

IBRAHIM: It's true, there were things I could no longer bear. And happiness was among them. Happiness is a very fickle mistress.

LIZA: Yes, but she travels easily, and she's as fickle in one place as she is in another.

IBRAHIM: I suppose that's true. I'll only be too glad when I put all of that past behind me.

LIZA: Not all the past, I should hope. Dreams and memories seem to me to be very useful things. They take you places you cannot go, and places you dare not. They are there when you're alone, and for a time can make you forget unhappiness ever existed.

IBRAHIM: You are still such a dreamy girl, aren't you, Liza?

LIZA: It will be interesting for you to live here in Mon Plaisir once more, surrounded by your boyhood memories. You may come to see yourself as a completely new and unexpected person.

IBRAHIM: That is what I hope for Liza. We shall see.

LIZA: Well, enough about the past. I have news for your future. At the Czar's behest I've spoken to Natalya.

IBRAHIM: Spoken to Natalya? About what?

LIZA: Don't worry, Ibrahim, I didn't speak for you, or mention marriage. I only talked about you to feel her out. And she finds you fascinating.

IBRAHIM: Fascinating? And what does she mean by fascinating?

LIZA: She thinks you are very good-looking. And when I told her about all the hardships and adventures in your life, she was in awe. She kept saying it, "fascinating."

IBRAHIM: I don't understand, Liza, what does she mean by fascinating?

LIZA: Well, Ibrahim, she's a young girl. She finds you attractive. She likes your manner and your appearance.

IBRAHIM: My appearance? Liza, you're being naïve.

LIZA: It is you who are being naïve, Ibrahim. Whether it is some fat Count, or some old, withered and aging Duke, or whoever it is, Natalya's marriage will be arranged. Appearances are the least of her problems. Natalya would be very lucky to have you for a husband.

IBRAHIM: I don't know, Liza. All this thinking about the future. I've never done it before. The future is very gray to me.

LIZA: Right now your future is that the Czar means for you to marry Natalya for your own good. Still Natalya is very young. She's just out of the convent. She has no experience. You will have to teach her how to love you, and you will have to wait for your pleasure until she learns. But, you are a man, a man of the world. You may look to other, more experienced women, until she does learn.

IBRAHIM: You mean take a lover? Marry Natalya and take a lover? I couldn't bear it. Liza, the intrigue would suffocate me.

LIZA: There are things far more suffocating than intrigues, Ibrahim. Life itself can be suffocating Sometimes we think too much about the future, and forget the moment. I think that people's attraction for each other should be explored. Don't you? Obviously, there's a reason for it. A connection, a need, something we want to discover for ourselves. We all need someone to talk to. To share our confidences and to be tender with. I've never had that with anyone, but you Ibrahim. I loved you then, I've loved you always, I love you now.

IBRAHIM: Liza, I don't know what to say? It's not that I don't want you. It's just that I don't know what I want. When you and I were children, playing together, touching each other, we were young and didn't know what we were doing. What could we have known about love? You were destined to be a Duchess, and me, the Czar's Negro. We are grown up now Liza.

LIZA: Men live in such perfect worlds. Ibrahim, listen to me. The wheels are in motion. There is no turning back for you now. I've had the rare honor of having breakfast with my prince this morning. My husband and your good friend Prince Menshikov. And between his scrawling on bits of paper, and his raging, he deigned to speak to me. And it was about you. He wanted to know about all your habits and your curiosities. Your ambitions, your fears. He means to thwart you, Ibrahim, by whatever means within his power. And he has that power, Ibrahim. The same power he has over you, as he has over me. We must be allies, Ibrahim. We must be friends.

IBRAHIM: I haven't been home but for a few months, and it seems like everything I've gone through before. Life is is nothing but duels and intrigues and war. I want no quarrel with Prince Menshikov, or you, or the Czar. I just want to come home. I need some peace, some time to think.

LIZA: And the Czar intends to stimulate your thinking. His majesty insists that at my husband's gathering tonight, that everyone should dance the minuet. The minuet is very popular with the Germans these days. And as Natalya's father hates the Germans, he doesn't allow her to learn it. If she dances poorly, she will be disgraced. And therefore the Czar has ordered her to come to you and learn.

IBRAHIM: To come to me? To learn the minuet, for tonight?

LIZA: She's just outside, waiting in my carriage with her dancing master now. He's a Swede, and they could hardly know how to do the minuet.

IBRAHIM: Liza, what are you doing?

LIZA: I'm trying to help you, Ibrahim. I'm trying to be your friend. I'm trying to tell you that, whenever you need me, whatever you need me for, I'll always be there. I'll go and get Natalya now.

(Liza exits. A pause. Enter Natalya.)

NATALYA: Lieutenant-Captain Petrovich, thank you so much for taking the time, and being so kind as to teach me the minuet. I'm sure you, who have been to Paris, must find it astonishing that a young lady of good family has no knowledge of such an elegant dance. But I assure you it is in no way because I'm incapable. Father simply wouldn't allow me to learn it. He thinks it's just another vulgar habit we've picked up from the Germans. Father is so old-fashioned. But tonight, tonight the Czar himself, insists that I dance. Father was very grave about it at first. But how could he refuse the Czar. And so here I am.

IBRAHIM: Not at all. It is an honor. But where is Liza? I thought she was with you.

NATALYA: The Grand Duchess has much to do to make ready for tonight. She sends her regrets. She looks forward to seeing you tonight and says that she was leaving me in very good hands. Her carriage'll await us later. And it is a very fine carriage too. Oh, I almost forgot. This is my dancing master, Gustav Adamych.

IBRAHIM: Gustav Adamych?

NATALYA: He's in the service of my father's estate.

GUSTAV: A pleasure to meet you my lord.

IBRAHIM: What's wrong with your leg, Gustav Adamych?

GUSTAV: There's a hole in it, my lord. A Russian hole. I was a soldier in the Swedish Army at the battle of Poltava. I was on the wrong side that day, and now I play music and teach dancing in St. Petersburg.

IBRAHIM: Better to live a long life as a crippled dancing master, than among your dead brothers in arms on the field of Poltava.

GUSTAV: You have a very good point, my lord.

NATALYA: Well, shall we begin. Gustav, watch closely, in case I forget any of my steps.

GUSTAV: Yes, my lady.

IBRAHIM: The minuet is very simple really. We begin in third position, left foot forward. Bend at the knees. Rise and step to the right. Bend again. Rise and step left. To the right. To the left. Good. Now, imagine the music and follow me. It is important that we look at each other at all times. And it is fashionable to engage in conversation while dancing . . . You dance very well, Natalya Gavrilovna. It is the custom in the minuet for the lady to choose a partner from among her admirers. As graceful and beautiful as you are, I'm sure you have many admirers from which to choose.

NATALYA: Well, there is Prince Dolgoruky, but my Aunt Tatyana says he is much too proud. Then, there are Shagin and Troekurov, who Auntie says are much too infected with the German spirit. Miloslavsky, she thinks is rich but stupid. And then there is Yeletsky, but Aunt Tatyana will have none of him.

IBRAHIM: You are very popular, Natalya. Even more popular than your Aunt Tatyana. And which of these gentlemen do you prefer?

NATALYA: I am in complete agreement with my Aunt Tatyana. Were it my choice to choose, I would have none of them. If I could choose for myself, I would rather someone who was tall, dark and graceful, dashing and brave. A military man I think

IBRAHIM: Forgive me, but I thought we were speaking of dancing, not courtship.

NATALYA: But dancing, Captain Petrovich, isn't it a game of love. How else is a young girl to know a man before they become husband and wife?

IBRAHIM: And what if the Czar himself, should make this match for you?

NATALYA: The Czar? Choose a match for me? I wouldn't know what to think. Yet, if the Czar should make the match, what could I do but say yes. No, it's too incredible. Father would be overjoyed. Aunt Tatyana would be ecstatic. Oh, please, Captain Petrovich, you must choose some other topic of conversation. This one is making me forget my steps.

IBRAHIM: Are you all right?

NATALYA: Yes. Only just let me catch my breath.

(Ibrahim sits Natalya in a chair.)

IBRAHIM: Gustav. There is water on the desk.

(Gustav brings the water to Ibrahim.)

IBRAHIM: Here, drink slowly.

NATALYA: Lieutenant-Captain Petrovich, why do you wear that cloth around your head?

IBRAHIM: This? This is the only thing I have left from the days when I was a boy in Abyssinia, in Africa. My mother weaved it for me. It used to fit around my waist. Now, it covers a wound. A scar from the war with Spain.

NATALYA: Hasn't it healed?

IBRAHIM: Yes, but the scar is very ugly.

NATALYA: May I see it?

IBRAHIM: The scar is hideous, Natalya.

NATALYA: Let me look. I won't be afraid.

(Ibrahim removes the cloth.)

NATALYA: Oh, Ibrahim, how you must have suffered.

IBRAHIM: The wound was less painful than being in a Spanish prison. They were particularly unkind to me. But that is long past now. Listen Natalya, may I speak freely?

NATALYA: Yes, Ibrahim, of course.

(Enter Korsakov.)

KORSAKOV: Oh, I'm sorry, Ibrahim. I had no idea you had company. And such beautiful company indeed. I only came down, because I thought it must be time to go to Prince Menshikov's.

IBRAHIM: Not at all, Korsakov. You are just in time. Natalya Gavrilovna, may I present my good friend Korsakov.
NATALYA: Korsakov?
KORSAKOV: Yes, Korsakov. And congratulations mademoiselle.
NATALYA: Congratulations? For what?
KORSAKOV: On being betrothed by the Czar to my good brother here, Ibrahim Petrovich Hannibal.
(Natalya faints. Blackout.)

END OF ACT I

ACT II

Lights up. A drawing room adjoining the ballroom in the Menshikov palace.

KORSAKOV: I'm sorry Ibrahim. I had no idea.
IBRAHIM: It's not your fault. How were you to know, that she didn't even know she was engaged to me.
KORSAKOV: She was bound to discover it sooner or later. Under the best of circumstances it still would have been something of a shock.
IBRAHIM: Yes, that the sight of me makes her faint. Is this how I am to live my life? I should have never come here. I should have stayed in Paris.
KORSAKOV: You were not so well off in Paris as here Ibrahim.
IBRAHIM: At least in Paris, I was free to defend myself. Here, nothing is real. I'm just helpless here. Wait. Here comes the Czar. I'll take this chance to intercede for you.
(Enter Peter and Gavril.)
PETER: Gavril Afanasyevich, my godson Lieutenant-Captain Ibrahim Petrovich. And who is this?
IBRAHIM: Godfather, I would like to introduce you to my old friend Korsakov from Paris. He is looking for a position.
PETER: Korsakov?
KORSAKOV: Yes sire.
PETER: What do you do Korsakov?
KORSAKOV: I am a poet your Majesty.
PETER: A what?
IBRAHIM: He is not really just a poet godfather. He's an improvisator.
PETER: Improvisator? What is that?
IBRAHIM: He makes them up as he goes along sire. Right there, on the spot.
PETER: Have you no trade?
KORSAKOV: No sire.
PETER: Well, you are a writer. We may have some use for you.
KORSAKOV: Thank you sire.
PETER: But there will be no rhyming, I promise you that.
KORSAKOV: Yes sire.
PETER: Leave us for now gentlemen. I have some important news for Gavril Afanasyevitch. And Ibrahim, come back shortly. I want to speak with you.
IBRAHIM: Yes sire.
(Ibrahim and Korsakov exit.)
PETER: My godson has grown into a fine young man, has he not?

GAVRIL: Yes sire. And what is the news you have for me sire?
PETER: It's about your daughter Natalya.
GAVRIL: Natalya?
PETER: I have decided on a match for her.
GAVRIL: Who, my lord?
PETER: My godson, Ibrahim Petrovich.
GAVRIL: The Negro?
PETER: Ibrahim Petrovich, my godson, yes. This displeases you?
GAVRIL: Oh no, your majesty, no. I am only too grateful. Ibrahim Petrovich, your godson, my son-in-law. It's wonderful, sire. Wonderful.
PETER: Good. I will have my godson call on you tomorrow. And if I can be of any help, with any of the arrangements or if you have any problems, now or in the future, you must come to me.
GAVRIL: Yes, sire. Thank you. You are too kind.
   (Enter Menshikov.)
MENSHIKOV: Bread for sale. Meat pies. Fruit tarts. Custards. Macaroons. Charlotte russe. Bread and pastry for sale.
PETER: Menshikov, you are a rogue and a rascal. Come here and embrace me my pastry cook.
MENSHIKOV: You see I still have a trade, my lord.
PETER: And lucky you are that you do. So, if I put you out, you won't starve. Sit down, so I can beat you in a game of draughts.
MENSHIKOV: There isn't a monarch in Europe who can beat this pastry cook at draughts.
PETER: We'll see about that. Sit down and play.
GAVRIL: If you will excuse me, sire, I will go and take my sister the news.
PETER: Yes, all right. We will see you later, Gavril Afanasyevitch.
GAVRIL: Yes, sire.
   (Gavril exits.)
MENSHIKOV: Gavril Afanasyevitch doesn't look very happy.
PETER: He looks happy to me.
MENSHIKOV: Perhaps I am wrong.
PETER: No doubt, you are. Your move, Menshikov.
MENSHIKOV: He has a very beautiful daughter.
PETER: Indeed? Has he now? Your move again.
MENSHIKOV: You know as well as I do, sire.
PETER: What are you sniffing out for now, Menshikov. You're up to mischief, I can see it in your eyes.
MENSHIKOV: Not me, my lord. I swear.

PETER: You swear? Menshikov, that is the most ridiculous thing I have ever heard you say. You swear? I will keep that in mind. What a joke. You swear. Now king me.
(Enter Ibrahim.)
PETER: Ibrahim! Come in here and save me. Menshikov has me in stitches. Come. I have news. I've spoken to the father. It's all settled. You're betrothed. She's yours.
MENSHIKOV: You're getting married, Ibrahim?
PETER: Yes. He's getting married to Natalya Gavrilovna.
MENSHIKOV: Afanasyevitch's daughter. I know the family well. Afanasyevitch's stepson, Valeryan, is in my Horse Guards Regiment in Moscow. A good family. Old and respected. Congratulations, Ibrahim. You have made yourself an auspicious move upward.
IBRAHIM: Thank you, prince.
PETER: You must call on your future father-in-law tomorrow. And make certain that you gratify his nobleman's pride. Leave your carriage at the gate, and walk through the courtyard. Talk to him about his service to the state, how he defended the palace from the Streltsi when the Czar was just a boy, how it was his musket ball that struck Charles at Poltava. All you have to do is listen to him, and you will make a lasting impression, I assure you.
IBRAHIM: Godfather, if I may be so bold. I have spoken with the girl and in truth I don't think she favors me.
PETER: These things take time godson. Patience. Tenderness. Trust. Indulgence. She will learn to love you as I do.
(The first strains of the minuet begin to play.)
PETER: What's this? The minuet? You were supposed to dance the minuet with Natalya. Servant!
(Enter Ivan.)
IVAN: Yes, your majesty.
PETER: Tell them to stop that music at once. And wait until I arrive.
IVAN: Yes, your majesty.
(Ivan exits. Peter takes Ibrahim by the arm.)
PETER: Coming, Alexander?
MENSHIKOV: I will be right behind you, sire.
(Peter and Ibrahim exit. Menshikov searches the drawing room until he finds paper and quill. He sits at the draughts board, clears it of checkers, and begins to write.)
MENSHIKOV: Betrothed to Natalya. It's perfect. Servant!
(Enter Ivan.)

IVAN: Yes, my lord.

MENSHIKOV: So, Ivan, how is it having a Negro for a master?

THE SERVANT/IVAN: It is my duty, my lord.

MENSHIKOV: Well, here is a little something that might help to serve your spite. I want you to take this letter to my footman. He is to deliver it to the commander of my Horse Guards Regiment in Moscow. It is for the release and transfer of a soldier named Valeryan. My footman is to personally see this soldier and tell him discreetly that the love of his life is about to be married to the Czar's Negro. Then we shall see if the young have any character. And if our aristocratic African duelist is as hot-headed as he is hot-blooded, we will have him in our snare. It's time he felt the Czar's wrath. Now go.

(Ivan exits. Enter Liza.)

MENSHIKOV: There is my lovely wife. Did you come to ask me to minuet?

LIZA: It is expected of us.

MENSHIKOV: I thought you would be dancing with your old Negro friend, Hannibal.

LIZA: He already has a partner.

MENSHIKOV: Yes. Your friend Natalya Gavrilovna. Do you know that the Czar has just betrothed her to him?

LIZA: Oh, what a surprise.

MENSHIKOV: It seems more like a pity to me.

LIZA: A pity? Why a pity?

MENSHIKOV: A pity for such a lovely girl to be married to a Negro.

LIZA: Would you prefer her to be married to a German?

MENSHIKOV: I like Germans. Germans are white.

LIZA: It is easy to see, my lord, why you dwell on such distinctions, as judgements of personal character and true honor are a complete mystery to you.

MENSHIKOV: You seem to champion the Negro. Perhaps you are right, and soon we are all destined to be close friends.

LIZA: I think not, my prince.

(Liza exits. Enter Gavril and Tatyana.)

MENSHIKOV: Congratulations, Gavril Afanasyevitch. And you may expect many more surprises in the weeks ahead.

(Menshikov exits.)

TATYANA: Congratulations? Surprises? What is he talking about?

GAVRIL: I don't know what he means. He was here when I was talking with the Czar. And it was not for nothing that the Czar called me aside. Guess what he wanted.

TATYANA: My dear brother, how should I know? I have no idea. Has he offered you a governorship somewhere, or an embassy?

GAVRIL: No. It concerns Natalya.

TATYANA: Natalya? No? She's getting married. And the Czar is her matchmaker. Am I right Gavrila? Why aren't you happy? You should be shouting to the roof. The Czar my niece's match-maker. Who is he? For whom did the Czar ask for Natalya's hand.

GAVRIL: Who is he? That's just it. You would never guess in a *million* years.

TATYANA: What is it Dolgoruky? Shagin, Troekurov? Oh, I hope not Troekurov. Miloslavsky? Who?

GAVRIL: No, none of them.

TATYANA: Who is he then?

GAVRIL: The Czar's godson, Ibrahim Petrovich.

TATYANA: The Negro? You will kill her. The very sight of him is too much for her. You will kill her. You want to marry your daughter to a bought Negro slave?

GAVRIL: He is no commoner. This man was the son of a sultan. So he was stolen, what of it? It's the fortunes of war. Of all the foreign monkeys that have come from abroad, he's more of a man than any of them. And what will the Czar say? How am I to refuse the Czar? He promises us his favor, his protection. We are under his authority, we must obey him in all things.

TATYANA: You will kill her. Kill her; do you hear me?

GAVRIL: Say what you will, I don't intend to quarrel with the Czar.

TATYANA: Oh dear God, what will become of the poor girl. Lord help and preserve us.

(Enter Peter, Ibrahim, Korsakov, Menshikov, Liza, and Natalya. Peter has Korsakov by the scruff of his neck.)

PETER: You are caught, sir, you are caught. You have done wrong. You did not follow the rules, so now you must be severely punished. Menshikov, fill me the Goblet of the Golden Eagle.

IBRAHIM: He didn't know, your majesty.

PETER: That is no excuse. This man is suppose to be a poet, yet he doesn't know a thing about polite society, such as ours. He did not make the three bows in the proper fashion when he took it upon himself to invite Natalya to dance, when in the minuet this right belongs not to the gentleman, but to the lady. Or to whomever I may choose. The Goblet Menshikov.

(Menshikov gives Peter a huge goblet filled with vodka.)

PETER: Now, I want to hear one of these poems you make up on the spot, and you must wash it down with this goblet of vodka. I am sure it will inspire you. Think of the end of your improvisation as down in the bottom of this goblet. And you may rhyme if you wish. Come on monsieur, drink up. Let us hear our improvisator.

KORSAKOV: Oh, you golden goblet
How came you to my hand
I thought I had enough of you
I merely came to dance
(Gulp.)
Your first taste was bitter
Bitter to the end
And as you trickle down my throat
I hope you'll be my friend.
(Gulp.)
Your second taste no better
No better than the first
And my stomach is beginning to tell me
It's going to get a good deal worst
(Gulp.)
Oh, to the bottom of this glass
I can't wait to go.
This liquid once was made to pass
From one damn dangerous potato.
(Gulp.)
What is the number, three or four
Or have I already gone past
Oh hell, who cares about the count
Let's have another slash.
(Gulp.)
Somehow this one's different
I must be near the bottom of the cup
And all of you are looking strange
You can barely all stand up.
(Gulp.)
I wonder what I'm thinking
I have the urge to bark
I'm getting drunk from drinking
And everything is going . . .
(Korsakov passes out/Blackout.)

. . .

Lights up: The sitting room of the Gavril's home. The adjoining room is Natalya's bedroom. Liza is sitting with Natalya.

GAVRIL: Has it been more than a week since Prince Menshikov's party. My, my, how the time passes. You and Natalya looked very handsome together.

IBRAHIM: Yes, Natalya dances very well. She learns quickly.

GAVRIL: Yes, and I'm afraid the fault is mine. I tell you, Lieutenant-Captain Petrovich, young people are spoiled beyond words nowadays. Young girls play the fool, and we encourage them. I can't seem to oppose these whims to learn foreign dances and wear these absurd German fashions, which seem to be worn for nothing more than for good people to laugh at.

TATYANA: People can't help but laugh, and feel sorry for these silly young girls today. With their hair done up as if they wanted castles on their heads. Their stomachs so laced in, it's a wonder that they don't break in two. And the petticoats with those ridiculous bustles that seem to go on behind them forever. Veritable martyrs, the poor dears, they can neither sit, nor stand, nor draw breath in those dresses.

GAVRIL: We Russian gentlemen have long since had our beards shaved and been forced to put on skimpy French jackets; it's no use in complaining about woman's frippery.

TATYANA: That's not what you say when Natalya orders new gowns every month, and throws away the one she's scarcely worn. In the old days a granddaughter used to inherit her grandmother's sarafan. Now, a young mistress wears a gown one day, and her maid wears it the next.

GAVRIL: Yes, it is a pity that the sarafan, and the hair ribbons, and the women's headdress are all gone now.

TATYANA: You must realize, Lieutenant-Captain Petrovich, it is difficult nowadays for husbands to keep their wives in hand. Wives have forgotten the words of St. Paul, "Woman revere your husbands." But no, they think of nothing but fine clothes and going to balls.

KORSAKOV: And what is the harm in young ladies attending the assemblies, madame? With whom would the gentlemen dance?

TATYANA: What is the harm? Why, it is unseemly, sir, for a Russian noblewoman to be in the same room with tobacco-smoking Germans and their rude servants. To dance and talk until all hours of the night with young men? And not with their relatives mind you, but complete and perfect strangers. Why, it's dreadful. It's the ruination of our Russian nobility.

GAVRIL: I don't care for the assemblies either. You may at any moment run upon someone who is drunk, or may be made drunk yourself, just for other people's amusement. Wouldn't you say that was true, Korsakov?

KORSAKOV: Touché, sir. You have hit the mark.

GAVRIL: I certainly hope it was not too hard on you, Korsakov. You were very drunk, I'm sorry to say but, you were at fault. I don't approve of the minuet, but I do know the rules. I'm afraid the Czar wants to deal with these silly transgressions of decorum quite severely. You were new to us and he wanted to make an example of you, by making you *drink* that big goblet of vodka, while reciting your poem.

IBRAHIM: Forgive me, Gavril Afayasyvitch, this is all very interesting, but may I know exactly what it is, that has made Natalya ill?

GAVRIL: A mystery. A complete mystery, brother Petrovich. The doctor said it was nerves. All the excitement and the sudden news. But, day by day she is getting on much better.

TATYANA: It's those tight-laced gowns. She can't breathe, the poor girl.

IBRAHIM: But how long before I can speak with her?

TATYANA: Natalya is still very ill. She's a delicate girl; it takes long for her to recover. She was always ailing and infirm as a child. Ever since she lost her mother, the poor thing. We are forever praying for her good health. You must be patient, Ibrahim Petrovich, Natalya is prone to be a weak and sickly young girl.

IBRAHIM: I have been patient, Tatyana Afanasyevna, for almost two weeks. If she's been ill all this time, perhaps it's something serious. Maybe we should summon the Czar's physician. Don't you think that would be wise Gavril Afansyevitch?

GAVRIL: No, no, brother Petrovich, not at all. Natalya is getting well. Don't worry, we'll prepare her and you shall see her this day. Go in, sister and see to Natalya. Make her ready to receive her fiancé.

TATYANA: But Gavril, he can't go in her bedroom and see her in her night clothes. We'll have to dress her. And you might as well know this takes considerable time with young girls nowadays

GAVRIL: Go on, sister. Make Natalya ready.

TATYANA: But, brother . . .

GAVRIL: Please Tatyana, do as I say.

TATYANA: Very well.

(Tatyana enters Natalya's bedroom.)

GAVRIL: You must please forgive my sister. Natalya is my only daughter, my only child. My sister's only niece. She only wants everything to be perfect

... If I may, Ibrahim Petrovich, could I have a word with you in private? If the good gentlemen here wouldn't mind?

IBRAHIM: Would you excuse us for a moment, brother?

KORSAKOV: As you wish, Ibrahim. I'll just go and have a pipe in the hall.

GAVRIL: Thank you, sir.

(Korsakov exits.)

GAVRIL: I almost hesitate to tell you this, Ibrahim Petrovich. And on my honor as a gentleman, what I'm about to tell you is something I in no way approve. But while Natalya was sick, in her sleep, in her delirium, she called out the name — Valeryan.

IBRAHIM: Valeryan?

GAVRIL: Yes. He was an orphan who was brought up in this house. His father was in the guards. He was one of the Czar's foreign mercenaries. A German. He saved my life during the Streltsi rebellion. When he died, the devil put it into my head to adopt that damned German wolf cub, his son. He and that Swede, Gustav, nearly blew up this place, firing off a toy cannon in this very room. For two years now, he's been off to the army. Natalya burst into tears saying good-bye to him. Sister love I thought. He, of course just stood there like a stone. It struck me suspicious at the time. Up to now she hasn't mentioned him. I thought she had forgotten all about him. But it seems she hasn't. But don't worry, it's all settled. I assure you, Natalya is pure, and she will marry you.

IBRAHIM: Is she in love with this boy?

GAVRIL: Love? What do young girls know of love. He's more like a wayward brother, than anything.

IBRAHIM: Then why are you telling me this?

GAVRIL: Because you should know. Chastity and modesty in a young girl are essential. To deceive you, would do you injury. Because I am a gentleman, and the one thing we have in common, Lieutenant-Captain Petrovich, is our honor.

(Tatyana appears from Natalya's bedroom door.)

IBRAHIM: Thank you, Gavril Afanasyevitch . . . but it seems you are wanted.

GAVRIL: Oh yes, it's my sister. My sister Tatyana. Excuse me. Excuse me, brother Petrovich. Forgive me please. I will be right back. Right back.

(Gavril exits with Tatyana into Natalya's bedroom. Enter Korsakov.)

KORSAKOV: Where is he?

IBRAHIM: In there with the sister.

KORSAKOV: I marvel, brother, at your patience. We've been listening for over a hour to that driveling, stuffy nonsense about the antiquity of the great

Lykov and Rzhevsky families. How painful it is for a woman to put on a dress, and that dancing with Germans will give you the plague. Were I in your place, for that old humbug and all of his family, including Natalya Gavrilovna with all of her delicate airs pretending to be sick, I would pick my nose and send it to them for their supper. Look at this place. Is this a sitting room for a young girl? Or a prison of mirrored vanity? Surely you're not in love with this little party dress?

IBRAHIM: I'm not marrying for love. This is for more practical reasons. If she has no positive aversion to me, I'm going to marry her.

KORSAKOV: Ibrahim, follow my advice for once. Give up this mad idea. Don't do it. Don't marry Natalya.

IBRAHIM: And why not? What am I supposed to do? Why should I always live alone, knowing nothing of the joys and duties of fatherhood and family, simply because I was born in another place?

KORSAKOV: But it seems to me, that for all this, she has no particular liking for you at all.

IBRAHIM: A childish objection, Korsakov. I've given up those charming delusions of love. In this world, it's enough if she's innocent and honest. I've had enough duels at dawn over another man's wife, not to want to grow my own set of horns. So I'll be content so long as she's true. And perhaps over time, with tenderness, trust, indulgence, she'll learn to love me.

KORSAKOV: Listen to yourself. You sound like an old cuckolded husband already. You haven't even married her yet, and already you're concerned about the girl's loyalty, and fidelity. Why do it? You're the godson of the Czar. Go to him. Talk yourself out of this mess.

IBRAHIM: I do not wish to go to the Czar for my every whimpering need. But, you don't understand that, do you? How could you? You already come from a noble family. Marrying Rzhevsky's daughter allies me to Russian nobility. To the land. I'd have a future. I won't be alien in my homeland anymore. The marriage gives me a place with honor.

KORSAKOV: But you, Ibrahim? You with your brooding, suspicious disposition? With that flat nose of yours, and your fat lips and fuzzy hair, to expose yourself to the dangers of matrimony in this society of provincialists. It was that way for you, even in Paris. Have you forgotten Countess Leonora already. Don't be a fool, Ibrahim. What makes you think you can ever have that kind of honor.

(Ibrahim strikes Korsakov.)

IBRAHIM: Thank you for your good and friendly advice brother, but you will remember the old proverb, "You need not trouble yourself to nurse other people's children."

KORSAKOV: You must be careful, Ibrahim, that you don't learn the truth of that proverb for yourself.

IBRAHIM: I already know it.

(Voices are heard from Natalya's bedroom.)

GAVRIL: He has been coming here to the house for two weeks, and he hasn't seen her yet! He may end up thinking that her illness is a sham, and that we are simply faking, trying to delay and get rid of him!

TATYANA: Well, it's true; isn't it?

GAVRIL: The Czar has already sent three times to inquire after Natalya's health! I told you before, I don't intend to quarrel with the Czar! Get her ready! I'm going out to tell him, he can come in! You have her ready! *(Gavril enters the sitting room.)*

GAVRIL: Thank heaven the worst is over. My daughter Natalya, she is much better now. Thank goodness. I'll take you to your betrothed immediately. She will be so glad to see you. Natalya has been waiting for this moment with all her heart.

IBRAHIM: Would you please ask your sister to come out. I want to speak with Natalya alone.

GAVRIL: Alone? This is just not done, sir. We are not Germans here.

IBRAHIM: You are my future father-in-law, Gavril Afanasyevitch. I must respect you. But, if honor is the one thing we share between us, then we both must uphold it.

GAVRIL: Very well. Tatyana! Come! Let Ibrahim Petrovich go in and see his betrothed.

(Tatyana enters the sitting room.)

TATYANA: You're not going in there with Natalya alone, are you?

GAVRIL: Tatyana, be quiet.

(Ibrahim enters Natalya's bedroom.)

KORSAKOV: Tell us a story, Gavril Afanasyevitch, about your exploits during the Streltsi rebellion. My generation knows so little about the days when Russia was struggling to give us all life.

GAVRIL: Well, if you think so, sir.

KORSAKOV: I do, Gavril Afanasyevitch, I do. Tell us a story. That's what we'll do to pass the time.

(Lights focus on Natalya's bedroom.)

IBRAHIM: I am sorry that you are so ill, Natalya Gavrilovna.

NATALYA: Thank you, Ibrahim Petrovich. I am much better now.

IBRAHIM: Good. Good. I was worried. I've been coming every day for the last two weeks to see you, but you were still very ill.

NATALYA: That's very kind of you, Ibrahim Petrovich.

IBRAHIM: Not at all, I was concerned. After all, when you first got sick, it was at Mon Plaisir when you came to see me.

NATALYA: Yes. I must have been coming down with something.

IBRAHIM: Yes, you must have. Yet, people say that you became ill when you heard that our marriage had been arranged.

NATALYA: I am not ill because of you.

IBRAHIM: Listen, Natalya, it is the Czar who says this marriage is arranged. And since he commanded it, I've come here every night for a fortnight to see you. And every night I think of it, marriage. It seems like such a long time, such a long way. All of our lives. And we hardly know each other . . . You must look at me, Natalya Gavrilovna, I could be filling your eyes for a long time. Do you want this marriage?

NATALYA: Yes.

IBRAHIM: My appearance is not disagreeable to you?

NATALYA: No.

IBRAHIM: Look at me!

NATALYA: No . . . your appearance is not disagreeable to *me*.

IBRAHIM: *If* it were not the Czar's wish, would you marry me?

NATALYA: But it is the Czar's wish.

IBRAHIM: But if it were not?

NATALYA: But it is.

IBRAHIM: Since it is the Czar's wish, then *is* my appearance disagreeable to you?

NATALYA: What the Czar wishes has no influence on your appearance. I only want to know when you wish to marry me.

IBRAHIM: And I want to know, if you wish to marry me, Natalya Gavrilovna.

NATALYA: Why are you doing this? It is the Czar's wish, and as everybody else, I wish to please the Czar. What do you want from me? If you don't want to marry me, then why are you here? I'm only a country girl. I've never even been to Moscow. I can't even read or write. That is the way it is with us young girls in Russia. We haven't any other life than to be women. What do I know?

IBRAHIM: Why did you come to see me the night of Menshikov's party? Was it really to learn the minuet?

NATALYA: It was Liza's idea mostly. It would have been a horrible shame not to have been able to do the minuet where the Czar was in attendance.

Why, the Czar commanded it. Commanded me. Liza said that you could teach me. I told her I would do anything not to be humiliated.

IBRAHIM: And what about that night we first met?

NATALYA: I came because you had just come from Paris. And yes it's true, I wanted to see you because I was curious. I wanted to meet the Negro of the Czar.

IBRAHIM: And did I meet your expectations?

NATALYA: Yes. You are dark and have woolly hair.

IBRAHIM: Woolly? Come, feel it, Natalya Gavrilovna. Take it in your hands. It's not woolly, it's hair. And did this darkness and this woolliness scare you?

NATALYA: No. It scared me that you had been to Paris, and knew what women wore underneath their dresses.

IBRAHIM: You were easily shocked. You are just a girl aren't you? Tell me straight Natalya Gavrilovna, tell me the truth. Do you love another? If the Czar's wish could be the same as Natalya Gavrilovna's wish, what would the Czar's wish be?

NATALYA: Lieutenant-Captain Petrovich, can I count on you?

IBRAHIM: You have my word of honor.

NATALYA: I do love someone, but it's no use. It's hopeless. Hopeless to think I could marry the boy I love. Father would never allow it. And do you know why? Because the boy I love is a German.

(Enter Valeryan.)

VALERYAN: So, at last I meet the creature in the flesh. You are the very monkey I came to see.

IBRAHIM: Who are you?

VALERYAN: I am the man who is for you, little tree ape.

(Enter Gavril, Korsakov, and Tatyana.)

GAVRIL: Get out! Get out of my house! Valeryan, get out!

IBRAHIM: Valeryan?

KORSAKOV: Come, Ibrahim. Let us leave this place.

VALERYAN: How could you do this, my lord. You a hero of the Streltsi rebellion, sire your daughter with a gorilla who will give you grandchildren with tails.

KORSAKOV: Come, Ibrahim, let's go.

TATYANA: Do something, Gavril Afanasyevitch, do something. Our lives are being ruined before our very eyes.

GAVRIL: Quiet sister. Take care of the child.

(Tatyana tries to restrain Natalya.)

VALERYAN: Are you a man, sir?

KORSAKOV: Why don't you just settle down, young man?

VALERYAN: Is this fop the owner of your tongue?

IBRAHIM: No, he is my second. He hands me my pistol every time some bastard bores me.

KORSAKOV: No, don't do it, Ibrahim.

VALERYAN: Your second? Yes, I accept.

IBRAHIM: No, it is I who accepts. I am the one who is insulted here, and being the injured party, the ground and the rules belong to me. Who will be your second?

VALERYAN: Gustav. Gustav Adamych.

GUSTAV: No, young master, please.

VALERYAN: Gustav Adamych will be my second. Weapons?

IBRAHIM: Pistols. Twenty paces.

GAVRIL: Please, Ibrahim Petrovich. Let this pass. Ignore him. I will take care of this.

VALERYAN: Place?

IBRAHIM: In the woods. The clearing in the grove of apple trees near Mon Plaisir.

NATALYA: Please Ibrahim Petrovich, don't shoot my Valeryan. I'll marry you, whatever you want.

VALERYAN: Time?

IBRAHIM: Dawn.

(Ibrahim exits.)

KORSAKOV: I advise you to make your peace with this world tonight, for you are most assuredly a dead man, young sir. I wish you would save us all the trouble and apologize.

(Korsakov exits.)

GAVRIL: Valeryan, you fool.

VALERYAN: Stepfather, Natalya and I are in love.

NATALYA: Valeryan!

VALERYAN: Natalya.

(Natalya and Valeryan embrace.)

TATYANA: Lord help us and save us.

GAVRIL: We're ruined. Ruined. Ruined.

(Blackout.)

. . .

Lights up. A dueling ground in the Russian woods. Lights up on Korsakov. Enter Ibrahim eating an apple.

IBRAHIM: Is he here yet?
KORSAKOV: No. He hasn't come. He's already late. Perhaps he won't come.
IBRAHIM: He'll come. He's young. He's in love. They always come. Apple, Korsakov?
KORSAKOV: No thank you, Ibrahim. I have no stomach for apples this morning.
IBRAHIM: How is it, your second time, Korsakov?
KORSAKOV: No better than the first, I'm afraid. I couldn't sleep. The waiting was driving me insane. Yet I wished that the dawn would never come. I kept thinking to myself that this may be the last day that I will ever see my friend.
IBRAHIM: The world is a dangerous place, Korsakov. It could be true for any day.
KORSAKOV: Is your honor so important to you?
IBRAHIM: It's not that honor is so important, Korsakov, it's simply all I have.
KORSAKOV: There is something I must tell you, Ibrahim.
IBRAHIM: What is it, Korsakov?
KORSAKOV: During the night I went for a walk to try and settle my nerves. But since I don't know St. Petersburg anymore, there was nowhere else for me to go but to come here. Tonight in this wood, I realized that I have not been a good friend to you, brother. After Valeryan called you all those awful names, "apes and monkeys," it struck me that for a brief moment, just before that, I treated you practically the same way. And this may sound utterly naïve and simple-minded to you, but it has occurred to me that you must endure this sort of thing all the time. I didn't know, Ibrahim. I didn't realize. I would have been more careful, but in truth I don't want to be careful, with you. I want to be carefree with you. You are my friend. But I know now that I have betrayed you with careless advice, and then stood by and did nothing while you were dishonored. Ibrahim, I know I have insulted you, and you may demand satisfaction from me at your pleasure.
IBRAHIM: You know, Korsakov, there is a relentless devil within me. Me and something *within* me, are always at odds. I cannot tell when it is I who is restraining myself, from when I am being restrained by the world. Who

put me in these chains? Bound me to this skin? This flesh? Was *it* me, or some others? Is *it* inside or is it out? I swear, I honestly cannot tell you. But there are times when I have moments that are truly noble. Where you grapple with your fears so severely, until you suddenly realize that these may be the last moments of your life. Then that life becomes fuller. More alive. More real. My title now is Lord of the duel. My estate spans for twenty paces over this ground. My future lies in the speed of a musket ball, and the fact that I happen to be a very good shot. What does it matter? There is only oblivion before me now. And if I'm as good a man to receive it, than I'm as a good a man to deal it out. I have no quarrel with you brother, because you are my friend.

KORSAKOV: If I am your brother, if I am your friend, then come. Let us just walk away from here now. Here, the penalty for dueling is death.

IBRAHIM: Death is the penalty in any case. I have nowhere else to go. Between he and I, one of us will leave this ground, and one of us will not. Nothing will live until then.

(Enter Valeryan and Gustav.)

VALERYAN: I beg your pardon. We seem to be a little late. I am at fault.

IBRAHIM: You shouldn't trouble yourself. It will never happen again.

GUSTAV: Good morning, sir. And how are you this very early morning?

KORSAKOV: Passable old gray beard, passable. I'm afraid that I have only had one other experience at this sort of thing. You were a soldier. You must be familiar with the affairs of honor. I would appreciate it, if you would take the initiative.

GUSTAV: Of course. Because Lieutenant-Captain Petrovich is the offended party, we must surrender to him the higher ground with his back toward the sun. I'm sorry young master.

VALERYAN: It's all right, Gustav. We must be fair.

GUSTAV: Give me your back, sir. Ready?

KORSAKOV: Ready.

GUSTAV: One, two, three, four, five, six, seven, eight, nine, ten. Ten paces. This marks the spot sir. This is where the gentlemen will discharge their weapons. Do you wish for me to make the call?

KORSAKOV: No. I'll do it. Gentlemen, if you please, the rules. "Terms of the duel between Lieutenant-Captain Petrovich of the Preobrazhesky Regiment and Lieutenant Valeryan of the Horse Guards Regiment: The rules. They are simple. You will go to your places and stand your ground. On the first command, you will cock and ready your weapons. On the second command you will aim your weapons. On the given signal you will

fire your weapons. Once both parties have fired their weapons, and there is no result, we will begin again and again, and again, until the affair of the duel has been satisfied. Gentlemen, take your ground please.
(Ibrahim and Valeryan take their ground.)

KORSAKOV: What do I do now, Gustav?

GUSTAV: Just give a signal, sir. Something they can see. A wave of your hand, a drop of a hat.
(Korsakov takes a handkerchief from his pocket.)

KORSAKOV: When I drop this handkerchief, gentlemen, you may fire. Ready. Aim.
(Enter Ivan.)

IVAN: Hold your arms, by order of the Czar.

IBRAHIM: So, it's you Ivan.

IVAN: They are here, your majesty!
(Enter Peter with pistol in hand.)

PETER: And what do you think you are doing, Ibrahim?

IBRAHIM: I am learning your lessons about politics, sire.

PETER: Politics?

IBRAHIM: Yes, sire. Politics. That great war within this little peace we are having. Surely you must know the circumstances. You are the Czar. Otherwise why are you here?

PETER: Is this how you are loyal to me? How you keep your word? How you betray me?

IBRAHIM: No one is more betrayed here than me, my sovereign. I did not heed your good advice, and was not a careful soldier. I have been unworthy of you. And I am here to correct that fault or pay the price.

PETER: There isn't any such price to pay. I told you before, there's no dueling in Russia. The penalty for the survivor is death.

IBRAHIM: Then you shall have to do your duty, sire.

PETER: I did not mean for this to be my lesson to you, Ibrahim.

IBRAHIM: Then perhaps, godfather, this will be my lesson to you.

PETER: Very well then. Don't let me interrupt you gentlemen. Please, continue on. Korsakov.

KORSAKOV: Yes, sire.

PETER: You have on velvet breeches, as even I don't wear. And I have greater means than you. That's extravagance. You must be careful I don't quarrel with you.

KORSAKOV: Yes, sire. Gentlemen, when I drop this handkerchief and it touches

THE NEGRO OF PETER THE GREAT

the ground, you may consider it the command to fire your weapons. Ready! Aim!

(Korsakov drops his handkerchief. Frozen in fear, Valeryan aims. Ibrahim awaits his fire in the height of contempt. Valeryan shoots and misses.)

IBRAHIM: *(Raising his pistol.)* Wait! Stop! Hold where you are! Stand your ground sir. It's my turn to fire. I still have the last shot.

(Valeryan prepares himself. He turns his body sideways and folds his arms across his chest, making himself the smallest possible target. Ibrahim fires, and Valeryan falls. The Czar aims his pistol at Ibrahim.)

PETER: It is I who has the last shot, brother. Look at what you've done, Ibrahim? You have just killed a Horse Guardsman. You a Russian soldier. The godson of the Czar. A Czar is not just a man. He is the state. And as the state he must keep all of his parts. But if he must lose any part of himself, then he must be the one who cuts it off. When you are wrong, I must punish you. You know this. You couldn't have won, so why did you do it? Why?

IBRAHIM: Life is hard being your ward, my Czar. All you want to give me, and all I want you to give me, we cannot have. I must have that for myself. I have my own laws.

PETER: You are speaking in the heat of the moment, Ibrahim.

IBRAHIM: A moment is all I have. And the good future you mean for me is bleak and bitter. Your good future, and your good intentions will ruin me. I cannot give you what you want. I want to, but I cannot.

PETER: How could you be so ungrateful? If you do not give me good reason Ibrahim, I will shoot you where you stand.

IBRAHIM: Have no fear, godfather. I will stand my ground.

PETER: Stand your ground? The ground on which you are standing is mine.

IBRAHIM: No, godfather. This ground is mine.

PETER: You are talking treason, Ibrahim. You, who I raised as a little boy, you are speaking treason to me?

IBRAHIM: It is no treason, godfather, but I am not your little boy anymore.

PETER: Is that so? Well, as you say, then I shall have to do my duty. *(Aiming his pistol at Ibrahim.)* And now, what is this lesson you were going to teach me, hey?

IBRAHIM: *(Leaning into the pistol barrel.)* How to live.

(Blackout.)

END OF PLAY

The Women of Lockerbie

Deborah Brevoort

2001 Onassis International Playwriting Competition winner, Silver Medal, Kennedy Center Fund for New American Plays Award, 2001

BIOGRAPHY

Deborah Brevoort is a playwright and musical theater librettist/lyricist who lived for many years in Alaska before moving to New York City. She is the author of numerous plays and musicals, including *The Women of Lockerbie*, which won the silver medal in the Onassis International Playwriting Competition in 2001 and the Kennedy Center's Fund for New American Plays Award. She is the librettist of *King Island Christmas,* with composer David Friedman, which won the 1997 Frederick Loewe Award and has had over thirty productions around the United States. An album produced by Thomas Z. Shepard was released by the King Island Company in November 1999. She and David are currently writing *Goodbye My Island,* a companion piece to *King Island Christmas.*

Deborah also wrote the book and lyrics for *Coyote Goes Salmon Fishing,* with composer Scott Richards, which won the 2001 Frederick Loewe Award. It was produced in 1996 by Stuart Ostrow and also at Perseverance Theatre in Juneau, Alaska. In 1998 she was given the Paul Green Award by the National Theatre Conference for her book-writing in the musical theater. Her play, *Into the Fire* won the 1999 Weissberger Award and is published by Samuel French. *Blue Moon Over Memphis,* her noh drama about Elvis Presley, won the 1994 Lee Korf Award. *Signs of Life* received a Rockefeller grant and was produced at the Perseverance Theatre. Deborah was one of the original company members with Perseverance Theatre. Since 1980 many of her plays and musicals have been produced there. Her website address is www.DeborahBrevoort.com.

CHARACTERS

MADELINE LIVINGSTON: A suburban housewife from New Jersey. Her twenty-year-old son Adam was killed seven years ago in the Pan Am 103 crash over Lockerbie, Scotland.

BILL LIVINGSTON: Her husband, father of Adam.

OLIVE ALLISON: An older woman, from Lockerbie. Leader of the laundry project. (See Historical Note, page 201.)

WOMAN 1 AND 2: Middle-aged women from Lockerbie.

HATTIE: A cleaning woman. From Lockerbie.

GEORGE JONES: The American government representative in charge of the warehouse storing the remains from the Pan Am 103 crash.

PLACE
The rolling green hills of Lockerbie, Scotland, where Pan Am Flight 103 crashed. There is a stream running between the hills.

TIME
December 21, 1995, the seven-year anniversary of the crash. The night of the winter solstice.

NOTE
There should be no intermission.

ACKNOWLEDGMENTS
The Women of Lockerbie was first written during a residency in Denmark, sponsored by New Dramatists and the Danish American Society. It was further developed through numerous readings at New Dramatists in addition to staged readings and workshops at the O'Neill, Shenandoah Retreat, Geva Theatre, Oregon Shakespeare Festival, and Bay Area Playwrights Festival.

During the course of the play's long development process, I received invaluable assistance from the wonderful actors at these theater companies, and more people than I can possibly mention here. I would like to thank in particular, however, Corinne Jacker, Gay Smith, Lue Douthit, Wendy Goldberg, Bob Small, John Steber, Todd London, Marge Betley, Lou Jacob, Liz Diamond, and my agent Beth Blickers for their invaluable advice, help, and support. My deepest debt, however, goes to Roberta Levitow, who's expert dramaturgy and generosity of spirit helped me to finally finish the play.

HISTORICAL NOTE
After the crash of Pan Am 103, the women of Lockerbie, Scotland, set up a laundry project to wash the 11,000 articles of clothing belonging to the victims that were found in the plane's wreckage. Once the clothes were washed, the women packed and shipped them to the victims' families around the world.

The Women of Lockerbie *is a work of fiction and does not purport to be a factual record of real events or real people. Although it is loosely inspired by incidents that did occur, the names, persons, characters, dates, and settings have been completely fictionalized, as have all of the dramatic situations.*

THE WOMEN OF LOCKERBIE

PROLOGUE

The play begins in darkness. Night has fallen. From offstage, a flashlight sweeps across the hills that are covered with patches of fog.

BILL: *(Off. Calls out.)* Madeline?
(There is a faint echo.) Madeline?!
(Bill Livingston and Olive Allison enter. Bill carries a woman's coat. Olive carries a flashlight.)

BILL: *(Calls.)* Madeline, sweetheart?
Where are you?
Answer me, Maddie!
Please!

OLIVE: *(Calls.)* Mrs. Livingston?
(Pause. Olive sweeps a flashlight over the hills.)

OLIVE: Are you sure she's out here?

BILL: Oh yes. I saw her run in this direction.
(He looks out over the hills.)
She's roaming the hills again
looking for our son's remains.
She's been roaming for two days now
ever since we got here.
Morning, noon and night
that's all she does . . .
(Pause.)
(Calls.) Madeline!
(Pause.)
It was all I could do to get her to attend the memorial service.
And now, she runs out of the church
before it's over.
Doesn't even put her coat on.
She'll die of exposure if we don't find her.

OLIVE: We'll find her. Don't worry.
I've lived in Lockerbie my whole life.
I know these hills like I know myself.
(Olive sweeps a flashlight over the surrounding hills.)

OLIVE: *(Calls.)* Mrs. Livingston?
    Come on, love.
    Come back to us!
    (Pause.)
BILL: It's a helluva night to be out.
    Cold and damp.
OLIVE: When the fog clings to the hills like this at night
    it means the morning will be clear.
BILL: *(Calls.)* Maddie?
    (Pause.)
    Maddie, honey?
    Answer me!
    Please!
    (Silence.)
    It's been seven years since he died in the crash.
    Seven long years
    and still
    she can't put aside her grief.
    I thought her sorrow would diminish with time.
    But it hasn't.
    It's as strong today
    as it was the day he died.
    I don't understand it.
    The other families have gone on with their lives.
    Why can't she?
OLIVE: The other families had a body to bury.
BILL: Yes. The body.
    Maybe if she had the body
    things would be different.
OLIVE: With a body
    she would have a coffin,
    or an urn,
    or a gravesite.
    A place to put her grief.
    But your wife has no such place.
    All she has is the sky
    where he vanished.
    The sky was not meant
    to be a burial ground.

It's too big
and when you store your grief there
it runs wild.

BILL: Yes.
And now that she's here in Lockerbie,
it's running even wilder.
It must be these hills . . .
They've unleashed a
frenzy
in her sorrow
that I've never seen before.
(Pause. He looks out over the hills.)
They've got a
strange
kind of
power
these hills
don't they?

OLIVE: Yes. They do.

BILL: And *beauty* . . .
Funny.
Beauty is the last thing I expected to find in Lockerbie . . .
(Pause.)
This is the first time we've come here.
I was afraid to bring her all these years.
I was afraid it would make her grief even worse.
And it has.
I don't know . . .
maybe I did the wrong thing
by bringing her here.
I just thought that
maybe
if she came to Lockerbie
on the anniversary
to attend the service
and see the monument
and meet the other families
maybe

then
she'll stop weeping.
(Pause.)
She's been weeping for seven years.
She lies on the living room couch and weeps.
All day.
She can't stop.
Or won't.
Our friends have given up.
They don't call or visit anymore.
Their patience is worn thin.
Mine is worn thin.
I didn't think it was possible
for two eyes
to cry so many tears.
But it is.
I have seen it.
I have seen an ocean pour from her eyes.

OLIVE: There is no greater sorrow than the death of a child.
BILL: Yes.
(Pause.)
He was our only child.
(Pause.)
He was twenty years old.
OLIVE: Adam Alexander Livingston.
BILL: You know his name?
OLIVE: Everyone in Lockerbie
knows the names
of everyone who died.
BILL: Everyone in Lockerbie is very kind.
You are very kind.
Thank you for coming here with me.
I'm . . . uh . . .
I'm at my wit's end here.
OLIVE: I know you are, love.
We all are.
(Flashlights sweep across the hills.)

FIRST CHORAL DIALOGUE

WOMAN 1 *(Off.)*: Olive?
WOMAN 2 *(Off.)*: Olive?
WOMAN 1 *(Off.)*: Olive?
OLIVE: Over here!
   (Olive flashes back with her light.)
WOMAN 2 *(Off.)*: Olive, is that you?
OLIVE: Aye!
   (The Women of Lockerbie enter, carrying flashlights.)
WOMEN: Hello.
BILL: Hello.
WOMAN 1: You're Mr. Livingston, aren't you?
BILL: Yes.
WOMAN 1: Are you all right?
BILL: I'm fine, thank you. It's my wife that's the problem.
WOMAN 2: Have you found her?
BILL: No. Not yet.
WOMAN 1: We saw her run from the church
   in the middle of the service
WOMAN 2: When they lit the candles
   and read the names of the dead
WOMAN 1: We were worried
WOMAN 2: We saw her roaming the hills
   this afternoon
WOMAN 1: Yesterday, too
   and the day before
WOMAN 2: Can we help?
BILL: Thank you, but I'm not quite sure what to do.
OLIVE: Why don't we split up and continue to look for her?
BILL: I don't know . . . this is the place she keeps coming back to.
   Maybe we should stay right here.
OLIVE: All right, then. That's what we'll do.
WOMAN 1: Olive, we just got word from Hattie down at the warehouse.
OLIVE: What's the news?
WOMAN 1: The mayor came out of the meeting with Mr. Jones.
WOMAN 2: He didn't succeed.
OLIVE: Has Mr. Jones announced yet what he's going to do?
WOMAN 1: No. But he revealed his plans to the mayor.

WOMAN 2: Olive . . .
>He's going to burn the clothes.

OLIVE: *Burn the clothes!?*

WOMAN 1: Yes.

WOMAN 2: Everything on the Shelves of Sorrow
>will be incinerated at dawn.

OLIVE: I was afraid something like this was going to happen.

WOMAN 2: *(To Bill.)* Now that the investigation is over
>and the evidence has been collected against the terrorists,
>they're going to burn the clothing of the victims.

BILL: I didn't know there was any.

WOMAN 2: There's quite a lot, actually.

WOMAN 1: Over 11,000 articles.

OLIVE: Why is Mr. Jones going to burn them?

WOMAN 1: "Government procedure."

WOMAN 2: "Blood and fuel contamination," he told the mayor.

WOMAN 1: *(To Bill.)* The women of Lockerbie have
>petitioned the American authorities in Washington
>to release the clothing to us.

WOMAN 2: We want to wash the clothes
>and return them to the victim's families.

BILL: Some families may not want them, you know.
>I know that I, for one, wouldn't want them.
>They'd just bring back things that are better left alone.

WOMAN 2: Each family can decide for themselves.

WOMAN 1: Besides, it's something we must do.

WOMAN 2: Not only for the families, but for ourselves.

WOMAN 1: We need to give love to those who have suffered.

BILL: Why?

WOMAN 2: So evil will not triumph.

BILL: That's very kind of you.

WOMAN 2: Not really.
>We're just doing what we want to.

WOMAN 1: What we would want others to do for us.

OLIVE: When evil comes into the world
>it is the job of the witness
>to turn it to love.

WOMAN 1: Aye.

OLIVE: We were the witnesses.

> We are simply doing our job.
> But

WOMAN 2: But

WOMAN 1: But

OLIVE: Your government has not been very responsive,
> I'm sorry to say.

WOMAN 2: They sent a man from Washington
> Mr. Jones

WOMAN 1: George Jones

WOMAN 2: To shut down the warehouse.
> He won't return our phone calls.

WOMAN 1: He's too busy to bother with us women.

WOMAN 2: He didn't even attend the memorial service.

WOMAN 1: He's only been in Lockerbie for two weeks.
> He doesn't understand the situation.
> He didn't see the destruction.

BILL: What can you do?

WOMAN 2: *(To Olive.)* Aye, what's the next step?
> Time's running out.
> In eight hours, the clothing will be burned.

OLIVE: Don't worry, Hattie and I worked out a strategy this morning.

WOMAN 2: *(To Bill.)* Hattie is the cleaning woman in Mr. Jone's office.

WOMAN 1: *(To Bill.)* She's one of us.

OLIVE: She's going to call Bishop Laing.
> He has offered to help.

BILL: Mrs. Allison. . .
> Please. Don't let me keep you.
> It sounds like you are needed in town
> with more important matters.

OLIVE: No. It's best that I work from behind the scenes.

WOMAN 1: *(To Bill.)* If Mr. Jones gets wind that Olive is around
> he'll call in Scotland Yard!

WOMAN 2: *(To Bill.)* The day he arrived in Lockerbie,
> she cornered him in the market!

WOMAN 1: *(To Bill.)* When he tried to get away,
> she grabbed his arm and started to yell!

OLIVE: I didn't yell.

WOMAN 1: Olive . . . dear . . . you yelled.

OLIVE: I spoke . . . forcefully.

DEBORAH BREVOORT

With great conviction.
WOMAN 1: *(To Bill.)* She terrified the poor man!
   (The Women laugh.)
OLIVE: He wouldn't listen to me!
WOMAN 1: Olive's going to stay in the background tonight.
WOMAN 2: Generals don't belong on the front lines anyway.
OLIVE: *(To Bill.)* Besides, I need to be here with you.
   Your wife's struggle with grief
   is the struggle we all share.
   It threatens to tear us apart, too.
BILL: It does?
OLIVE: *(Pause.)* Aye.

FIRST EPISODE

MADELINE: *(Off.)* Adam?
BILL: Maddie?
WOMAN 1: Is that her?
BILL: Yes. Maddie! Over here!
WOMAN 2: Where is she?
BILL: On the other side of that hill.
OLIVE: There she is now.
   (The Women shine their flashlights, catching Madeline as she comes over the hill.)
MADELINE: Adam?
WOMAN 1: Poor thing.
WOMAN 2: Look how she wanders
   Her spirit broken
WOMAN 1: It breaks my heart to see her
WOMAN 2: She is a like a tree
   that's been struck by lightning,
WOMAN 1: split down the middle with grief.
MADELINE: Adam?
BILL: Maddie! Over here!
   (Bill runs to the top of the hill to meet her.)
MADELINE: He's here, Bill.
   Adam is here
   on the other side of that hill.

  I can feel him.
BILL: Maddie, put your coat on.
MADELINE: When I walked over that hill
  I could feel him.
BILL: Well, good.
MADELINE: If only I could find him!
  If only I could find some part of him.
  A *bone*.
  The bone
  from his *chin*.
  I would know it if I saw it!
  He had such a
  strong
  firm
  chin . . .
  What I would give . . .
  And what I would give to talk to him.
  Even if it was only to say
  "Pick up your socks!"
  And to hear him say, *"Mom!"*
  Remember how he would say that?
  He would rolls his eyes at me and say *"Mommmmm!"*
BILL: Yes, I remember.
  I also remember how mad you got
  when he did that.
MADELINE: I never got mad.
BILL: You always got mad.
  You would shoot him a look
  and say, "Don't *Mom* me!"
  (Madeline heads back up the hill.)
BILL: Where are you going?
MADELINE: To find him.
  (He stops her.)
BILL: You won't find him, Maddie.
  There is nothing to find.
  The bomb went off in the compartment
  under his seat.
  Everyone in that part of the plane vanished.
  You know that.

MADELINE: There's got to be something of him somewhere!
(Madeline breaks away and runs up the hill.)
BILL: Maddie, please!
OLIVE: Mr. Livingston.
You can't reason with grief.
It has no ears to hear you.
Let her walk the hills
and tread her grief into the ground.
(Slight pause.)
Do you think you should go with her?
BILL: And do what?
OLIVE: Walk the hills . . .
Tread the ground a little yourself, perhaps?
BILL: If I do that, I'll just make matters worse.
OLIVE: All right then.
We'll stay nearby
and wait for this
to run its course.
(Offstage, a church bell rings.)
WOMAN 1: The Candlelight procession has begun.
They're walking to the town square
for the all-night vigil.
WOMAN 2: Some are going up to Lamb's Hill
to pray at the stone wall.
Used to be
we would celebrate on that wall.
Remember?
WOMAN 1: Aye. The solstice.
WOMAN 2: The winter solstice.
WOMAN 1: Every December 21st
we'd go up there and light a bonfire
then sit all night
and wait for the return of the sun!
WOMAN 2: And when it appeared
we'd pop the cork
and toast the coming of spring!
WOMAN 1: Things are different now.
WOMAN 2: December 21st is no longer a day of celebration.
It's a day of mourning.

WOMAN 1: A day when we pray for the dead.
BILL: Funny.
    The solstice is not something
    we celebrate in New Jersey.
    Don't know why.
OLIVE: It's because you're in the middle, love.
BILL: The middle?
OLIVE: Of the earth.
    Away from the extremes of
    darkness and light.
    (Madeline appears again at the top of the hill.)
WOMAN 1: *(Whispers.)* Look. Your wife.
WOMAN 2: What is she doing?
    (Madeline walks back and forth along the top of the hill. She looks into the sky and speaks silently to herself. The Women and Bill watch her from a distance.)
BILL: She's talking to herself again.
    She's been doing that a lot lately.
    I come home from work to find her
    sitting at the window
    talking
    to the sky.
    And late at night
    she wanders through the house
    talking to Adam
    as if he were there in the room . . .
WOMAN 1: What does she say?
BILL: She goes over and over
    the moment she heard the news.
    Over and over the moment of his death.
    Just like she's walking these hills now,
    but with words,
    going over and over
    the same ground.
OLIVE: Grief needs to talk.
BILL: I've stopped listening.
    I can't take it anymore.
    (Pause.)
    We live in silence.

>We go whole days and nights
>without saying a word to each other.

WOMAN 1: Let us talk to her.
>Maybe she'll listen to us.

WOMAN 2: And let us listen to her.
>We haven't heard her story before.
>What is old to you is new to us.

WOMAN 1: Who knows?
>We might hear something in what she says
>that can help her close the door on grief.

BILL: By all means. Go ahead.
>I'll give anything a try.

WOMAN 1: *(Calls out.)* Mrs. Livingston?

WOMAN 2: *(Calls out.)* Mrs. Livingston, may we talk to you?
>*(Madeline stops walking.)*

MADELINE: You want to talk to me?

WOMEN: Yes.

MADELINE: Want to talk to the crazy lady, huh?

BILL: Maddie, please.

WOMAN 1: No, that's not why we're here.

MADELINE: It's all right if it is.
>It's all right, too, if you think I'm crazy.
>Because I am.

WOMAN 2: We don't think you're crazy.

MADELINE: I'm roaming the hills looking for my son's body.
>Only a crazy person would do something like that.

OLIVE: Or a mother.

MADELINE: I'm not a mother anymore . . .

WOMAN 2: Mrs. Livingston?

WOMAN 1: Talk to us. Please.
>Tell us your story.

WOMAN 2: Tell us where you were
>and what you were doing
>when it happened.

WOMAN 2: We need to hear it.

WOMAN 1: And we need to tell our story, too.

OLIVE: Seven years ago
>life as we knew it came to an end
>and we are still suffering.

MADELINE: I was in the kitchen.
>I was baking a pie for Adam.
>A pumpkin pie, to welcome him home.
>The TV was on.
>I listen to it when I'm cooking.
>It was tuned to a soap opera.
>"All My Children."
>One of the couples was fighting.
>The woman was pregnant.
>She wanted to get an abortion.
>"Don't be a fool!" I say to the woman.
>"Have the baby!"
>I sprinkle flour on the counter
>and roll out the pie dough.
>I roll it once in each direction.
>Like this . . .
>*(She rolls.)*
>The way my mother taught me.
>And then
>Ted Koppel comes on the air.
>I know immediately that something is wrong.
>You only hear Ted Koppel's voice at night
>never in the day.
>He said:

BILL: "We interrupt this program . . ."

MADELINE: I thought,
>"Oh dear,
>Something awful has happened.
>What a shame.
>And so close to Christmas."
>I grab more flour and sprinkle it.
>I roll the crust.
>I hear . . .

BILL: "Pan Am 103."

MADELINE: The pie dough sticks to the rolling pin.

BILL: "Pan Am 103 was last seen in a fireball over Scotland."

MADELINE: I double over.
>I sink onto the kitchen counter.
>My face presses into the pie dough.

214 DEBORAH BREVOORT

It is cold on my nose and cheek.
I cannot stand up.
I grope the counter
for something to hold on to.
My arm hits the flour bin.
It crashes to the floor.
My feet are covered with flour.
I reach for the handle
on the refrigerator.
I pull myself up.
And there
in front of me
is a note
held by a magnet
that says
"Adam. 7PM. JFK. Pan Am 103."
(Madeline sinks to the ground, overcome with grief.)
I live in New Jersey!
I have two cars in the driveway!
This was not supposed to happen to me!
(Long pause.)

WOMAN 1: You think the worst can't happen.

WOMAN 2: You think that it won't.

WOMAN 1: But then, one day, it does.

OLIVE: The "poor soul" on television
is suddenly you

WOMAN 1: And the faraway disaster
lies in the flour that falls
on your kitchen floor.
(Olive lifts Madeline back to her feet. She takes a candle from her coat pocket and offers it to Madeline.)

OLIVE: Let's light our candles
Shall we?
I brought them from the church.
We'll keep our vigil here
together
in this place where your son died.

MADELINE: No!
(Madeline breaks away.)

Lighting candles will give me no comfort!
(Madeline runs to the other side of the hill.)
(Olive turns back to the others.)
OLIVE: I could use the comfort of a candle.
WOMAN 2: I could too.
(Olive lights her candle. The Women light their candles from hers.)
OLIVE: Mr. Livingston?
BILL: Please.
(Bill takes a candle from his coat pocket. Olive lights it.)

FIRST CHORAL ODE
"GRIEF"

(Olive watches the flame on her candle.)
OLIVE: Death is a guest whose visit is short
When it comes to your house
it never stays
WOMAN 1: It just pokes its head in the door
to drop something off!
WOMAN 2: . . .and is gone.
(Slight pause.)
WOMAN 1: But Grief . . .
(Slight pause.)
OLIVE: Grief is a guest who stays too long.
Its visit turns from days
WOMAN 2: into weeks
WOMAN 1: into months
OLIVE: into years.
WOMAN 2: It takes over your house
and will not leave.
OLIVE: It wears a dark coat.
WOMAN 1: It sleeps in your bed all day
and sits in your chair all night.
WOMAN 2: It rearranges your closets
and cupboards.
WOMAN 1: It leaves dirty dishes
in the sink.
WOMAN 2: Wherever you go

> it follows.

WOMAN 1: Whatever you do
> it watches.

OLIVE: It hovers behind you
> looking over your shoulder
> so you cannot forget
> that it's there.

BILL: Yes . . .
> *(They stand in silence, looking at their candles.)*

SECOND CHORAL DIALOGUE

WOMAN 2: I was driving to the filling station.

WOMAN 1: I was walking the dog.

OLIVE: I was baking a pie, like your wife.

WOMAN 2: Suddenly the sky turned red.

WOMAN 1: The ground shook.

OLIVE: The pie fell.

WOMAN 1: The tree at the end of the lane burst into flames.

OLIVE: I ran to the door.

WOMAN 2: I slammed on the brakes.

WOMAN 1: I turned and looked.
> My neighbor's rose garden
> was on fire, too.
> Green bushes
> with
> wee
> buds
> of fire
> where the flowers should have been.

WOMAN 2: I jumped out of the car.

OLIVE: I ran out of the house.
> There
> on top of the hill
> was a suitcase.
> *(Slight pause.)*
> A red suitcase
> *(Slight pause.)*

> Sitting there
> as if someone had
> set it down.

WOMAN 1: People were running from their homes
> screaming and crying.

WOMAN 2: Gordon MacPherson
> was kneeling in the street
> holding the body of his daughter.
> His wife was beside him
> pushing her fists
> into her eyes.

WOMAN 1: When I got to my house
> the lights were still on
> but the roof was gone.
> I unlatched the gate
> and stepped into the yard.
> Someone yelled

OLIVE: "Don't go in there!"

WOMAN 1: But I didn't listen.
> I had to see what had happened.
> I pushed open the door.
> Inside my living room
> was a pile of bodies.
> *(Pause.)*
> 71 bodies still strapped to their seats.
> *(Pause.)*

WOMAN 2: Suddenly there were helicopters
> and police sirens.
> Down on Lockerbie Lane
> Christmas carols were playing.

OLIVE: And up above
> letters
> from mailbags
> fell
> from the clouds.

WOMAN 2: They drifted
> to the
> ground
> and covered

the street
like snow.
(Pause.)

WOMAN 1: We saw the wreckage.

OLIVE: The things they couldn't show on TV.

WOMAN 2: We saw the bodies

WOMAN 1: and the body parts

OLIVE: strewn
like litter
along the streets.

WOMAN 2: And we saw the faces.

WOMAN 1: Oh God, the faces.

OLIVE: The faces of the dead.

WOMAN 1: It's the faces that haunt me the most.

WOMAN 2: Some had been asleep when it happened.
Their faces were peaceful.

WOMAN 1: But others were awake.
Their faces were frozen
in horror
and disbelief

OLIVE: They knew.

WOMAN 2: Yes, they knew.

WOMAN 1: You could tell they knew what was happening.
(Pause.)

WOMAN 2: I would rather spend my life
hauling bricks on my back
then to carry within me
just one of the memories
I have from that day.

WOMAN 1: Bricks would be lighter
and easier to bear.

WOMAN 2: Aye.

OLIVE: Aye. Memory is a heavy burden.
It's a sack you can't set down.
You carry it with you wherever you go
and it weighs on you
even when you sleep.

SECOND CHORAL ODE
"LOCKERBIE"

The Women are suddenly thunderstruck with the realization that this has happened in Lockerbie.

WOMAN 1: We live in Lockerbie.
OLIVE: Lockerbie
WOMAN 2: Lockerbie, Scotland
    A tidy little town
    with rolling green hills
OLIVE: North of the Solway Firth
    in the Dumfries region
    of the Scottish lowlands
WOMAN 1: Where the Annan River
    meets the Kinnel and the Moffat
OLIVE: But not exactly.
WOMAN 1: No, not exactly
    we're off to the side a bit
    off the beaten path
WOMAN 2: far away from the troubles of the world.
OLIVE: Trouble just doesn't come to Lockerbie, Scotland.
WOMAN 2: There's nothing for it to do here
WOMAN 1: except graze with the sheep
    or take tea in the afternoon.
OLIVE: But one day
WOMAN 2: Yes, one day
    in an instant
WOMAN 1: in a blink of an eye
    a twist of fate
    rained
    twisted metal
    on our roofs
OLIVE: The fog that clung to our gentle hills
    turned to smoke
    and the gentle rain falling from the sky
    turned to blood.
    (Pause. Bill blows out his candle.)
    (Pause. The Women watch him.)

WOMAN 1: Mr. Livingston?
WOMAN 2: Mr. Livingston, are you all right?
BILL: Oh, yes. Yes. I'm fine.
WOMAN 1: Have we upset you?
BILL: No. No. I just . . .
    didn't know.
    That's all.
    (Madeline appears at the top of the hill.)
OLIVE: Your wife. Look.

SECOND EPISODE

Madeline walks back and forth talking to herself. The Women and Bill watch her.

MADELINE: I never should have let him study in London.
    I never should have let him go so far from home.
    He was too young.
    Much too young to go so far from home.
    I should have made him wait for a year.
    I should have been more firm.
    I should have said no.
    I should have just said
    "*No, no, no* you cannot go!"
    Oh God,
    Why didn't I say that . . . ?
    (She wanders, distraught.)
    And why did I choose Pan Am over Delta?
    There were two boxes on the application form!
    Why didn't I
    check
    the *box*
    for Delta?
    (She stands still for a moment, then suddenly starts to walk again, traversing the hill, heading toward Bill and the Women.)
    And I should have let him stay an extra day with his friends!
    But I said:
    "No, I want you home for Christmas

I want you home for the party
You need to hang the Christmas lights for your father
your father has a bad back and he needs you to help him."
(Pause.)
Oh God . . .
(She traverses the hill again, distraught.)
And why did I plan the party for Friday?
I should have planned it for Saturday!
If I had planned the party for Saturday
he wouldn't have been on that plane.
He would have come home a day later.
He never would have died.
Yes, if I had planned the party for Saturday,
he never would have died . . .
(Bill approaches her gently.)

BILL: Maddie. . .
we couldn't have the party on Saturday.
Remember?
Saturday was Christmas eve.
We never had the party on Christmas eve.
We always had the party the day before.

MADELINE: You can have a party on Christmas eve!

BILL: Yes, but we never did that.

MADELINE: He could have flown on Delta! —

BILL: — You didn't like Delta —

MADELINE: — I could have said,
"*No*, you cannot go to London."
I could have said
"*Yes*, you can come home whenever you want!"

BILL: You let him go because you loved him
And you brought him home because you missed him.
You did what any mother would do!

MADELINE: *I* should have hung the Christmas lights!

BILL: Maddie . . .

MADELINE: I could have gotten up on that ladder myself!

BILL: I wouldn't have let you!
Maddie!
There was nothing you could have done to stop this.
This tragedy didn't happen because of you.

      Get ahold of yourself!
      (Madeline turns and heads back to the hills.)
BILL: Maddie!
      Come back, please!
      (Pause.) Maddie?
      (Pause.) Sweetheart?
      (Pause.) Please?
      (Madeline disappears over the top of the hill.)
BILL: Oh God. She's getting even worse.
      (Bill stands with his back to the Women, watching where Madeline has gone.)

THIRD CHORAL DIALOGUE

OLIVE: Our lives are made of choices
      Hundreds of little choices
      that determine our fate
      each
      with a consequence
      we cannot see.
WOMAN 1: You check the box for Delta
      and your son lives.
WOMAN 2: You check the box for Pan Am
      and he dies.
WOMAN 1: You walk the dog early one day
      and escape the disaster that falls on your house.
WOMAN 2: Or you go to the filling station
      before you go to the market
      and find yourself standing
      in the middle
      of the wreckage.
WOMAN 1: Choices.
WOMAN 2: Such *little* choices . . .
WOMAN 1: That create such big results.
OLIVE: You duck into a doorway
      to get out of the rain . . .
      and meet your future husband!
WOMAN 2: You take the train
      instead of the bus

    and meet a long lost friend
    you haven't seen in years!
WOMAN 1: Sometimes I wonder
    if the choices you make
    are yours at all . . .
WOMAN 2: Or if they're made by something else.
    Something greater, like God.
WOMAN 1: Yes.
    Sometimes it seems that these things are fated.
WOMAN 2: Fated, yes.
    Meant to happen.
    (Bill turns around to face the Women.)
BILL: And sometimes it seems that they're not.
    Sometimes it seems they're not meant to happen at all.
    They just do.
    For no reason.

THIRD EPISODE

Madeline storms down the hill.

MADELINE: If I ever meet his killers
    I will kill them.
    No.
    I will *more* than kill them.
    I will torment them.
    I will inflict on them
    the measure of pain
    they have brought to me.
BILL: Maddie!
MADELINE: They should suffer!
    At the very least
    their suffering should equal
    the suffering they've caused!
BILL: You can't repay endless suffering.
MADELINE: Oh yes you can!
    You know how?
    With *endless pain!*

That's how!
And let me tell you,
Pain
is a
gentle
word
to describe what I would do to them
if I ever got the chance!
I would bind their hands and feet
with *wire!*
I would cut them with sharp knives!
I would grind cigarettes into their eyes —
BILL: — Madeline! Stop!
What's got into you?
This is a vigil!
We came here to find peace!
MADELINE: I want justice!
I won't find peace until there is justice!
BILL: That's not justice.
That's revenge.
MADELINE: Those men killed your son!
They killed 259 people!
They destroyed our lives!
BILL: I know, but —
MADELINE: — How can you be so calm!
BILL: Because rage won't bring him back!
Honey, look, I know you're angry —
MADELINE: — You're goddamn right, I'm angry!
I didn't deserve this!
BILL: No you didn't.
None of us did.
MADELINE: I was a good mother!
And a good wife!
And a good neighbor!
I made cookies for the bake sale!
I gave money to the swim team!
I remembered birthdays!
When someone got sick
I made chicken soup!

>   I *pitted cherries* and *peeled grapes*
>   to make your favorite pie!
>   And this is how I'm repaid?
>   *This* is what I get?!
>   For being thoughtful?
>   For being a good person?
>   For leading a good life?
>
> BILL: Honey, I know.
> MADELINE: No, you don't know!
> BILL: Yes, I do.
>   It's not fair.
>   But Maddie.
>   Life's.
>   Not.
>   Fair.
>   At some point, you have to accept that.
>   You have to move on.
> MADELINE: *Move on?*
>   To *what?*
>   What *is* there in a day
>   that's worth moving on to?
>   Breakfast?
>   Lunch?
>   Dinner?
>   Driving the car?
>   Talking on the phone?
>   Playing bridge?
>   No.
>   I don't know how anyone could *move on*
>   after something like this!
> BILL: I moved on.
> MADELINE: You didn't love him as much as I did!
> BILL: Maddie!
> MADELINE: If you did, you wouldn't have gotten over it so fast!
> BILL: Maddie, that's not true!
>   You know that's not true!
> MADELINE: You just go on as if nothing has happened!
> BILL: What am I supposed to do?
>   Stop living?

Spend my days weeping on the couch like you?
MADELINE: You didn't cry at the funeral!
You didn't cry when you got the news!
You didn't cry at all!
BILL: How could I, Maddie?
I had to do everything!
I had to do everything
to keep *you* from falling apart!
I had to send the medical records to Scotland.
I had to talk to the friends and neighbors
I had to talk to the reporters
who stood on our lawn with *cameras*
taking pictures of my grief!
I even had to take his Christmas presents back to the mall
because *you* couldn't stand the sight of them under the tree!
Do you know what that was like?
Can you even imagine it?
Try!
Try to imagine it, just for a moment!
(Madeline runs back to the hills. Pause. Bill turns back to the women.)
BILL: What do you say to the sales clerk?
What do you say to the sixteen-year-old school girl
standing behind the counter at JC Penney's
who smiles at you and asks
"Why are you returning the sweater, sir?"
Do you tell her?
What do you say?
I just looked at her.
I could tell it was her first job.
Her face was round and soft.
Her hands were still chubby, like a child's.
What do you say to someone so young and innocent?
"This was for my son, but he died?"
"He was blown to bits by a bomb?"
"The plane he was taking home for Christmas . . . *crashed?*"
What do you say?
What do you say to the pretty young girl
with red and green ribbons in her hair?
I said.

"My son . . ."
(Pause.)
I cannot tell her.
I cannot show my grief,
because to do so would take her innocence from the world.
I just said. . .
"My son doesn't need it anymore."
And then I breathe a sigh of relief
because I think I've gotten through it.
But I haven't.
Oh no!
It doesn't stop there.
She smiles and says
"Would you like to exchange this for something else?"
(Pause.)
Do I want to exchange this for something else?
(Pause.)
Oh . . . yes.
Oh, yes, yes, yes, I do.
Oh, what I would *do*
to turn this in for something else.
But I say,
"No. No, thank you . . .
Your store doesn't carry what I want or need right now.
Just give me the credit, please."
And then I go to the next store.
To return the Nikes.
And the next store
to return the pajamas
And the next store
to return the bathrobe and the blue jeans and the bike helmet.
(Pause.)
I go to six stores before the day is through.
I have that same conversation in every single place.
(Pause.)
She's right.
I didn't show my grief.
I couldn't.
I had to keep myself numb just to get through it.

>   *(Pause. He turns around and looks in the direction of the hills.)*
>   *(Calls.)* Maddie?
>   *(She doesn't answer.)*

OLIVE: She went to the other side of the hill
to keep her vigil in the dark.
(Bill turns around and looks at the Women.)

BILL: I . . . I'm sorry . . .
I . . .
Oh God.
God.
I don't know what to do.
(He sits on a rock by the stream.)
(Olive gives Bill her candle. Then, she pulls a small book out of her pocket. She opens it and reads. The following Ode is addressed to Bill.)

THIRD CHORAL ODE
"FAITH"

OLIVE: *(Reads.)* The dark forest leads to an open field
The dark valley rises to a mountain
where the sun shines bright.
Spring follows winter
and morning, the dark night.

WOMAN 1: There's an order in the world.
An order behind the chaos and the violence.

WOMAN 2: And there's a purpose.

WOMAN 1: Yes.

WOMAN 2: If the sun never set
we would find no beauty in the sunrise.

WOMAN 1: If the night was full of light
we would not see the stars.

OLIVE: And if hatred never pierced our hearts
we would not know the power of love.

WOMAN 1: These things are given to us for a reason.

OLIVE: Though the reason is never made fully clear.

WOMAN 1: They are given to us so we may learn and grow.

WOMAN 2: And no one is given a burden
that they are unable to bear.

WOMAN 1: You have to trust in this.
WOMAN 2: Yes.
WOMAN 1: Trust in the rising sun.
    and in the stars that shine at night.
OLIVE: Trust in the strength of love
    to overcome the awesome power of hatred.
WOMAN 1: Trust.
WOMAN 2: Yes, trust.
OLIVE: And believe
    that behind the suffering of the world,
    there is a purpose
    to everything.

FOURTH DIALOGUE
"THE AGON"

Bill responds to the Women.

BILL: I want to believe that.
    I want nothing more than to believe
    that this has happened for a reason.
    But I can't.
    I just . . . *can't.*
    To believe that would mean that Adam died
    just so I could learn and grow.
    And that's not true.
    There is no lesson so important
    that it was worth the price of his life.
    To believe that would mean
    that I am at the center of the universe
    and that all things happen for my benefit.
    And they don't.
    The events of the world . . .
    the horrors . . .
    just happen.
    And they happen for *no reason.*
    The only thing you can do is accept that
    and carry on the best you can.

Just . . . accept the suffering that comes to you
and find some way to keep going.
Love helps.
Goodness and kindness do too.
But the only reason they are in the world
is not because God gave them to us
but because along the way people discovered
they can make our lives a little easier to bear.
(Pause.)
If there is a God . . .
and sometimes when I lie in bed at night
I think that there isn't . . .
But *if* there is,
he is absent from the world
and pays no attention to the needs of men.
(Pause.)
(Bill stands up.)
Excuse me. I need to be alone
I'm going to walk these hills for awhile . . .
(Bill blows out the candle that Olive gave him and exits.)
(The Women watch him disappear over the hill.)
OLIVE: Oh God . . .
  His words leave me with nothing to hold on to.
WOMAN 1: Aye, they fill me with doubt, too.
  (Olive blows out her candle.)
WOMAN 2: Olive?
WOMAN 1: Love? Are you all right?
OLIVE: My faith is hanging by a thread
  again
  ready to break . . .
  (Slight pause.)
  How easily my faith is broken . . .
WOMAN 2: Mine too.
  (Slight pause.)
  It breaks often, my faith.
WOMAN 1: I lose it at night when I'm lying in bed.
OLIVE: I lie awake at night too.
WOMAN 1: But in the morning
  when the first rays of sun hit my window . . .

it is restored.
WOMAN 2: But then the night . . .
WOMAN 1: The night . . .
OLIVE: The night comes again so quickly, doesn't it?
(Pause.)
WOMAN 1: Funny.
The world won't let you keep your faith
But it won't let you lose it, either.
WOMAN 2: No
OLIVE: No. *(Slight pause.)* So, what do you do?
WOMAN 1: I bake scones.
WOMAN 2: I clean the house.
My house has been spotless for the last seven years.
WOMAN 1: And I always bake extra.
So I can give them to other people.
(Pause.)
OLIVE: I have to do something.
I'm going to the warehouse.
I've got to get the clothes.
I have to find a way out of this dark valley
before the night is through.
(The Women blow out their candles and exit.)
(Silence.)
(The wind blows softly.)
(The fog moves slowly across the hills.)

FOURTH EPISODE

George Jones enters, walking quickly.

GEORGE: Goddamn it!
Goddamn those goddamn women!
(He stops to look behind him.)
Jesus H. Christ.
Reporters!
They called in the *goddamn reporters!*
(He continues walking again, then stops. He looks out over the hills. He's fear-

ful of this place and starts to whistle to himself. Then, he checks his watch and exits.)

(Hattie enters, running. She carries a mop. She shivers from the cold.)

HATTIE: Oh Hattie!
Hattie! You're a fool!
Grabbed your mop but not your coat!
You're going to freeze to death, you are
unless Mr. Jones goes back to the warehouse quickly!
(From offstage, a whistle.)
(Hattie stops.)
(Another whistle.)
(Hattie peers in the direction of the whistle.)

HATTIE: Always whistling that Mr. Jones.
Whistle, whistle, whistle.
It's enough to drive a person mad.
(She watches him.)
What in the devil is he *doing* out here?
(Pause. She watches him.)
Roaming the hills?
Hmmm. . .
Maybe he's having a change of heart, he is
and came out here to have a think on it.
(George enters again. Hattie runs up the hill, trying to hide. George sees her.)

GEORGE: Who is that?
(George runs after her.)
Hattie?
(George catches her.)
Hattie!
What are you doing out here!
(Hattie starts to furiously mop the grass.)

HATTIE: Just cleaning up a bit, Mr. Jones.

GEORGE: Hattie, you're mopping the *grass.*

HATTIE: Aye, it's gotten muddy, sir.
From the rains.
I thought if I attacked the problem at the source
I could cut down on the mud
gettin' tracked across your office floor.

GEORGE: You followed me out here didn't you.

HATTIE: Why, Mr. Jones, I would never think of doing such a thing!

GEORGE: You've been spying on me ever since I got here.
　　Always swishing your mop outside my door
　　listening to my conversations!
HATTIE: I swish my mop to clean the mud you track on the floors, sir!
GEORGE: Do you remember the oath you signed with the American government?
HATTIE: Oath, sir?
GEORGE: The paper you signed. When you took this job.
HATTIE: Aye, sir, I seem to recall some paper.
GEORGE: In that paper, there was a provision for spying.
　　Do you remember that provision, Hattie?
HATTIE: I'm sorry, sir, but I don't.
　　You see, I don't read.
GEORGE: You don't read, huh?
HATTIE: No. I'm just a cleaning woman, sir.
　　The only thing I know how to do is mop floors.
GEORGE: Then what are those books you've always got in your pocket?
HATTIE: Books, sir?
GEORGE: Yes, *books*.
HATTIE: Oh, the books.
　　They're . . . picture books, full of pictures.
GEORGE: They're not picture books.
　　They're *romance* novels.
　　I see you sneak into the broom closet to read them.
　　And I hear you *sighing* in there when you do.
HATTIE: I don't sigh, sir!
GEORGE: You sigh. You sigh for the romance when you read those books.
HATTIE: No, sir. You're wrong.
　　I weep.
　　And not for the romance,
　　but for the lack of it.
GEORGE: Weep, sigh, it's all the same to me.
　　But you *read*.
　　And you read that oath before signing it
　　because I saw you read it.
HATTIE: No sir! I didn't! I was just moving my eyes!
GEORGE: Do you know what Washington does to spies, Hattie?
HATTIE: No.
GEORGE: They put them in jail.

234　DEBORAH BREVOORT

HATTIE: Oh.
GEORGE: Consider this a warning.
Stop spying.
Or I'll have Washington put you in jail.
(Bill enters from the hills.)
BILL: Hello?
GEORGE: Hallo?
(Hattie runs to him.)
HATTIE: Help!
GEORGE: Hattie, get back here!
HATTIE: He's going to put me in jail, he is!
GEORGE: Hattie!
BILL: Who's going to put you in jail?
HATTIE: Mr. Jones! He's accusing me of being a spy!
BILL: Mr. Jones?
The Mr. Jones?
GEORGE: You've heard of me?
BILL: Oh yes. The women have told me all about you.
GEORGE: Oh no. Are you a reporter?!
BILL: No. I'm a tourist.
GEORGE: What are you doing here?
BILL: I'm . . . visiting my son. For the holidays.
GEORGE: Oh! Well, good. Well, look. Don't listen to what the women say about me. They've got it all wrong.
HATTIE: *(To Bill.)* And I say, sir, that the women have got it right.
He's a bully, he is.
GEORGE: — I am not!
HATTIE: — And he ought to be ashamed of himself, picking on an *old woman* like me!
GEORGE: I didn't "pick on her!"
HATTIE: *(To Bill.)* He was picking on me, sir, right before you got here.
He chased me over that hill!
GEORGE: I didn't chase you over the hill!
HATTIE: Him, a *full-grown man,* chasing me, *an old woman* —
GEORGE: *(To Bill.)* — I didn't chase her! —
HATTIE: — and then *scaring* me half to death by threatening to put me in *jail!*
GEORGE: *(Explodes.)* I'm not going to put you in jail!
(Hattie smiles sweetly.)
HATTIE: All right, then.

THE WOMEN OF LOCKERBIE

I'll be on my way, sir, now that that's settled.
(Hattie promptly turns to exit.)
GEORGE: Wait a minute! Hattie!
HATTIE: Yes, Mr. Jones?
GEORGE: Where are you going?
HATTIE: Back to the warehouse.
GEORGE: To do what?
HATTIE: To mop the floor.
GEORGE: What floor?
HATTIE: The floor in your office.
GEORGE: Stay out of my office.
HATTIE: But there's mud in your office, sir. You didn't wipe your feet —
GEORGE: — I don't want you going into my office!
Do you understand?
HATTIE: Yes, sir.
GEORGE: All right.
(Hattie exits.)
(Calls after her.) You may leave!
(They watch her go.)
GEORGE: These women are driving me crazy!
Look.
Let me give you a piece of advice
about the Women of Lockerbie.
Don't be fooled by the lace on their collars.
Or the flowers on their teacups.
They're not the sweet little old ladies they appear to be.
They're tigers.
And they're ferocious.
You know what they just did?
They called in the television crews!
The *networks*.
The *American* networks.
They're all down at the warehouse
with their reporters
waiting for a statement from me!
And that's not all.
There are two hundred women with them!
Two hundred women!
With *candles*.

They're trying to create
an international incident, these people.
BILL: But I thought Lockerbie was already an international incident.
GEORGE: Lockerbie? Hardly!
The world has forgotten all about Lockerbie.
They forgot about it two weeks after the crash.
But if those women get it back in the news . . . !
Well, then it will be. And then I'll *never* get out of here!
BILL: You don't like it here?
GEORGE: What's to like?
Lockerbie is the Siberia of the State Department!
But.
You have to "do your time" in burgs like this
before you get the better assignments.
Me, I'd rather be someplace else.
You know, places like . . .
Kuwait . . .
Tel Aviv . . .
The hot spots.
And if I handle this right, I just might get there.
BILL: Then why are you doing it, if I might ask?
GEORGE: You mean this business with the clothes?
BILL: Yes.
GEORGE: I have orders from Washington.
They want things wrapped up here.
Quickly.
So that's what I'm doing.
Look. This whole affair has gone on long enough.
These people should just get over it.
It's been seven years.
I mean . . . *move on* for God's sake!
Get a life!
I've tried telling them that,
but of course, they won't listen.
They sent the mayor to see me.
They sent the *bishop,* for God's sake.
Next, they'll probably send in a *mother!*
(He groans.)
The mothers are the worst.

They come clutching the baby pictures.
Johnny blowing out the candles on his birthday cake.
Timmy smiling with his mouth full of braces.
They think the world should stop just because
little Timmy got braces!
The mothers will drive you crazy.
There is always a mother
who makes it impossible to do your job.

BILL: What about the fathers?

GEORGE: Oh, I have to deal with them too.
But men . . .
Men are different.
Thank God.
You can always reason with a man.
At least they don't shove those pictures in my face.
(Bill pulls out his wallet and opens it.)

GEORGE: What do you have there?

BILL: My son's school picture from the third grade.
With his mouth full of braces.
Look.
(Bill shoves the picture in George's face.)

GEORGE: *(Pause.)* Was your son . . . uh . . . on board?

BILL: Yes.

GEORGE: Oh. *(Pause.)* I didn't know . . .

BILL: His body was never found.
He's still . . . out here . . . somewhere.

GEORGE: *(Pause.)* I'm . . . sorry.
(Pause.) Um. What was his name?

BILL: Adam. Adam Alexander Livingston.

GEORGE: Oh, yes. Yes. I, uh, seem to recall it . . .

BILL: And here is a picture when he hit a home run.
In the Little League.
The game was tied and the bases were loaded.

GEORGE: Yeah?

BILL: Yeah! He brought them all home.
(He laughs softly with the memory.)
And here. . .
here. . .
is the ticket stub

238 DEBORAH BREVOORT

from the Yankee game I took him to on his last birthday.
I just found this a few minutes ago,
in the pocket of my coat.
Funny.
I haven't worn this coat in years.

GEORGE: Well, hey.
Hey, hey, hey, that's great.
So your son was a Yankees fan?
(Bill nods.)

GEORGE: Helluva team, the Yanks.
Helluva owner.
I like George Steinbrenner.
Always have. Always will.
Man knows how to run a team.

BILL: Yes. Yes he does.
(Pause.)
Mr. Jones.
Do you have children?

GEORGE: No. No, I don't.
Don't have a wife.
Well, I had one.
Had *two,* actually.
But we never got around to having kids.
You know.

BILL: Then it might be hard for you to understand
the loss that a parent feels . . .

GEORGE: They say there's nothing worse.

BILL: They're right. There isn't.
(Pause.)
See that hill?

GEORGE: Yeah.

BILL: My wife is on the other side of it.

GEORGE: Right now?

BILL: Yes.

GEORGE: Doing what?

BILL: Looking for my son's remains.

GEORGE: *(Slight pause.)* You're kidding.

BILL: No.
(George rolls his eyes and whistles.)

GEORGE: Women. You know?
BILL: They're not the only ones who feel loss.
　　Men do too.
GEORGE: Not like that.
BILL: No, not like that.
　　That's the difference, I guess . . .
　　The women show it and the men don't.
　　And they show it more because we don't.
　　It's not fair, really, now that I think about it.
　　The women have to do their own crying
　　and also, the crying for the men . . .
　　(Pause. He reflects for a moment on this realization.)
　　When Adam died . . .
　　I cut off the pain.
　　I had to.
　　I couldn't take it.
　　But then. . .
　　I didn't feel anything else either.
　　Just now
　　when I was walking these hills
　　and found this ticket stub from the Yankees,
　　I felt something.
　　For the first time in years.
GEORGE: You did, huh.
BILL: Yes.
　　(Slight pause.)
　　Look at this thing.
　　(He holds up the ticket stub and looks at it with astonishment.)
　　It's a piece of paper
　　A *little* piece of paper.
　　Who would have thought
　　that a
　　little
　　piece
　　of *paper*
　　like this
　　could have that kind of power?
　　(Pause.)
　　Those clothes aren't just clothes.

240　DEBORAH BREVOORT

They're not *things*.
They have *life*.
Just like this piece of paper.
Please.
Reconsider your decision.
Release the clothes to the women.
GEORGE: Look . . . I wish I could, *really*, but —
OLIVE: *(Off. Calls.)* — Mr. Livingston?
BILL: Over here!
GEORGE: Who's that?
BILL: The women.
GEORGE: The *women?!*
Oh shit!
Look, I've got to go, I'll see you later —
(George starts to run off.)
(The Women enter.)

FIFTH EPISODE

OLIVE: Mr Jones!
(George stops. He turns around and feigns surprise.)
GEORGE: Oh! Mrs. Allison! Hello!
OLIVE: Hello.
GEORGE: Mrs. Allison, what are you doing out here? In the middle of the night?
OLIVE: I could ask the same of you.
GEORGE: Well, yes, I suppose you could.
(Pause.)
OLIVE: So . . . ? What are you doing here Mr. Jones?
GEORGE: Just getting a little fresh air. And you?
OLIVE: I'm looking for you.
GEORGE: Oh. Well, look, I'm sorry, but I'm afraid I've got to go —
OLIVE: — Mr. Jones —
GEORGE: — I've got an appointment —
OLIVE: — In the middle of the night?
GEORGE: Yes, as a matter of fact.
OLIVE: It's two o'clock in the morning, Mr. Jones.
GEORGE: Not in Washington, Mrs. Allison.
(Pause.)

So, if you'll excuse me . . .
OLIVE: No, I won't.
GEORGE: I'm afraid you'll have to.
OLIVE: I need to talk to you.
GEORGE: I'm a busy man, Mrs. Allison.
OLIVE: And I'm a busy woman.
GEORGE: You certainly are. You've been busy tonight, at any rate.
OLIVE: I have something very important I need to discuss.
GEORGE: As far as I'm concerned, there's nothing to discuss.
(George starts to exit — quickly.)
OLIVE: Why are you afraid of me?
(George stops.)
GEORGE: I'm not afraid of you, Mrs. Allison.
OLIVE: Then why are you running away?
GEORGE: I'm *not* running away. I'm simply in a rush to get back to the warehouse. I've got a conference call with Washington, if you must know. To discuss the situation here.
OLIVE: What situation?
GEORGE: You know very well what situation.
OLIVE: There are many, Mr. Jones.
GEORGE: I'm talking about the *circus* going on down at the warehouse. With the reporters. And the women with candles.
Very well done, I might add. But it won't work.
OLIVE: I didn't create that situation. You did.
GEORGE: I did nothing of the sort.
OLIVE: Did you think you could burn the clothes and not have anyone notice?
GEORGE: I didn't think it would turn into an international incident, if that's what you mean.
OLIVE: If you release the clothes, it won't be.
GEORGE: I won't be bullied, Mrs. Allison.
OLIVE: I'm not bullying, Mr. Jones. I'm begging.
(Olive falls to her knees at his feet.)
Please. Release the clothes.
Don't burn them.
GEORGE: Mrs. Allison . . . now, wait . . . Don't do that . . .
OLIVE: The families need them.
We need them.
GEORGE: Mrs. Allison, here, get up . . . *please* . . . get up . . .
(He helps Olive back to her feet.)

Look . . .
I would like to release the clothes.
Really. I would
But I can't.
They're contaminated.

OLIVE: How can they be contaminated, Mr. Jones? They're *seven* years old.

GEORGE: They've been sealed in evidence bags ever since the crash. They've never been washed.

OLIVE: We'll wash them.

GEORGE: I'm sorry, but I can't let you do that.

OLIVE: Why not?

GEORGE: Because. Whenever there is an incident at altitude —

OLIVE: — I'm sorry . . . a . . . what?

GEORGE: An incident at altitude.

BILL: A plane crash.

GEORGE: . . . Right.
Involving an American aircraft
outside of the United States,
the State Department has certain policies.
Certain *procedures*.
For disposal and containment.
And releasing the clothing of the victims to civilians
is not one of them.

OLIVE: Make an exception.

GEORGE: I can't make an exception.

OLIVE: Mr. Jones, you can always make an exception.

HATTIE: That's right! And the State Department allows for exceptions too! It says so right here in their regulations!
(Hattie pulls a piece of paper out of her pocket.)

GEORGE: I thought you said you couldn't read, Hattie!

HATTIE: I lied.

GEORGE: Look, the regulations don't apply here.
This is a foreign policy matter.
Every action here must be
weighed according to a whole different set of criteria.
And *justified*.

WOMAN 2: Well, that's no problem, Mr. Jones. We've got the perfect justification.

GEORGE: Oh you do, huh.

THE WOMEN OF LOCKERBIE 243

WOMAN 1: Yes, we do.
GEORGE: And what's that.
THE WOMEN: Love!
GEORGE: Ladies . . . I can't use *love* as a justification.
OLIVE: Why not?
GEORGE: Because love is not a good enough reason!
OLIVE: There is *no better reason* than love!
GEORGE: Tell that to my boss.
OLIVE: I will. Where is he?
GEORGE: Look . . . excuse me for being blunt.
   But you're getting too caught up in your emotions
   to see the big picture.
   Try to consider my perspective for a moment.
   I have a responsibility here.
   A responsibility to reduce the trauma
   that has already come to this community
   And to look out for its welfare.
   For your welfare.
OLIVE: The Scottish people are quite capable
   of looking out for our own welfare, Mr. Jones.
   We don't need you, or the American government to do that for us.
HATTIE: This is why no one likes Americans, sir.
   You think you know what's best for everyone!
WOMAN 2: Aye. This is *Scotland!*
WOMAN 1: The American government should have
   no say about what happens over here!
GEORGE: The bomb was an attack on the American government, ladies.
   We have *everything* to say about it.
   Look.
   You have no idea what you're asking for.
   Let me spell it out for you.
   The clothes are contaminated.
   They're covered in *blood.*
   A *lot* of blood.
   Blood from *259 people.*
   And that's not all.
   There are . . . guts on those clothes.
   Guts.
   Do you understand?

The clothes are not a pretty sight.
I can't let anyone see them!
I can't let *you* see them!
I mean, ladies, trust me
it will make you *sick* just to look at them.
They made *me* sick.
And you don't want to touch them, either.

OLIVE: Mr. Jones you seem to forget
that we were here when the crash occurred.
The things we have already seen
are worse than those clothes.

WOMAN 2: The things we have *touched* are worse, too.
(Slight pause.)
Mr. Jones . . .
(Slight pause.)
I picked up *body parts.*
(Pause.)

WOMAN 1: I did too.
I found a woman's hand
and a
child's leg
in my garden.
I picked them up with my own two hands
and carried them down to the morgue.
(Pause.)

GEORGE: You did?
(Pause.)

WOMAN 1: *Yes.*
(Pause.)

OLIVE: Everyone did.
(Pause.)

GEORGE: You are very strong.
I wouldn't have been able to do that.

OLIVE: Sure you would have.
You find the strength to do what you have to, Mr. Jones.

GEORGE: I still have the families to think about.
They haven't seen what you've seen.
The sight of the clothes
— washed, or unwashed —

could be devastating.
BILL: Why don't you let the families decide that for themselves?
GEORGE: I don't want to open old wounds.
OLIVE: But you won't, Mr. Jones. You'll heal them.
GEORGE: Well, that's where you and I disagree.
If you ask me, the best way to heal a wound
is to leave it alone.
And that's what I intend to do.
I'm sorry.
I know that's not what you want to hear.
But that's the way it is.
So, if you'll excuse me,
I've got to go.
I'm late for my conference call.
(George begins to exit.)
OLIVE: Mr. Jones, wait!
GEORGE: I'm sorry, Mrs. Allison.
That's my decision.
I'm not going to discuss it any further.
Hattie?
HATTIE: Sir?
GEORGE: If you want to keep your job, I expect to see you back at the warehouse in ten minutes.
HATTIE: Yes, sir.
(George exits.)
OLIVE: But — Mr. Jones!
WOMAN 2: Let him go, Olive.
OLIVE: Mr. Jones!
WOMAN 1: His mind is made up, love.
You can't change it.
OLIVE: But — he —
Oh!
Men like that!
How can he do that?
(Shouts after George.)
Mr. Jones! Mr. Jones!
WOMAN 1: Steady yourself, love.
WOMAN 2: Getting upset won't do any good.
OLIVE: We can't let him do that!

WOMAN 1: You can't stop him, love.
WOMAN 2: You've done everything you possibly could.
HATTIE: Not *everything*.
WOMAN 1: What do you mean, Hattie??
HATTIE: *(Slight pause.)* We can just take them.
WOMAN 1: *Take* them?
WOMAN 2: You mean, the *clothes?*
HATTIE: Yes.
WOMAN 1: But . . . How do we do that?
HATTIE: I'll let you in through the back entrance. Where there isn't a guard.
WOMAN 1: And then what?
HATTIE: We take the clothes and bring them back here!
WOMAN 1: But Hattie!
    There are 11,000 pieces of clothing!
    We can't just carry 11,000 —
HATTIE: — Sure we can!
WOMAN 2: *How!?*
HATTIE: Because there will be 200 of us carrying them!
    I'm going to open the front gates.
    and let the crowd of women inside, too.
    (Slight pause.)
    In front of the reporters and the *cameras* . . .
WOMAN 1: Hattie, you'll be arrested.
HATTIE: Yes. I know.
    You will be too.
    But the clothing won't be burned.
    Not if the telly is showing pictures of
    200 grandmothers going off to jail.
OLIVE: You're right!
    Come on, let's go.
HATTIE: No. You stay here.
OLIVE: But —
HATTIE: — We need you out here.
    To talk to the reporters
MADELINE: *(Off. Calls out.)* Adam?
BILL: Oh no.
HATTIE: What was that?
BILL: My wife.
MADELINE: *(Off. Calls out.)* Adam?

HATTIE: We've got to go.
OLIVE: Hattie, wait —
HATTIE: — We don't have much time.
   Come on!
   (Hattie and the Women exit quickly.)
BILL: I hope this works.
OLIVE: I do too . . .
BILL: What will you do if it doesn't?

SIXTH EPISODE

MADELINE: *(Off. Calls out.)* Adam?
OLIVE: Where is she?
BILL: Right there. She's coming over the hill.
   (Madeline appears at the top of the hill. She watches the Women exiting in the distance. She doesn't see Olive and Bill.)
MADELINE: They're gone.
   (Pause.)
   Gone.
   They lit their candles and went back to town . . .
   (Pause.)
   They have forgotten you, Adam.
   Just like the world has forgotten.
   (Pause.)
   But I remember.
   And these hills remember too.
   Look how black they are . . .
   Even the moon won't shed it's light upon them . . .
   (Madeline goes to the stream. She stands very still, looking at the water.)
   The water's black, too. . .
   Black water running between black hills . . .
   (Pause.)
   Such a thin line
   of darkness
   between the living and the dead . . .
   (Pause.)
   How quickly you passed . . .
   One moment here.

(Madeline steps to the other side of the stream.)
The next moment there.
(Madeline steps back to the other side of the stream.)
Here.
(Then she steps across it again.)
There.
(She steps back and forth across the stream several times in silence.)

BILL: *What* is she doing?
OLIVE: Jumping back and forth across the stream . . .
BILL: She's losing her mind . . . !
(Madeline crosses the stream.)
MADELINE: Living.
(Madeline crosses the stream.)
Dead.
(Madeline crosses the stream.)
Living.
(Madeline crosses the stream.)
Dead.
(She stands very still and doesn't cross the stream again.)
Dead.
(Pause.)
Dead, dead, dead.
(Pause.)
What
is it like
to be dead?
(Pause.)
What
was it like . . .
when you crossed the line
and passed to the other side?
Were you drinking a coke?
Eating your peanuts?
Taking a nap?
Or were you talking . . . ?
Having a nice conversation
with the woman right beside you?
Mrs. Corcoran.
Yes, Doris Corcoran, her name was.

She was a teacher
from Syracuse University
What were you saying to her?
Were you talking about London?
Christmas?
College?
Changing your major to math?
(Pause.)
And what . . .
did you
do
the moment it happened . . . ?
Did you grab Mrs. Corcoran's hand?
Hold on to the arm rests?
Close your eyes and pray?
Or did it happen too fast
for any of that?
And what happened next?
Adam . . .
What
happened
next?
What did you do?
Where did you go?
You must have gone *somewhere*
You have to be *someplace* . . .
(Madeline turns to go back to the hills.)

BILL: Oh God . . .
What do we do?
OLIVE: I think we should try and talk to her again.
BILL: There is nothing we can say that will turn her from this.
OLIVE: There's got to be. Come on.
(Bill doesn't move.)
OLIVE: The last leg of a journey
is always the hardest, Mr. Livingston.
When you climb a mountain
the rocks at the top are steeper
than the ones you climbed before.
This is where the tests are.

The tests of love.
(Olive approaches Madeline.)
OLIVE: Mrs. Livingston?
MADELINE: I thought you were gone.
OLIVE: No. I'm here with your husband.
   We need to talk to you.
MADELINE: I don't want to talk.
   Leave me alone.
BILL: Maddie —
MADELINE: — Go away!
   There is nothing you can say
   that will make me forget him!
BILL: I don't want you to forget him.
   I want you to stop adding to the wreckage!
   Your grief is destroying our lives!
   It's destroying *me!*
   What would Adam think if he saw you like this?
MADELINE: He would think that his mother loved him!
   He would think, "Well at least *my mother* doesn't forget!"
BILL: I haven't forgotten him, Maddie!
MADELINE: You cleaned out his room!
   You gave away his belongings!
   You took away every sign that you ever had a son!
BILL: I did that for you.
MADELINE: You didn't do it for *me!*
   You did it for *yourself!*
BILL: I did it to help *you* stop grieving!
MADELINE: You did it to avoid feeling any grief *yourself!*
   The only thing you did for me was make it even harder!
   (She walks away from him.)
BILL: Maddie!
MADELINE: Go away!
BILL: Maddie, wait!
   Maddie! Look!
   (He fishes the Yankees' ticket out of his pocket.)
BILL: I found something of Adam's . . .
   (She stops.)
MADELINE: You did?
BILL: Yes.

MADELINE: What?

BILL: This.

MADELINE: What is it?

BILL: Come here and I'll show you.

(Madeline comes back to him.)

BILL: Look.
>It's the ticket stub from the Yankees' game
>I took him to on his birthday.

(She takes the ticket.)

MADELINE: Where did you find this?

BILL: In the pocket of this old coat.

MADELINE: Where's the other ticket?
>There should be two.
>Not just one.

BILL: Well, I only found this one, Maddie —

MADELINE: — If it was in your pocket, it's not Adam's.
>It's *yours*.

BILL: Yes, but —

MADELINE: — I don't want anything of yours!
>I only want something of Adam's!

(She throws the ticket on the ground and walks away from him. He follows.)

BILL: Maddie!

MADELINE: Go away!

(Bill grabs her.)

BILL: God you are stubborn!

MADELINE: Let go of me!

BILL: You hold on to your grief too hard!
>Why do you hold on to your grief so hard!

MADELINE: It's the only thing I have left to hold on to!

BILL: You have *me!*
>Hold on to *me!*

MADELINE: I don't want you!

(She pushes him away.)

OLIVE: Don't turn your hatred toward your husband, Mrs. Livingston.

MADELINE: You stay out of this!

OLIVE: He's all you've got left.

MADELINE: Who are you anyway?

OLIVE: I'm only trying to help.

MADELINE: I don't want your help!

OLIVE: You need help —
MADELINE: — You don't know what I need!
OLIVE: — Yes, I do —
MADELINE: — Go away —
OLIVE: — No —
MADELINE: — This has nothing to do with you! —
OLIVE: — It has everything to do with me —
MADELINE: — You have no idea what I've been through! —
OLIVE: — Yes I do! —
MADELINE: — You didn't lose a son in the crash! —
OLIVE: No, I lost a daughter and a *husband!*
Your son's plane fell on my farm
and killed my family!
My daughter is dead!
My husband is dead!
A plane full of *Americans*
killed everyone I love!
I hate Americans!
You started this whole thing, you know!
You bombed that passenger jet from Iran!
You shot down a plane full of innocent people!
Lockerbie was the revenge for that!
You probably don't even know about it!
You were too busy baking your pies
and driving your cars
and living in your big houses
to pay any attention!
You Americans!
A bunch of cowboys
galloping through the skies
dropping bombs!
I hate you!
I hate you for this!
(Olive charges Madeline and starts to hit her. Women 1 and 2 enter.)
WOMAN 1: Olive!
WOMAN 2: Olive!
WOMAN 1: Olive, stop!
WOMAN 2: Olive, what are you doing?!
WOMAN 1: Olive!

(Olive and Madeline fall to the ground.)
OLIVE: Oh . . .
WOMAN 2: Olive . . .
OLIVE: Oh . . . my . . .
WOMAN 1: Come on, love.
> Get up.
> Love?

(Olive and Madeline lie in a heap on the ground.)
OLIVE: I . . .
> Oh my . . .
> I . . .
> Oh God.
> I need to wash.
> I . . . the clothes.
> Where are the clothes?
> I need to wash.

WOMAN 2: We don't have the clothes Olive.
OLIVE: . . . You don't?
WOMAN 1: No.
MADELINE: What clothes?
WOMAN 2: From the crash.
MADELINE: There are *clothes?*
WOMAN 2: Yes. But we don't have them.
WOMAN 1: We were inside the warehouse, Olive.
WOMAN 2: We got all the way
> to the Shelves of Sorrow.

WOMAN 1: But we were caught.
WOMAN 2: They let us go
> but Hattie's been detained.

WOMAN 1: And that's not all . . .
> *(Slight pause.)*

WOMAN 2: The fuel trucks have arrived.
OLIVE: . . . Fuel trucks?
WOMAN 2: Yes. They're starting the incineration now.
WOMAN 1: They won't wait until morning.
WOMAN 2: They're burning the clothes tonight.
> *(Madeline gets up.)*

WOMAN 1: Mrs. Livingston?
> *(Madeline doesn't answer. She starts to exit in the direction of the warehouse.)*

WOMAN 2: Mrs. Livingston, where are you going?
  (Madeline exits.)
OLIVE: Wait . . .
WOMAN 1: Mrs. Livingston, wait.
OLIVE: Mrs. Livingston?
WOMAN 2: She's gone, love.
  (Olive gets up off the ground. She starts to exit in the direction of the warehouse.)
WOMAN 1: Olive, wait.
WOMAN 2: We're coming with you.
OLIVE: No.
WOMAN 2: But Olive . . .
OLIVE: *No.*
  (Olive exits.)
WOMAN 1: Mr. Livingston, what's going on?
WOMAN 2: What happened?
  (Bill doesn't answer.)
WOMAN 2: Mr. Livingston?
  (Bill picks up the ticket stub lying on the ground. He looks at it for a moment, then puts it in his pocket. He starts to leave.)
WOMAN 1: Mr. Livingston?
  Where are you going?
  (He stops.)
BILL: To get my things at the hotel.
  I'm leaving.
WOMAN 2: But why?
WOMAN 1: Your wife will need you when she gets back.
BILL: No she won't.
  (Bill turns to leave again.)
WOMAN 2: Mr. Livingston —
WOMAN 1: — Wait —
WOMAN 2: — Mr. Livingston, what happened?
  (Bill stops.)
BILL: My wife doesn't want me anymore.
  She doesn't love me anymore either.
  In fact, she hates me.
  And what's worse . . .
  (Pause.)
  I hate her too.

THE WOMEN OF LOCKERBIE 255

WOMAN 2: Of course you do. That's only natural.
BILL: Natural? To hate my wife?
WOMAN 2: You have to hate someone.
WOMAN 1: If you don't, you'll turn your hatred against yourself.
WOMAN 2: Mr. Livingston . . .
    Hatred is love that's been injured.
WOMAN 1: If you have hatred in your heart
    it means you have love in it also
WOMAN 2: Your hatred will turn again to love.
    And your wife's will too, when she heals.
BILL: But she won't heal.
    She refuses to.
WOMAN 2: She will. You just have to wait.
BILL: I've been waiting for seven years!
WOMAN 1: Maybe waiting's not enough, love.
    Maybe you need to do something else.
BILL: Like what?
WOMAN 1: Like . . . grieving . . .
    (Pause.)
WOMAN 1: You didn't let yourself grieve . . .
    (Pause.)
WOMAN 2: If you let yourself grieve
    maybe your wife will let herself heal. . . .
    (Pause.)
WOMAN 2: Here. Sit down.
WOMAN 1: Yes. Sit here with us.
    Please.
WOMAN 2: Don't go back to the hotel.
    Your wife may not need you right now,
    but we do.
BILL: You do?
WOMAN 1: Yes. We are frightened.
BILL: I guess I'm a little frightened too . . .
    (Pause.)
    All right.
    (They sit on rocks. They sit in silence for a moment.)
WOMAN 1: I'm shaking.
WOMAN 2: I'm shaking too.
    (Pause.)

WOMAN 1: Oh God . . . the things we have seen tonight . . .
BILL: Yes.
WOMAN 2: Yes.
    It was our first time in the warehouse.
WOMAN 1: Our first time in the Shelves of Sorrow.
WOMAN 2: It was like living once again through the horror.
WOMAN 1: We walked through the wreckage . . .
    past the metal
WOMAN 2: Mountains of metal
    stacked higher than the hills.
WOMAN 1: I felt so small walking past them . . .
WOMAN 2: When we entered the shelves
    with items from the cabin
    I cried
WOMAN 1: I did too
    when I saw the seat cushions
    covered with blood
    and the pillows and the blankets
WOMAN 2: and the trays from the seat backs
    piled neatly in a stack.
WOMAN 1: How *neatly* everything is stacked
    on the Shelves of Sorrow.
WOMAN 2: Yes.
    So . . . orderly.
    And arranged.
WOMAN 1: Everything
WOMAN 2: marked
WOMAN 1: with a number.
    (Pause.)
HATTIE: *(Off. Calls out.)* Mr. Livingston?
WOMAN 1: Hattie?
HATTIE: *(Off. Calls out.)* Mr. Livingston!
    (Hattie enters running.)
HATTIE: Your wife! Your wife, she —
BILL: — What?! —
WOMAN 2: — What is it!? —
HATTIE: She's gone wild!
BILL: Oh no.
WOMAN 1: What happened, Hattie?

WOMAN 2: Tell us what happened!
>*(Hattie tries to catch her breath.)*

HATTIE: When she arrived . . . !
>At the warehouse . . . !
>Olive was with her . . . !
>The crowd parted
>as they walked to the gate . . . !
>When Olive and your wife saw the fuel trucks
>lined up at the warehouse
>they fell to their knees
>and started to wail.
>The crowd of women
>fell to their knees, too
>and wailed with them,
>two hundred women
>kneeling at the gate and wailing
>until the night air was filled
>with the cries of the Women of Lockerbie.
>And then . . . !
>The fuel trucks stopped their engines.
>The door to the warehouse opened.
>Mr. Jones stepped outside.
>He ordered the fuel trucks to begin.
>But the drivers got out of their trucks!
>Mr. Jones marched over to the drivers
>and ordered them again.
>But they folded their arms
>and refused to move!
>And then . . . the cameras started flashing!
>The reporters called out his name!
>And the women wailed even louder!
>Mr. Jones stood nose-to-nose
>with the drivers
>and then . . .
>suddenly!
>*turned*
>and walked to the gate!
>When he saw Olive and your wife
>kneeling on the ground,

he just stood there
and looked at them
for a long, long time.
And then . . .
he reached in his pocket
pulled out a *key*
and unlocked the gate!
He lifted the two women from the ground
and threw open the gates for the others to enter.
And then, with television cameras flashing all around him
he led all of the women into the warehouse.
When they got to the Shelves of Sorrow,
Olive and your wife searched
for a bag with your son's name.
But there was none.
They searched through the boxes.
Nothing
When they got to the shelf marked "Unidentified Remains"
your wife ripped open the bags
the bags full of bloody scraps
looking for a scrap of your son
And still, she couldn't find one.
And then, she went wild.
She stormed through the warehouse
pulling items from the shelves
She knocked down a stack of dinner trays
and the passenger seats
She threw them on the floor!
She threw down the "overhead bins" too
And a sink from the galley
And a television monitor
She punched through the television monitor!
And then, she fell to her knees
and pounded the ground
and started to scratch herself.
She scratched her arms
and her chest
and her breasts
until they were bleeding . . .

SEVENTH EPISODE

Madeline enters walking slowly. Her chest, arms, and neck are covered with blood from scratching herself. She walks very slowly to downstage center. She stands very still, looking out over the hills.

MADELINE: There is nothing of Adam's
on the Shelves of Sorrow . . .
(Pause.)
But . . .
(She suddenly laughs joyfully.)
I can feel him!
He's here . . .
in my arms . . . sleeping!
He's sitting on my lap . . .
(She touches herself, then laughs softly.)
Feeding at my breast . . .
Pushing out
from my womb
into the world . . .
(Pause. Madeline looks at her hands.)
The day he was born
his feet were as long as my little finger.
Do you remember Bill?
Remember how little they were?
I spent *hours* looking at his toes . . .
so
tiny . . .
And then
suddenly!
he was *sixteen!*
One morning I went to his room to wake him for school.
His foot was sticking out from the covers.
It was big.
Twice the size of mine.
And there was hair
on his big toe . . .
Three
little

hairs
that announced
his arrival
into manhood.
(Long pause.)
(Olive enters with a bag of clothing.)

WOMAN 1: Olive . . .

WOMAN 2: The clothes . . .

OLIVE: Yes. I've got the clothes.
Mr. Jones released them.
And he opened the gates too.
I don't know why. But he did.
(She sets down the bag of clothing. The women gather around it.)

OLIVE: All this time
I've been trying to turn their hatred into love.
I didn't know
until now
that the hatred I needed to turn
was my own.

HATTIE: Hatred, Olive? In you?

OLIVE: — Yes. There's been hatred in my heart
ever since this happened.
And bitterness and rage . . .
And it's time for me to get rid of it.
(Pause.)

HATTIE: There's hatred in my heart, too.

OLIVE: Is there, love?

HATTIE: Aye. But I thought I was the only one who was feeling it!

WOMAN 1: Oh no!

WOMAN 2: No!

WOMAN 1: I hate the men who did this!

WOMAN 2: I hate them too!

WOMAN 1: We all do!
(Pause.)

OLIVE: Well, then.
Evil has triumphed here after all.
Hasn't it?
(Pause. The Women take this in.)
(Olive crosses to Madeline.)

OLIVE: Mrs. Livingston . . .
　　You're bleeding.
WOMAN 2: Yes . . . She's hurt herself
OLIVE: *(Gently.)* You need to wash, love.
WOMAN 2: *(Gently.)* Yes. Come to the stream, Mrs. Livingston.
WOMAN 1: *(Gently.)* Let us wash you.
MADELINE: No.
　　(Madeline opens her blouse to expose her chest, covered with scratches.)
　　This
　　is his
　　gravestone.
　　I want everyone to see it.
　　(Slight pause.)
　　My body will be a monument
　　to his memory.
　　I want everyone who looks at me
　　to see what happened to my son!
OLIVE: *(Gently.)* Your son deserves a better monument than that.
　　That . . . *(Indicating her wounds.)*
　　is a monument to his killers.
　　A monument to violence.
　　Scratch marks and sorrow are not
　　a fitting memorial for your son.
　　(Pause.)
　　Just as a heart full of hatred is not worthy
　　of my husband and daughter.
　　(Pause.)
　　We are going to wash the clothes, Mrs. Livingston.
　　And when we do,
　　we will make our hearts pure again.
　　That will be our monument to those who died here.
　　Will you join us?
　　(Pause. Madeline doesn't answer.)
　　(George Jones enters carrying a suitcase.)
GEORGE: This is your son's.
　　I found it with the luggage.
　　His clothes are still inside,
　　just as he packed them.
　　(George sets it down in front of Bill.)

I thought you should have this.
(Long silence as Madeline and Bill look at the suitcase.)
(George starts to leave, but stops when Madeline crosses to Bill and takes the suitcase.)
(Madeline starts to open it, then stops.)
(She looks over at Bill.)

MADELINE: Do you want to open it, Bill?

BILL: Yes, Maddie. I think I need to do that.
(She sets the suitcase down gently in front of him.)
(Pause. Bill slowly opens the suitcase.)

BILL: Look.
The T-shirt he always slept in . . .
(Madeline takes out the T-shirt.)

MADELINE: Oh, look at this thing!
Full of stains and holes.
I told him not to take this to London!
But I guess he snuck it into his suitcase . . .
(Madeline looks at the T-shirt.)
Look. Inside.
(They look inside the shirt.)

BILL: His name.
You always put his name on everything.

MADELINE: He got so mad at me when I did that!
(Bill takes another shirt out of the suitcase.)

BILL: Maddie, look.
A T-shirt he got in London . . .
(Pause.)
He put his name inside it too.
(Bill weeps openly for the first time.)
(Madeline comforts him.)

GEORGE: So . . .
if you'll excuse me. . .
I've got to go.
There's a press conference.
I've got to make a statement
and somehow salvage this situation.
(George starts to leave. Olive stops him.)

OLIVE: Mr. Jones?

GEORGE: Yes, Mrs. Allison?

OLIVE: What are you going to say?
　　In your statement?
GEORGE: I don't know yet.
　　But it won't be about *love,*
　　I can tell you that.
OLIVE: Why don't you say something about hatred, then?
GEORGE: *Hatred?*
OLIVE: Yes.
GEORGE: Like what?
OLIVE: Like . . . "Hatred will not have the last word in Lockerbie."
GEORGE: That might work.
　　It would certainly make a good headline.
OLIVE: Yes, it would.
　　Especially since it's true.
GEORGE: Well, yes, yes, I suppose it is.
　　(Pause. George thinks.)
　　All right, Mrs. Allison.
　　That's what I'll say.
　　Thank you.
OLIVE: Thank you.
　　(George reaches out and gives Bill an awkward pat on the shoulder.)
　　(George nods "good-bye".)
GEORGE: Ladies.
　　(George Jones exits.)
　　(Olive kneels by the bag of laundry. The Women gather around her. Olive reaches out and touches the bag.)
OLIVE: It's hard not to hate.
　　And it's harder yet to love
　　when hatred's been awoken in your heart.
　　But that's what we must do, isn't it?
　　(Slight pause.)
　　Act with love in the face of our own hatred.
WOMAN 1: Aye.
WOMAN 2: Aye.
HATTIE: Aye.
　　(Pause.)
OLIVE: Let the washing begin.
　　(Olive slowly opens the bag. The Women look inside, but stop. They are overcome by the sight of the clothes.)

WOMAN 2: Oh God.
WOMAN 1: Oh God.
  (Olive closes the bag.)
MADELINE: What is it?
OLIVE: I . . . I don't know if I'm strong enough to do this . . .
  (Long Pause.)

FOURTH CHORAL ODE
WASHING

(Madeline goes to Olive. She gently takes the bag and opens it for her. When Olive doesn't reach inside, Madeline takes out a piece of clothing and hands it to her. Then, she takes out a piece for each of the women. She takes one for herself, then leads Olive and the women to the stream.)
(They kneel.)
(Madeline is the first to wash. The others follow.)
(They wash.)
(They wash.)
(They wash in silence for a long time.)
(The stage slowly floods with light.)
(It is dawn.)
(The hills, which were black in the night turn green with the morning light.)

END OF PLAY

Millennium 7

Edgar Nkosi White

To Albee

BIOGRAPHY

Edgar Nkosi White is a playwright and author. He has attended NYU and Yale School of Drama and his plays have been performed in New York, at The Royal Court, Riverside Studios, and at the Edinburgh Festival. His first novel, *The Rising,* described the Caribbean experience in America and Britain. Born in Montserrat, he lived in New York for many years. He is currently working on a novel entitled *The Pygmies and the Pyramid.*

His plays include *The Nine Night* (Methuen Press), *Lament For Rastafari,* and *Redemption Song* (Marion Boyars Publishers). Most recently his plays *Marion Anderson* and *The Love Song for Langston Hughes* were performed at the Schomburg Center for Culture and Art in New York. He has had four plays performed at the Joseph Papp Public Theater, as well as at Café La Mama.

CHARACTERS
- RACHEL FLEISHMAN: a resident in a nursing home. In her seventies. Still defiant. Has humor, wit, and fear.
- NAOMI: A black former Bell Telephone worker, now a resident in nursing home. She is early seventies. Eyes still bright. Lives for Sunday visits from her son. Wants to believe that nursing home is only temporary.
- MITCH: Naomi's son, age thirties. Newly arrived black bourgeois achiever trying to survive success. Works for Disney. He needs and fears the weekly visit to nursing home.
- GOLEM: Guard at nursing home.
- WINGATE (THE FLASHER): Resident in nursing home (mid-seventies), has no visitors.

SETTING

An expensive nursing home in Manhattan where the borders of peoples lives intersect.

TIME

The frightening present.

MILLENNIUM 7

ACT I
SCENE ONE

Music intro: Vivaldi: "The Four Seasons"

RECORDED VOICE: *(English woman.)* "Welcome to Millennium Gardens where your loved ones will always get the very best in care and service."
(At rise we see the wraith-like figure of an old woman dressed entirely in black with hair now gone white, she blazes across stage in her motorized wheelchair smoking cigarette vehemently. Examines objects on table with great suspicion, discovers open Bible. Circles this strange object slowly then begins to read.)

RACHEL: "I shall do the thing which goodness is" *(Pauses.)* What the hell does that mean? The thing which goodness is? I bet you it's that woman. Like some hen. Whenever she gets up she leaves a Bible behind her like an egg. At least I leave cigarette butts not Bibles. *(Pause.)* Sundays. I hate them! *(Enter Naomi. Black, age about seventy, but youthful in face with smooth, unwrinkled skin. They watch each other a moment. She picks up Bible and begins to read.)*

RACHEL: You could say good morning you know.

NAOMI: Excuse me?

RACHEL: I said you could say good morning, there are people here you know.

NAOMI: Really, where?

RACHEL: Right here.

NAOMI: Well you never know with you people.

RACHEL: Which people?

NAOMI: *Old.* I'm talking about old people like you . . . For months I've been speaking to you, sometimes you grunt, other times you don't even do that, so I just said to hell with it.

RACHEL: Well you should keep trying.

NAOMI: Oh yeah, why?

RACHEL: Because I'm worth it that's why.

NAOMI: Says who?

RACHEL: Says who, says me, that's who. Rachel Fleishman. I think I'm worth it.

NAOMI: You would. Okay Rachel. Why all of a sudden today you feel like speaking?

RACHEL: That boy who comes here on Sunday, that's your son?

NAOMI: Yeah, that's my Mitch.

RACHEL: I had a son, he used to come on Sunday too. Then he died . . . in *The Towers* . . . so . . . he don't come no more. Now it's just Sunday. All day long.

NAOMI: The Towers. I'm sorry I . . .

RACHEL: Why, it's not your fault. You're not God are you?

NAOMI: You never know what somebody's going through.

RACHEL: Don't worry about me, I'm all right except on Sundays. I'm not so good with them.

NAOMI: I don't know what I'd do if anything happened to Mitch.

RACHEL: Smoke . . .

NAOMI: Did you see my walker?

RACHEL: Over there in the corner.

NAOMI: I don't know why they make us use these things . . .

RACHEL: Because they don't want us to fall on our ass and maybe sue them that's why.

NAOMI: Most the people in here are so gaga they wouldn't be suing anybody.

RACHEL: Did you see the Golem?

NAOMI: Which Golem?

RACHEL: The guard.

NAOMI: Not for a while, why, you need him?

RACHEL: That's all right I'll find him.

NAOMI: Rachel, how long have you been here?

RACHEL: Me, about three years. Give or take a century.

NAOMI: I've been here two months. Seems nice.

RACHEL: *(Shrugs.)* It's all right if you like prisons.

NAOMI: It's not like that. Come on, everybody's very friendly . . . well almost everybody.

RACHEL: Alice in Wonderland! Listen, what do you think the owners of this place just decided one day: "Hey, you know what. We just love elderly people. Wouldn't it be nice to maybe get a bunch of them together so we can look after them. Watch them grow, like plants?" You think that's what happened? Come on, it's a business. A business. We live longer these days. They need someplace to put us. A warehouse.

NAOMI: Gee, I wouldn't say that.

RACHEL: No, of course you wouldn't. I guess you must have fell in love with the advertisement they do with that English broad they use: "Welcome to Millennium Gardens Nursing Home where your loved ones will always get the very best in professional care. A little taste of paradise right here on earth." And they got the Vivaldi music going like mad in the background to sucker you.

NAOMI: Well it takes all kinds to make a . . .

RACHEL: Zoo. Look, I smoke, all right?

NAOMI: Certainly, if you like.

RACHEL: I like. *(Pause.)* Once I had a son, now I have cigarettes.

NAOMI: *(Moves to television.)* You don't turn it on?

RACHEL: What?

NAOMI: The TV. You don't look at it?

RACHEL: Nothing on there's worth seeing. Mostly I watch myself and think. See from here, it's like a mirror.

NAOMI: *(Walks over.)* Let's see.

RACHEL: Look from back here. What do you see?

NAOMI: *(Looking.)* I see . . . two old women.

(They look at each other.)

RACHEL/NAOMI: Maybe we better turn it on! *(They laugh together.)*

RACHEL: Your son he brings you things?

NAOMI: Bring me things? Yeah, I try to tell him not to but he always does anyway.

RACHEL: He could maybe pick me up something?

NAOMI: Like what?

RACHEL: Naturally I'd pay him back of course.

NAOMI: Rachel, what would you like him to bring for you?

RACHEL: I don't know, flowers maybe, or something to help me sleep.

NAOMI: Help you sleep, he's not a doctor.

RACHEL: Doesn't matter he's a man, he'll do.

NAOMI: You want to share my son?

RACHEL: Just on Sunday.

NAOMI: Why?

RACHEL: Unless somebody ask, they don't give a damn about you in this place, that's why. If no one visits you it means you're dead, believe me.

NAOMI: But how would that work, I mean obviously they would know that he's my son.

RACHEL: Look, maybe he comes. He stops at the front desk and says he's here to see Mrs. Fleishman this week . . .

NAOMI: You. But they know he comes for me?

RACHEL: So what, one week he's here for you one week for me. So?

NAOMI: I don't know it sounds pretty crazy to me.

RACHEL: Forget it then. *(Turns her wheelchair with her back to Naomi.)*
NAOMI: Listen don't be getting an attitude. Most the time you don't even have anything to say to me and now all of a sudden I'm suppose to just give up my son? I don't think so.
RACHEL: What about all those Bibles you keep drowning us in?
NAOMI: All what Bibles, only have two. One in French and one in English. You have to keep your mind busy or else it rots, you should too.
RACHEL: It's already too busy. I need to get it to stop working over time. Anyway what does your book say about giving?
NAOMI: It's sacred.
RACHEL: So?
NAOMI: Yeah lady but you talking about my son, I don't play that.
RACHEL: For God sake, I'm not going to eat him. Look, do you know how hard it is for someone like me to even ask . . . someone . . . like you?
NAOMI: *(Looks at her.)* Someone like me, what . . . No, how hard is it?
RACHEL: Very.
NAOMI: You manage.
RACHEL: Just. So, will you ask him?
NAOMI: We'll see.
   (The guard enters, looks in.)
RACHEL: Golem, where've you been? Wait!
GUARD: Busy now Mrs. Fleishman.
   (He exits. She follows after him in wheelchair.)
RACHEL: Wait I need to see you don't run off. Golem . . . Golem?
   (She exits following him.)
NAOMI: Hey, you all right?
   (Darkness.)

SCENE TWO

The time is several months later. Naomi enters carrying a vase of flowers. She sees Rachel and pauses.

NAOMI: *(Aside.)* At first I couldn't even get the woman to speak. Now she won't leave me alone. Every minute now it's something. They expect you to be smiling and cheerful all the time. Oh well, I guess I asked for it. Now she even has my son working for her. *(Aloud.)* Hi there. They never change the water for these flowers do they.

RACHEL: They hardly change our water you think they're going to worry about flowers?

NAOMI: Oh, by the way, did you see my walker?

RACHEL: In the corner where you always leave it.

NAOMI: Darn thing's a nuisance. I don't know why they have to make us use them. They don't like it when we lose our walkers.

RACHEL: Lose your mind but not your walker. Look at that guy over there, is he walking or dancing? God!

(Man in corner with walker.)

NAOMI: *(Looks.)* Leave him alone, he's trying. And my glasses. You see my glasses?

RACHEL: Wait a minute, what am I, your caretaker? You probably left them in the dining room when you were eating lunch. That's what you usually do. I don't know why you don't just get a chain and wear them around your neck like me. See. This way you can't lose them.

NAOMI: I don't like chains around my neck. *(Pause.)* You wouldn't understand.

RACHEL: Don't start. And by the way, is this your Bible?

NAOMI: Oh yeah, probably.

RACHEL: Oh yeah probably? Why is it that you're always leaving Bibles everywhere. I swear you're like a damn hen. Whenever you get up, there's a Bible. What is it with you?

NAOMI: I've only got two.

RACHEL: Well they multiply like rabbits then because I keep seeing new ones. Stop trying to convert me, will you. I'm a Jew. Stop being a pain in the ass . . .

NAOMI: Who wants to convert you?

RACHEL: Thank you. Enough already.

NAOMI: I've got two Bibles, one in French and this one in English.

RACHEL: What you doing with a French Bible?

NAOMI: I don't know. I thought it might be fun to have a new language. I never had time before to do anything for me. You know what I mean? A new challenge. *"Puis je vis"* "Then I saw" *"Un ciel nouveau et une terre nouvelle"* "A new heaven and a new earth."

(She smiles filled with joy, Rachel looks at her in disbelief.)

RACHEL: Me, start learning French. Now? For what, where am I going to, France?

NAOMI: You can never tell.

RACHEL: Honey, I know where I'm going and it's not France, believe me.

NAOMI: You have to keep finding ways to keep the mind excited.

RACHEL: It's already too excited.

NAOMI: Excited, not frustrated. That's why you smoke so much.

RACHEL: Don't start with the cigarettes again. My choice okay?

NAOMI: Fine, *(Sings.)* "Puff the Magic Dragon, lived by the sea . . ." My grandson sings that.

RACHEL: Hey, if I choose to smoke that's my business.

NAOMI: Is it?

RACHEL: Yes. Stop trying to convert everybody. You're as bad as those damn Jehovah Witness people who come scratching here at the door every Sunday annoying people.

NAOMI: Listen Rachel, nobody's trying to convert you. No, no. Tell you what, you keep smoking like a good girl *(Pause.)* until you kill yourself, all right? No problem. "Pas probleme!"

RACHEL: *(Slowly.)* My choice!

NAOMI: Fine, but tell me, did you ever stop to consider that maybe I don't *choose* to inhale that all the damn time. *(Pause.)* Look at that, you see you? You got me cursing on the Lord's day. God, I know you sent this one to test me Lord. Just to teach me great patience, and I fail *every* time.

RACHEL: Me, test you! Anyway what's the difference, you curse every other day don't you?

NAOMI: Sunday's different.

RACHEL: Yeah, it's longer. *(Screams.)* And they don't give any goddamn medication on Sunday.

NAOMI: Good, you can go one day a week without tranquilizers.

RACHEL: First of all, they're not tranquilizers, they're painkillers, and no I can't.

NAOMI: Can't what?

RACHEL: Do without them.

NAOMI: What are you, a drug addict?

RACHEL: No, *old.* That's what I am. Old.

NAOMI: Nonsense, you're just as old as you feel.

RACHEL: Exactly the problem.

NAOMI: Oh shut up, you love complaining. Here read the newspaper and keep quiet.

RACHEL: I used to be able to do the crossword in a half hour flat. A half hour. In ink no less. Now I'm lucky if I can remember my own name. It's not fair.

NAOMI: What's not fair?

RACHEL: It's my birthday *(Pause.)* again.

NAOMI: Really? Fantastic, why didn't you tell Mrs. Willis, the recreation therapist?

RACHEL: Are you crazy? That's the last thing I need. Mary goddamn Poppins. Running around with her balloons and whistles and little party hats.

NAOMI: Oh come on she's nice. She would have had a party for you.

RACHEL: A party. Just what I need. Let's all get together and watch me dying. Old Wingate running around exposing himself and Martha from the seventh floor dribbling ice cream. Please. I'm going to go upstairs and sleep until tomorrow.

NAOMI: What in the world is your problem? How old are you for God sake?

RACHEL: Too old. You know what I realize now?

NAOMI: What?

RACHEL: It's only once a week that my mind works clear. One day a week that the world makes some sense. You spend the entire week waiting for *that* day but of course it never comes on the same day twice. So God tricks you into hope.

NAOMI: I'm going to tell Miss Willis your birthday's next week. We'll have a big party.

RACHEL: *(Ignores her.)* I need medication.

NAOMI: You said they don't work anyway so why you taking them?

RACHEL: *(Whispers.)* That's not the point. Listen as much as they charge for this place I want every damn thing that I'm entitled to. Everything. *(Yells.)* Cheap bastards! They charge for aspirin even. The only thing they give you free is a lousy can of Insure. The chocolate one tastes like . . .

NAOMI: I heard the racket you were making in the lunchroom today. What was all that about anyway?

RACHEL: The chicken.

NAOMI: Chicken?

RACHEL: Did you see the size of that leg they gave me?

NAOMI: What was wrong, yours wasn't cooked or something?

RACHEL: You don't give anything that huge to a lady. You cut it up.

NAOMI: Wait a minute, that's what the hell you were so upset about?

RACHEL: I'm sorry, I have a certain standard. That's the way I was raised, I can't help it.

NAOMI: "I have a certain standard," the little Jewish princess. Boy, are you spoiled.

RACHEL: You do not give a lady something that looks like it belongs in *Jurassic Park*.

NAOMI: Listen girl, there's people outside eating out of garbage cans. There's starvation right outside our window. Homelessness everywhere.
RACHEL: There may be but I don't choose to know them. Do you mind?
NAOMI: What would you like to do with them?
RACHEL: Who?
NAOMI: The homeless.
RACHEL: I don't know, it's not my problem. I have enough to do trying to keep . . .
NAOMI: Should we shoot them?
RACHEL: Shoot who?
NAOMI: The homeless.
RACHEL: I don't want to shoot them, I just don't want to know them that's all. Hey, want to know the best way to help the poor? Don't join them.
NAOMI: No feeling.
RACHEL: Sure I feel, *(Pause.)* gypped. The point is I'm *not* homeless. I'm paying good money to live here. They didn't take me in because they like me.
NAOMI: *(Dismissal.)* Let's forget it.
RACHEL: *(Chases behind her.)* Anyway why am I the Wicked Witch of the West just because I don't like the way they serve food here?
NAOMI: What you expect, joy unspeakable?
RACHEL: Yeah, I could do with a little joy unspeakable.
NAOMI: Be glad you're eating.
RACHEL: At these prices I don't want to just be eating. I expect to eat well. *(Shouts.)* This place is a damn ripoff. I will not be ignored.
NAOMI: It's a nursing home not a hotel. Hello! Besides, they let you get away with murder. You're the only one who gets to keep a piano in her room.
RACHEL: Which, by the way, they make me play in the closet so as not to disturb people. You do too much of that in the closet stuff and you start to get a little wacko, you know what I mean . . .
NAOMI: Be grateful.
RACHEL: For what a goddamn piano?
NAOMI: No, *hands* that can still move.
(Enter guard. He looks around.)
GUARD: Hello. Everything all right? What's all the yelling?
RACHEL: And now the Golem.
GUARD: Hello Mrs. Fleishman, by the way the name is Ted.
RACHEL: At these prices the name's Golem
GUARD: Have it your way. So what's the problem?

NAOMI: No problem Ted.
RACHEL: So who we arresting today, widows or cripples?
GUARD: I'm a guard, Mrs. Fleishman, not a cop.
RACHEL: I see, crippled widows!
GUARD: Just a guard. I'm just here to help you.
RACHEL: Yeah, help us stay here.
GUARD: Help you not to hurt yourself.
RACHEL: Bye, Golem.
GUARD: *(Whispers.)* How come you don't call me that when you need a little favor, like a little something from the liquor store. Not so hoity-toity then, right?
RACHEL: A gentleman wouldn't mention it.
GUARD: True, but then again a lady wouldn't ask.
RACHEL: Golem!

(He exits.)

NAOMI: Why do you always call him that?
RACHEL: Because that's what he is, a goddamn Golem.
NAOMI: He's just a guard. He's nice.
RACHEL: For you everybody's nice. I don't like being in prison, sorry.
NAOMI: We're not in prison.
RACHEL: Oh no? Try leaving. We create them and then they take us over. Like Frankenstein. That's why I call him Golem.
NAOMI: The guard's for our own protection.
RACHEL: Yeah well, don't protect me so good.
NAOMI: You know people wander in and out of here.
RACHEL: He's not for keeping out. He's for keeping in, all right? Look, I'm a grown woman. If I want to walk in the street, I don't need any Golem standing in my way.
NAOMI: If you wanted to walk, I'm sure they'd let you.
RACHEL: Okay honey, time for a reality check. Nobody in here just goes for a walk, all right? They've got electronic sensors attached to our wristbands. Remember Mr. Jenkins, he thought he was walking to the corner for a soda. The next thing he knew he was in handcuffs.
NAOMI: Rachel, it wasn't a soda he went after, it was his brother, in Brooklyn . . .
RACHEL: Whatever, anyway they brought him back.
NAOMI: The truth was his brother didn't want to see him.
RACHEL: Face it this place is a prison. Worse, a bone yard where your family sticks you so they don't have to deal with you anymore.

NAOMI: My son Mitch comes.
RACHEL: You don't know how lucky you are.
NAOMI: Oh yes I do.
RACHEL: When they see nobody comes, that's it for you kiddo. Don't tell me we're not prisoners. I woke up one day and found myself inside this body. No parole on this sentence.
NAOMI: Listen, do you know who you are?
RACHEL: Yes, unfortunately.
NAOMI: And you know *where*.
RACHEL: Yeah, I know who and I know where, what I don't know is *why*.
NAOMI: Hey, two out of three ain't bad. You're still ahead. Read your paper and leave me alone
(Enter Wingate, a male patient in his seventies. He has a far-away look and a pixie-like grin. He wears a pair of gloves with open fingers like a bike rider.)
NAOMI: *(Laughing.)* Look, here's your friend.
RACHEL: Oh Jesus, not him again. Goddamn Harpo What do you want? Get out of here before I run you over with my wheelchair.
WINGATE: Hello, hello. Is it well?
NAOMI: Pull up your pants Mr. Wingate. Now he's somebody who doesn't even know *where*.
RACHEL: Horseshit! He knows.
NAOMI: The poor man loves to expose himself.
WINGATE: Birdie. *(Reaches inside pants.)*
NAOMI: No Mr. Wingate, nobody wants to see your little birdie today.
RACHEL: Don't try it Wingate. Take it out and you lose it! *(Lifts her cigarette lighter that has an extra high flame.)*
NAOMI: Rachel, you wouldn't.
RACHEL: Just try it buddy. You'll have roasted weenie, I swear.
WINGATE: Bye bye!!
(Wingate pulls up pants and exits hurriedly.)
NAOMI: You're terrible.
RACHEL: *(Laughing.)* I was waiting for him. Waiting.
NAOMI: Poor guy.
RACHEL: Yeah, he's nice too, right? I need a drink.
NAOMI: They don't open the bar until 3, today.
RACHEL: Everything moves so slowly on Sunday.
NAOMI: I used to love my Sundays.
RACHEL: Yeah, I remember growing up, we used to get the papers. My dad

would save the puzzle for me. Hell, no one else was interested but me. I was still bright then.

NAOMI: Did you get in your mother's bed on Sunday with the paper? We did.

RACHEL: No, my mother was not the let's-all-get-in-bed type. Hell, I don't even think my father got in bed with her unless he had to.

NAOMI: Well he must of at least once. You're here.

RACHEL: Four times. Three brothers and me. My father used to say that the only thing wrong with me was that I was a girl. What he used to call me? Oh yes, "God's little joke."

NAOMI: Your father again.

RACHEL: I was the one with the brains. He knew it, but you see in a Jewish family, girls aren't suppose to run the business, just run their husbands.

NAOMI: I like it.

RACHEL: He gave everything to Stanley, the eldest. Now he was nice. Dumb, but nice. Daddy lovingly described him as: "Not the sharpest pencil in the box" Stanley.

NAOMI: *(Laughing.)* Your father was something else.

RACHEL: Listen, they gave my brother everything. All he had to do was not screw up. We would have been millionaires by now if he just held on. In one year he managed to go through fifty thousand dollars. As if that wasn't enough, he sells off all our real estate for nothing. All he had to do was wait. It's worth five times the amount now. No, not my brother, Stanley the asshole.

NAOMI: So what did your father say?

RACHEL: Nothing, Stanley at least was a son. Me, all I get is the twenty-second course on money.

NAOMI: Twenty seconds?

RACHEL: Like this: "Sweetheart, funny thing about money" "Yeah?" I said. "Yeah. It goes . . . fast. No matter how much you got it goes, so you better marry rich, kiddo."

NAOMI: That's it?

RACHEL: He must have figured anymore would have just confused me.

NAOMI: Marry rich.

RACHEL: That's right. We're not talking mystery here. Basic logic. Get the girl married. My mother saw to everything. It was her wedding. She was so happy she'd finally found a lawyer for me. "You can let him know you have brains now, it's too late, he's married you." Just one problem.

NAOMI: What?

RACHEL: By then I'd played dumb so long that I couldn't speak.

NAOMI: You?

RACHEL: I'm serious. Hey, you had to be so careful, men crumble easy, then they run.

NAOMI: You just have to give them an image, which doesn't scare them too much. You know, slightly lost but full of trust. I was pretty good. Hey, Rachel look: *(Performs the wide-eyed stare of the "Young White Girl.")* Check the walk. *(Slightly mincing step.)* Look! You'll have to *imagine* the flex of the hair.

RACHEL: Good, very good. You'd have done well as a Jewish princess.

NAOMI: So anyway you wouldn't exactly say you married for love.

RACHEL: Love. What love? That was Loretta Young and Ronald Coleman wasn't it? Maybe Bogart and Bergman . . . Hollywood.

NAOMI: Greta Garbo.

RACHEL: Just to be able to get the hell out my mother's house. That's what I loved. The size of the diamond on my finger. I don't know, is that what you mean? "Love."

(She looks at ring.)

NAOMI: I was in something. Must have been love. He sure didn't have anything else to give me. Not that he didn't try. He was West Indian.

RACHEL: Was or is?

NAOMI: Oh he still is. They don't change, honey. Not big on conversation. They like their dinner ready and your legs spread open.

RACHEL: Oh!

NAOMI: Never ask them where they're going or when they're coming back and you'll be all right.

RACHEL: So what happened?

NAOMI: I asked.

RACHEL: Fatal?

NAOMI: Very. His name was Pilgrim. I kept waiting on the Progress.

RACHEL: Cute.

NAOMI: Always called him Mr. Pilgrim. He made sure there was food in the house. He wasn't mean just stubborn. His grandfather died from sugar, mine died from cotton. We understood each other. He said one thing that made sense: "Don't grow old where they don't forgive age." He wanted to go back home. His head was full of dreams.

RACHEL: So who left who?

NAOMI: I don't know. After the second illegitimate daughter and a third son showed up. I asked him when he planned on telling me. He said, "So what's wrong. They happen before you so why I should tell you?" I said well if you can't see why, what's the sense. We're just strangers.

RACHEL: At least you had Mitch.

NAOMI: I always wanted a son.

RACHEL: One's no use to you, you need more. They die on you. You need a spare.

NAOMI: They're not tires, Rachel.

RACHEL: With one you end alone. Friends? *(Laughs.)* You can forget them.

NAOMI: You had friends who used to come all the time, I remember you told me . . .

RACHEL: Honey, when the money goes, they go. At first they came to the nursing home just to look. Curiosity. It was different when I was still Park Ave. Then it was every Thursday night get together. That was culture night. The 92nd street Y, or Lincoln Center. Music, plays, folk songs; anything just so long as it's "cultural." Girl's night out. *(Music: Folk Songs of the Auverne. Natania Davrath.)* There was Penny Aaronson and Gloria Gerstein, Hannah and Verna. Some were widows, some spinsters. We promised we'd always support each other and what happened?

NAOMI: Rachel, *you* drove them away. You told them not to come anymore.

RACHEL: Nursing home takes all the money and gives you an allowance like some kid. Yes, just enough to buy cigarettes . . . Just enough so that you can smoke yourself to death. You know why I do this? It's the one freedom I've got left. *(Stands, flings pack of cigarettes.)* I hate it. I'm a grown woman not a child. Don't try to potty train me goddamn it! *(Cries.)*

NAOMI: Rachel, stop. It's all right. Don't cry.

RACHEL: I don't cry. I. don't cry.

(Enter guard.)

GUARD: Is she okay?

RACHEL: I don't need anything yet Golem. Not yet. Get the hell out of here! You don't come when I call you.

NAOMI: It's all right, go.

GUARD: Are you sure, maybe I should call . . .

NAOMI: It'll be okay. She's having a birthday.

GUARD: Oh. Okay . . . Listen she thinks I'm like here to persecute her or something. I'm not. Me personally I couldn't care less if she wants to go out. God forbid she was like my mother or something. Even might be me in here. I'm just doing my job, all right. Right now I need this. Try get her to see that, okay? I'm no . . . what?

NAOMI: Golem.

GUARD: Yeah. *(He exits.)*
NAOMI: Come on girl, sit down.
RACHEL: Wow, I'm sorry. I don't do this.
NAOMI: It's Sunday.
RACHEL: Yeah, that must be it.
RACHEL: You know, it's not that I don't want to see friends. It's just that if they come at all it's only to show how much better than you they're doing. I hate that. Everything's like a contest. They want to see who can outlive each other.
NAOMI: Wouldn't you if you could?
RACHEL: I'd like to think that I'm not that crass.
NAOMI: Get a chance we're all that crass, trust me.
(They play the game of Operator.)
RACHEL: Hello operator?
NAOMI: Yes.
RACHEL: Give me God. You know Golem, the guard that you think's so nice?
NAOMI: Yeah.
RACHEL: Well he gets vodka for me.
NAOMI: I know.
RACHEL: You know? You're not suppose to know until I tell you.
NAOMI: I'm God. I'm suppose to know.
RACHEL: Stop knowing things before you should. It's bad manners. They're borders you don't go beyond.
NAOMI: Sorry but it's not good to ask them to do things for you. They know your business then.
RACHEL: You have your son to ask, who do I have? Don't judge me.
NAOMI: I'm not.
RACHEL: I created him by asking him to do things for me, then one day I couldn't stop asking, know what I mean?
NAOMI: So stop
RACHEL: Just say no, right? What am I going to do take up bowling? *(Suddenly.)* Where's my cigarettes?
NAOMI: You mean your one act of freedom? They're over there in the corner.
RACHEL: *(In child's voice.)* Can you get them for me please?
NAOMI: No, if you're well enough to smoke them, you're well enough to get them yourself.
RACHEL: God, so touchy she is!
(Rachel picks up cigarettes. To the left of stage is the area that is the elevator.

We see Wingate walking confused. We hear the recorded sound of the elevator door opening and closing.)

RACHEL: Oh God, not him again.

NAOMI: He keeps walking in and out of the elevator. He doesn't know where he is?

RACHEL: Is that us Naomi . . . God, is that us?

(The two stare at the figure of Wingate. Darkness.)

SCENE THREE

Sometime later. Music of Pablo Casals playing: Goyaesca. *The two women dance together. Rachel in her wheelchair, Naomi with her walker, holding it like a lover. Rachel circles around her. Wingate enters room, stands apart, and mimics them dancing.*

NAOMI: That was nice.

RACHEL: At least they have music hour on Sunday.

NAOMI: We should go sit with the group next door.

RACHEL: Never, I'll die first. You go.

NAOMI: They talk about us you know.

RACHEL: Let them.

NAOMI: They say we're antisocial.

RACHEL: Better than brain-dead. I'd rather sit with my album.

NAOMI: Wingate wants to hold the elevator for you but you never get on.
(She does exercises with the walker while Rachel sits with photo album.)

RACHEL: You know, I guess it's harder for them.

NAOMI: Them who?

RACHEL: Men.

NAOMI: Oh, that them.

RACHEL: Must be hell for a man to get old and can't use his willie anymore.

NAOMI: Yeah, I guess so, considering that's all they've got. *(Pause.)* God that sounds terrible! That's how they see themselves though. You know what I mean?

RACHEL: Women are used to peeing on themselves. Men aren't.

NAOMI: *(Laughing.)* I never thought of it like that. That says it all.

RACHEL: Well that's why they go gaga first I mean look at this place.

NAOMI: First they go gaga and then they go . . . period.

RACHEL: We give . . . they give up.

NAOMI: Well they sure use those willies while they've got them, tell you that much. Don't feel so sorry for them.
RACHEL: You know I think my father played around, I mean I don't have any real proof because my mother never named names.
NAOMI: No White House tapes?
RACHEL: No, but I think there was a lot of *shtupping* going on.
NAOMI: *Shtupping?*
RACHEL: Yeah, you know *(Makes gesture of copulation.)*
NAOMI: What?
RACHEL: Come on you know.
NAOMI: Oh!
RACHEL: He'd smile to himself a lot. I mean a man doesn't have to be particularly bright to get through life, look at my brothers, they're classic examples. Put it this way, brains never got in their way.
NAOMI: I hear you.
RACHEL: Then there was my husband, Harold. He was never particularly intelligent but he was a damn good lawyer. If you doubted him, *you* felt guilty.
NAOMI: You mean like he had authority.
RACHEL: Here, look at him.
NAOMI: Good-looking man.
RACHEL: Yeah, that's it, authority. He could lie and get away with it. Lied to me. Lied to everybody, *(Pause.)* even himself, couldn't help it.
NAOMI: Why you say that?
RACHEL: Never mind. Doesn't matter. What time is it?
NAOMI: Four.
RACHEL: Our son's late.
NAOMI: He'll be here.
RACHEL: How do I look?
NAOMI: You look fine.
RACHEL: It's just that I hate to look just any how, if he's coming. I mean . . . you know, he respects me. He's very polite your son.
NAOMI: It's good to take pride in yourself.
RACHEL: Well I figure if he comes all this way to see *us* . . . I mean *you,* the least I can do is try and look presentable.
NAOMI: Sure.
RACHEL: I used to do that for my son.
NAOMI: You really loved him didn't you.
RACHEL: Died on me. Bastard . . .
NAOMI: Rachel!

RACHEL: *(Shrugs.)* Not him. God. They should make them to last longer than their mothers. Survive terrorists.

NAOMI: They're not batteries, Rachel. Not batteries not tires. They're no guaranties.

RACHEL: Easy for you to say, you've never lost anything.

NAOMI: You don't know that.

RACHEL: I sound angry?

NAOMI: Yes.

RACHEL: Not allowed, right? Should've had two though, just in case, but who knew. Who knew anything.

NAOMI: No refunds.

RACHEL: I entered marriage dumb. The house my husband bought us was so big I couldn't even find the kitchen. Not that I would have known what to do in there anyway. Thank God for Hilda. The maid. She was colored. *(Naomi looks at her, she shrugs.)* What? What I do now?

NAOMI: Nothing, nothing.

RACHEL: What can I tell you, if she was Chinese I'd of said Chinese. Whatever. She cooked, thank God, I couldn't. She did everything. I played my piano.

NAOMI: *(Frosty.)* Lucky you!

RACHEL: Lucky me? Believe me, you don't want to know.

NAOMI: Please, give me a break will you. I didn't have anybody cooking and cleaning for me, you know what I'm saying? I went to work at that damn telephone company for twenty years.

RACHEL: Nothing wrong with working. Work builds character. I'd of worked but nobody would let me.

NAOMI: Well they damn sure let me!

RACHEL: Oh.

NAOMI: I'd still be working if they didn't play their little games.

RACHEL: Which one, they play so many.

NAOMI: "You're part of the family, Naomi, we love you forever Naomi." They had me teach this young college kid the systems. He looked so lost I even shared my lunch with him. Three months later this kid has my job. *Bye!* Can't believe it. I know that's what led to my heart attack. They didn't just stab me in the back, they had me sharpen the blade for them.

RACHEL: They had you teach him and then gave him your job?

NAOMI: Yeah, the sneaky . . .

RACHEL: Go on say it.

NAOMI: Bastards.

RACHEL: There, now, doesn't that feel better?

NAOMI: No, but its a start.

RACHEL: They just downsized you that's all.

NAOMI: To you it's just a word. To me it was a life.

RACHEL: Naomi, it's not a life, it's just a goddamn job that's all. Don't confuse them.

NAOMI: The funny thing is that I never felt safe. For years, I was so careful to not get involved with office politics. Never criticize. Good slave. Then just when I started to relax . . . wham!

RACHEL: Maybe you should of got involved with the office politics. Listen, when you find yourself in a whorehouse, spread your legs.

NAOMI: Your father?

RACHEL: Yeah, how'd you guess.

NAOMI: Great. What's the time?

RACHEL: Almost five.

NAOMI: He's really late.

RACHEL: This is the time my Bobby would come. He always made sure he came late. I don't think he could do more than an hour with me.

NAOMI: Don't say that.

RACHEL: Listen, sometimes it's hard for *me* to do more than an hour with me. *(Lights cigarette.)* I'm no walk in the park, I know it. He came because he knew he was the last of the family.

NAOMI: That's the one thing I've always admired about the Jews.

RACHEL: *(Aside.)* Why do I think that I'm not going to want to hear this?

NAOMI: Family. Always good to your families.

RACHEL: *(Laughs.)* So naïve.

NAOMI: What, not true?

RACHEL: Some Jews and some families, people are people. What do people care about first? Themselves. Period, end of story. It's me me me me me.

NAOMI: Really?

RACHEL: My family pretended there was no problem. We lived in Maryland. Can you imagine me in Maryland?

NAOMI: Yeah, with George Washington and the Delaware.

RACHEL: Damn few Jews in Delaware and those who were, were like us. In serious denial. My father never mentioned it at the dinner table. I grew up thinking I was Shirley Temple.

NAOMI: Shirley Temple! Well let me not laugh, I knew I wasn't but I'd have liked to have been.

RACHEL: What the hell, why should we lie to each other, we're going to be dead soon.

NAOMI: You're going to be dead soon, I'm going to live forever.

RACHEL: My husband Harold came from the same kind of family, very conservative. The only difference was that he really felt guilty about doing nothing. He had a Dybbuk riding him.

NAOMI: A what?

RACHEL: A Dybbuk, an evil spirit . . . As a matter a fact he had quite a few of them riding him . . . I was too dumb to know. I stayed in the big house . . .

NAOMI: With Hilda, the maid.

RACHEL: Right, and I had Bobby, which made everybody very happy. I mean I presented him with a son and not a *problem*. Everything was great . . . I thought.

NAOMI: Hey, you did all right.

RACHEL: That's what I said until one day, I came home early. It was a Thursday Hilda's day off. I came in and pushed open the door and ran into my first problem.

NAOMI: Yeah?

RACHEL: There was my husband in bed with another man.

NAOMI: Jesus!

RACHEL: No it definitely wasn't him.

NAOMI: What did you do?

RACHEL: I ran, I just ran. I couldn't deal with it. I don't remember anything. All I know is that I ended up back in my mother's house. Don't ask me how because to this day I blocked it out. All I remember was trying to tell her what happened and her saying to me . . .

NAOMI: Divorce him.

RACHEL: Are you crazy? No way. She remained perfectly calm. She says: "You couldn't have seen that dear. You just imagined it." I said what are you talking about? I know what I saw, I'm not crazy.

NAOMI: She thought you were lying?

RACHEL: Wait. She says: "Honey, it doesn't make any sense to have seen what you thought you saw."

NAOMI: Not make sense?

RACHEL: Right, because if you did see what you *thought* you saw, it would just lead to problems, problems for everybody. I said, but if I stay with this man, this whole marriage would be built on a lie? She says, *"So,* what you expect, Shirley Temple?"

NAOMI: Wow!

RACHEL: I said yeah, dammit. That's what I expect. That's the way you raised me. "Well you're not, okay! No Shirley Temple. So as long as he gives you everything and doesn't beat you, you go back there and forget everything."

NAOMI: And you did?

RACHEL: *(Nods her head.)* I had to for my son's sake.

NAOMI: You sure?

RACHEL: What do you mean if I'm sure? All right, I went back for my son, my mother, my friends, everybody.

NAOMI: Did you go back for Hilda the maid's sake?

RACHEL: You're laughing at me.

NAOMI: No I'm not.

RACHEL: *(Yells.)* For myself all right! I went back for myself. Let me tell you the kind of sweetheart my husband was. If you challenged him or gave him too much trouble, he'd have you committed to some nuthouse.

NAOMI: Come on Rachel.

RACHEL: What you think I'm lying? He was a lawyer for God's sake. A lawyer. You know how many did that to their wives to shut them up. Please. I went back and learned how not to see too much.

NAOMI: Think Bobby knew about his father?

RACHEL: Bobby? Bobby was good at not knowing things too.

NAOMI: He had a good teacher.

RACHEL: I'll never know for sure. Never mentioned it to me. He joined the Air Force when he was finished high school and went overseas for six years. Then when he came back here he worked with the Naval Academy. He was hardly ever here. Then one day he says to me that he wants to ask me something about his dad.

NAOMI: And?

RACHEL: And what? I panicked. I never found out what it was because I had this stroke the day he came home.

NAOMI: The same day?

RACHEL: Swear to God, I don't remember a thing. I think I was so wired up that I just collapsed. You figure it, I can't. I give up.

NAOMI: That is really weird, Rachel. Too weird.

RACHEL: Don't you think I know that. There I was dead to the world. It was perfect. Just the way my mother always wanted me to be. In a coma.

NAOMI: She didn't really want you in a coma.

RACHEL: No, just comatose.

NAOMI: So you never spoke with Bobby about . . . ?

RACHEL: By the time I recovered I was in here. We never spoke about it and then he died in the Towers disaster that day. We never got a chance to really discuss anything. I was the one that was suppose to go first. I mean what damn sense does this make. None. Why take him and leave me?

NAOMI: He loved you.

RACHEL: The mother's suppose to go before the child. Right?

NAOMI: Life doesn't behave itself . . . sometimes.

RACHEL: You know this is the first time that I ever told anybody what really happened.

NAOMI: I know.

RACHEL: Listen you can't tell anybody, right?

NAOMI: Do you think I would, that's what you think of me?

RACHEL: No, but . . . *swear.*

NAOMI: Rachel, who the hell would I tell?

RACHEL: *Swear.*

NAOMI: All right I swear.

RACHEL: God, what did I do? What did I do? I should have never told you.

NAOMI: Rachel calm down, listen . . . no . . . you'll never forgive me if I tell you this.

RACHEL: What?

NAOMI: No, I can't, you're not going to like this.

RACHEL: I hate it when people do that. Tell me already!

NAOMI: Okay . . . listen, I'm sorry to tell you this but . . . nobody really gives a shit!

RACHEL: *(Confused.)* What are you talking about . . . nobody really gives a . . . ?

NAOMI: Your life, your big secrets and revelations. What I mean is . . . Where is your husband?

RACHEL: Harold? He's dead.

NAOMI: And your mother and father?

RACHEL: They're . . . dead.

NAOMI: And your son, Bobby. God bless him

RACHEL: Gone . . . they're all gone.

NAOMI: So who in the world could I tell, who even knew them?

RACHEL: *(Pauses.)* There're people who know *me.*

NAOMI: Yeah but . . .

RACHEL: Yeah but what? Are you trying to tell me that my life doesn't matter?

NAOMI: Oops. Sorry, of course not. It matters very much. I swear I won't tell a soul. Okay? Just stop.

RACHEL: Stop what?

NAOMI: Beating up on yourself.

RACHEL: Stop and do what. What am I going to do with myself?

NAOMI: Try living.

RACHEL: I live with my memories.

NAOMI: So get new ones, new memories.

(Takes album from her and closes it. Enter Mitch. Early thirties, already slightly balding with a constantly amazed look on his face. He enters running and uncomfortable. He carries attaché case.)

MITCH: *(Quick kiss.)* Mom, how you doing?

NAOMI: Notre fille!

MITCH: Sorry I'm late. How you doing Mrs. Fleishman?

RACHEL: Me? Irrelevant mostly and you?

MITCH: What?

NAOMI: Don't bother with her, she's fine. *(Pause.)* So, you made it.

MITCH: Sorry I'm late. I got . . . lost I guess.

NAOMI: Lost?

MITCH: Well, it's hard to explain. I forgot where I was going.

RACHEL: How could you forget?

MITCH: Yeah I know. Here, I bought these for you. *(Gives packages.)* I couldn't remember if I was on my way to work or on my way home.

NAOMI: Honey, you're working too hard. For real. You need to slow down.

MITCH: I found myself falling asleep at the wheel. Wasn't for a really loud commercial on the car radio, I might of been . . . well you know. In an accident.

(Naomi and Rachel exchange looks.)

RACHEL: Jesus!

MITCH: So I pulled over at a gas station, but then I couldn't remember where I was going, that's when I started to panic.

RACHEL: I know the feeling.

(In background we see Wingate, stepping on and off elevator.)

MITCH: That never happened to me before, ever.

NAOMI: What did you do?

MITCH: I remember they said something about you should breathe in a paper bag, but I didn't have one, so I breathed into my attaché case.

RACHEL: Mitch, it's not quite the same thing.

MITCH: I know, anyway it slowed me down enough to notice the *Sunday Times* and remember what day it was. If it's Sunday, then I must be coming to see you.

RACHEL: You should do endorsements.

NAOMI: It's not funny, I think you're in trouble.

MITCH: I'm okay.

NAOMI: Were you and Sylvia arguing again?

MITCH: Arguing? No, no more so than usual. No crisis situation or anything. I mean things are down to a dull roar.

RACHEL: A good way to describe marriage. A dull roar?

MITCH: Mom knows what I mean.

NAOMI: Know what it is? You're always moving house. Every other year now you two keep moving further and further away into the suburbs. No wonder you lose yourself. You're trying to vanish.

MITCH: I just went kind of crazy.

NAOMI: But what happen, why today?

RACHEL: Sunday's a good day for crazy . . .

MITCH: I've been doing too much overtime.

NAOMI: Too much *Sylvia!*

MITCH: Stop it Mom! I've got to go to the bathroom. Open your presents I brought them for you.

(*He exits.*)

RACHEL: See, I told you, men aren't use to peeing on themselves . . .

NAOMI: She's killing him?

RACHEL: Who? Oh you mean the wife?

NAOMI: Sylvia.

RACHEL: Leave it alone, Naomi. They don't like it when you interfere.

NAOMI: Would you?

RACHEL: No.

NAOMI: She's pushing him to a breakdown.

RACHEL: Well it's his.

NAOMI: It's the kid. That's why he stays. In a way it's my fault. I taught him to always look after family. Be responsible. Don't stray like his father.

RACHEL: Mr. Pilgrim?

NAOMI: Right, at least you listen. I think I taught him too well.

RACHEL: You should have given him classes in Sylvia.

NAOMI: I couldn't. Five years ago she opened her legs and by the time he found his way out . . .

RACHEL: He was married and a daddy. But didn't he know to use something?

NAOMI: He did use something, but it wasn't his head.

RACHEL: *(Laughing.)* Not that head anyway.

NAOMI: Men are so dumb. There's a million ways to get them.

RACHEL: Hey, you only need one.

(They laugh as Mitch, "the good son," enters.)

MITCH: That's better. You're laughing, did you open your presents?

NAOMI: No son, we were waiting for you. Isn't he generous Rachel?

RACHEL: And handsome, very handsome.

MITCH: Go on, open them.

(They tear open packages like children at Christmas and find Disney sweatshirts.)

NAOMI: Oh look, Mickey Mouse

RACHEL: And I got Donald Duck.

MITCH: *(To Rachel.)* I know you only wear black. Yours was a little more difficult to get.

NAOMI: *(Kissing him.)* Oh, thanks sweetheart.

RACHEL: Yes Mitch, come get yours from me.

MITCH: *(Gets kiss.)* It's nothing. I mean, I work for them. It's the least they could do for God's sake.

NAOMI: Did you eat?

MITCH: I'm fine.

NAOMI: Here.

(Reaches inside pocket of sweater and produces chicken leg wrapped in foil.)

MITCH: Thanks, mom.

NAOMI: I saved it from lunch.

RACHEL: I would have saved mine for you but I had a hernia.

MITCH: What? I'll have it later.

RACHEL: The sweatshirt's nice, did you make them?

NAOMI: You think he sews?

RACHEL: I don't know. So what do you do for Disney?

MITCH: What do I do? Graphics. Graphic imaging.

RACHEL: Oh.

NAOMI: "Oh." Like she knows what the hell you're talking about.

RACHEL: What am I a dummy you draw things, right?

MITCH: Yeah, that's it.

RACHEL: But you didn't draw "Mickey" because then your name would be Walt and you'd have so much money that nobody could even talk to you.

NAOMI: He'd also be dead. Do you know how long ago Disney croaked?

MITCH: Please, we don't refer to his passing as "croaked."

NAOMI: Whatever.

RACHEL: Disney, don't they own the world or something?
MITCH: Most of it, yeah. Me, I work with computers. I come up with a lot of special effects stuff.
NAOMI: He's really good. He lives in front of the computer.
RACHEL: I don't understand those things.
NAOMI: I was just getting really good when they downsized me.
RACHEL: Shrunk!
NAOMI: Not funny.
MITCH: I used to love the computer.
NAOMI: I remember the first one I got you. You stayed in your room for days at a time. I used to wonder what in the world is this boy doing in there?
RACHEL: A real wizard right? He's got the look.
MITCH: Now I can't stand them.
NAOMI: What happened?
MITCH: I feel like I'm being erased.
NAOMI: Erased?
MITCH: I can't explain it. I'm sitting there, right? Sometimes ten hours at a time I sit there . . . disappearing. They pay me well. I'm lucky I guess. You know how many people would like to work for Disney?
NAOMI: *(Whispers.)* He's the only one in his department.
RACHEL: Only what?
NAOMI: You know, black.
RACHEL: *(Whispers.)* Oh, is that good? Sometimes being the only one's not all that great.
MITCH: You got that right. I'm suppose to come up with new ideas, new concepts but . . . not too new. Know what I mean?
NAOMI: In other words don't scare them too much.
MITCH: Right. And the money's good, I guess. Its funny, I should be happy . . . it's just that money, you know . . .
RACHEL: Goes?
MITCH: Yeah. Sylvia's got Garth in this special school . . .
NAOMI: Kid's just five years old.
MITCH: I mean it's a good school and all . . .
NAOMI: But it's expensive as hell.
MITCH: Now I did overtime last week. I got an extra thousand dollars. I say to Sylvia. "Gee, I guess we can afford to go to a movie this weekend." Not funny. She has zero sense of humor when it comes to the kid. I mean she's like . . .
NAOMI: Try, *crazy.*

MITCH: Crazy. Let's say she's not big on objectivity where he's involved.
NAOMI: He's just a kid for God sake. One kid. He's got enough toys to open a factory. I said to her, Sylvia, why don't you make a little money, open a day care. God knows you've got enough junk here . . . That one didn't go down real well either.
MITCH: He's a special kid.
NAOMI: Spoiled
MITCH: Very gifted.
NAOMI: Rotten!
MITCH: *(Eating chicken.)* Maybe I will have this now. Sylvia makes these special salads.
NAOMI: Yeah, I bet the refrigerator stays full of them. You're not allowed to get rid of them right away. You have to wait two weeks.
MITCH: Okay, homemaking is not her specialty.
NAOMI: The place looks like a war zone, and this is *with* a maid.
RACHEL: Oh you've got one too?
NAOMI: Yeah but it's different from your time, now they come from South America.
RACHEL: Does she do windows? Hilda, she drew the line at windows.
MITCH: I don't know, I'm never home when she's there. I'm always doing overtime in front of the computer . . . falling asleep. Trying to make enough for this . . . *(Pauses suddenly.) Jesus!*
NAOMI: What?
RACHEL: It's the chicken, right?
MITCH: I'm starting to hate my kid *(Throws away chicken.)* What kind of a sick person am I? How can you hate your own child?
NAOMI: Easy if he's a spoiled brat who has temper tantrums and screams for an hour straight without stopping.
RACHEL: What! He does that?
NAOMI: Girl, please, don't even get me started.
MITCH: That's when he's acting out.
NAOMI: See, he don't do that nonsense around me. He saves all that for mummy and daddy. Him and I had this discussion before and he knows that I will beat his behind in a minute. That boy got good sense when he's ready.
MITCH: We can't do that.
NAOMI: Listen Mitch, you better do something quick-fast-and-in-a-hurry because that child is about to make your life a living hell.
MITCH: She's talking about putting him in therapy.
NAOMI: She the one needs to be in therapy.

MITCH: Fall asleep at the computer. Lock the door so the boss doesn't find me.
RACHEL: You know sometimes they like that, finding you asleep at your desk. Shows that you're really . . .
NAOMI: Dumb!
MITCH: I'll be all right
NAOMI: My behind!
MITCH: Maybe if we had another one there'd be a kind of balance. He'd learn to share.
NAOMI: Look how he started off, you videoed the birth. Had a damn film crew there.
MITCH: That was my idea, at least I think it was . . . I don't even know anymore.
NAOMI: The kid starts life as a movie star. Now he even has his own cell phone to report on the maid.
RACHEL: One son's not a good idea.
MITCH: But she can't have anymore. We've been trying. We've got this specialist who made up this chart for us. You know based on her cycle. She beeps me at work. I come home . . . It's crazy.
NAOMI: Wait a minute, wasn't she the one who wanted you to have a . . . what you call it?
MITCH: Vasectomy. Right, she said I was being inconsiderate because I wasn't willing to sacrifice anything.
NAOMI: Now she's ready to go the other way.
MITCH: And I'm not producing fast enough for her. And it's funny because when I'm home I feel like I'm an intruder. As if I don't belong there.
RACHEL: Maybe you don't?
MITCH: What?
NAOMI: Belong there.
RACHEL: You just entered the middle class. Welcome!
MITCH: Stop it will you.
RACHEL: You don't know whether you're coming or going. You got your life divided into boxes.
NAOMI: The only place you *can't* sleep . . .
MITCH: Is at home.
RACHEL: Tell me something, do you still enjoy doing it . . . you know . . .
MITCH: Doing what?
NAOMI: She means sex. With Rachel it's always sex.
RACHEL: Yeah, like you're not interested, right?
NAOMI: Me? Anyway, it's different, he's my son.

RACHEL: Our son. Well?

MITCH: That's kind of personal.

RACHEL: Listen, at this point that's all we've got is other people's *personal*.

NAOMI: I use to have some good personal stuff once . . . I think.

RACHEL: *(To Mitch.)* So?

(Two sets of eyes stare at him.)

MITCH: Well, before we got married we couldn't get each other's clothes off fast enough, you know what I mean?

RACHEL: Vaguely!

MITCH: I'm talking anywhere, cars, elevators, movies. Anywhere. And then we got married and things changed.

RACHEL: Slowly?

MITCH: No, instantly.

NAOMI: The baby came.

MITCH: Wasn't just that, I mean true to say we didn't plan on the baby.

NAOMI: You didn't anyway.

MITCH: What?

NAOMI: Nothing, go on.

MITCH: First we argued about the vasectomy and why I didn't do it. Now we argue because she wants another baby and can't seem to have one.

NAOMI: This is so crazy. Time was when black people couldn't spit without getting pregnant. I know that was my greatest fear when I was young. That kept my behind very quiet. Now a days you got specialist with charts. You calling each other up on beepers to make appointments to conceive and what? Nothing's happening.

MITCH: You know what it's like having a woman pointing her finger in your face and saying:

(The two women encircle him. Rachel in wheelchair, Naomi with walker.)

NAOMI/RACHEL: *Produce!!!*

RACHEL: *(Laughing.)* Have you tried oysters? Joking. Look, just stop trying so hard.

MITCH: She spends all this money on Health Foods. I've still got a knot in my stomach.

NAOMI: Stress! You're giving yourself an ulcer.

MITCH: It's my ulcer, I own it.

NAOMI: Claim your ulcer.

(Sound of beeper going off. Mitch checks number.)

RACHEL: God, I hate those things,

NAOMI: Let me guess. . . . .

MITCH: Sylvia, I better check see what she wants. *(Starts to exit with phone.)*
NAOMI: *You,* in a bottle.
  (As *Mitch exits he encounters Wingate who is carrying a huge Pampers for adults. He offers it to Mitch.*)
MITCH: No thanks. Damn, my cell phone's dead.
RACHEL: And take him with you will you.
NAOMI: My son.
WINGATE: Who?
NAOMI: Him, my son.
MITCH: Come show me the phone.
WINGATE: *(Looking at sweatshirt.)* Mickey Mouse!
  (They exit.)
RACHEL: Should get one for everybody in here. It's already Disneyland.
NAOMI: That girl's driving him nuts. It's my fault. I never taught him about women.
RACHEL: He wouldn't have listened, anyway. Men always trip over their third leg.
NAOMI: He's starting to look old, already. I don't want to see my son looking old.
RACHEL: Listen, it takes a lifetime to learn anything that's any use. By the time you know something, you're locked up in a nursing home and it's too late.
NAOMI: Well I'm not locked up.
RACHEL: Dream on kid.
NAOMI: And I damn sure am not going to let her kill my son.
RACHEL: What can you do.
NAOMI: Watch.
  (Mitch enters.)
RACHEL: Everything okay?
MITCH: Yeah, she just wants me to stop at the market on the way home. Some soy milk and some iceberg lettuce.
NAOMI/RACHEL: For the salad!
MITCH: Yeah.
NAOMI: Um . . . Mitch guess what Rachel was saying?
MITCH: What?
NAOMI: She doesn't think that we can go outside of here. Tell her, she's wrong, right?
RACHEL: Yeah Mitch, tell me how wrong I am.
MITCH: Well . . . somebody kind of has to sign you out.
NAOMI: What do you mean kind of sign me out?
MITCH: You know, sign you out.
RACHEL: Ah-hah!

NAOMI: Why?

MITCH: Why, what?

NAOMI: Why does somebody have to do that?

MITCH: Well because . . . that's the way it is. It's for your protection.

RACHEL: Kind of.

NAOMI: So now tell me good so that I can understand. Unless you sign for us we can't move?

MITCH: They don't want patients just roaming the streets.

NAOMI: So we *are* prisoners?

MITCH: No, patients.

RACHEL: And patients must be patient.

MITCH: *(Gathering things.)* Anyway, I've got to get myself back to Mt. Vernon. Long day tomorrow. Got to get some rest.

NAOMI: Not in Mt. Vernon you won't *(Pause.)* So it's true, we can't leave.

MITCH: No, well not exactly. Anyway, what's the problem?

NAOMI: *(Flings sweatshirt.)* Here, I'm not ready for Disneyland yet.

RACHEL: Ah, venom!

MITCH: Mom, please I really don't need this today. I've got enough problems.

NAOMI: Well I'm sorry that my life is causing you problems.

MITCH: That is not what I said!

NAOMI: Cause yours sure caused me some.

MITCH: See, now why you even want to go there? You're going to work the guilt, right? Look, I come to see you every week, regular as clockwork.

NAOMI: Okay, and?

MITCH: If you say you need tennis balls to stick on your walker so that it won't scrape the floor. I bring them don't I?

NAOMI: Yes Mitch you do.

MITCH: Whatever you say you need, I bring for you.

NAOMI: Yes you do *(Pause.)* and then you leave.

MITCH: I leave? Yeah I leave, what do you expect. What do you want me to do, move in?

RACHEL: That wouldn't be so bad.

MITCH: Well, I'm very sorry but I have a life.

NAOMI: Yes well guess what, I'd like one too.

MITCH: *(Frantic.)* What the hell more can I do? Everybody keeps wanting more from me. There's nothing left.

NAOMI: Never mind, go on, you have to get back to Mt. Vernon.

MITCH: Right! *(Long pause while the two women stare at him.)* Look, do you know what I had to go through to even get you in this place?

NAOMI: You mean talking me into prison.

RACHEL: *Ow!*

MITCH: *(Gives Rachel filthy look.)* Do you mind staying out of this, please? *(Back to mother.)* No, I mean getting them to admit you here. Its very expensive here you know.

NAOMI: Expensive! I never asked to come here you know. You want to talk expensive? Do you know how much I spent on that art college you went to? The one with all those rich white students. You know how hard it was to send you there? My ass having to work on that Bell telephone plantation did that. *That's expensive.* It cost one heart.

MITCH: See, more guilt.

NAOMI: No, truth, so don't even try it. You told me to give up my apartment.

MITCH: You had to climb three flights of stairs, for God sake. You couldn't keep doing that after the heart attack.

NAOMI: I could have got something for seniors on the ground floor. You said it would be better to be somewhere with a trained staff to care for me.

MITCH: And so, was I wrong?

NAOMI: Better for who? Not me. You could have left me right where I was. At least the freedom was mine. Let me walk slow if I have to but let me walk.

(Finding the temperature suddenly a little hotter than she can handle, Rachel begins to wheel away slowly.)

RACHEL: Well, I think I'll go up and sleep off the rest of the birthday.

NAOMI: No you're not.

RACHEL: I'm not?

MITCH: Look, we all need to take a time out.

NAOMI: That's what you do to kids, give them a time out when they misbehave. You must think I'm Garth.

MITCH: Oh, for God sake. Will you stop it!

NAOMI: It's okay. You go home to Sylvia.
  (Stretches and sings.)
  "I *sing because I'm happy*
  I sing because I'm free
  His eyes are on the sparrow"

MITCH: Please give us a break. Don't start with the singing.

NAOMI: *"And I know he watches me"*

RACHEL: Boy, I thought my mother was good.

MITCH: All right mom, there's something you want. What is it?

NAOMI: I want out.

MITCH: What do you mean, out?
NAOMI: Out of here.
MITCH: You want to go for a walk now?
NAOMI: I'm not Lassie. I want to leave here.
MITCH: Leave here?
MITCH: For what?
NAOMI: For good.
MITCH: You want to change nursing homes?
NAOMI: No, I want to change my life.
MITCH: Change what life? . . . Look, if you're thinking of . . . no way! Sylvia would never . . .
NAOMI: Are you crazy, do you think I would ever live with Sylvia with her tired self and that spoiled-behind son of yours? No way.
MITCH: Well then where would you go?
NAOMI: Rachel and me will find something together.
RACHEL: *(Just about to lights cigarette begins to choke.)* Rachel and you . . . what?
NAOMI: Look Rachel, you've been complaining all this time about . . .
RACHEL: Okay so I *kvetch* a little but . . . what the hell would I do?
NAOMI: I don't know teach piano maybe. Watch people's children. I don't know. Something, anything.
RACHEL: But who would take care of me?
(Naomi gets up and pushes Rachel's wheelchair to mirror.)
NAOMI: Look at yourself. You're not the little Jewish Princess anymore. All your life you've been complaining that you wanted to work but no one would let you. Never let you use your brain. Well . . . ?
RACHEL: Stop with your judging already. Remember what it says in that book of yours.
NAOMI: Yeah, *judge pas!* but get up off your ass.
MITCH: This is crazy. I think you need a sedative. I'm going to get the nurse. *(He exits.)*
NAOMI: Give it to that wife of yours. You can stick it up her . . .
RACHEL: Naomi, I'm an old woman. Old.
NAOMI: Look Rachel this is your birthday I don't have anything else to give you except a chance. Don't you start wimping out on me too. What's the worse that could happen to you out there?
RACHEL: Out there? I don't know. It's so dangerous
NAOMI: And?
RACHEL: Well I mean you don't know, anything might happen.

NAOMI: Yeah, that's the beauty. A chance for change. Danger and excitement. Here you know exactly just what's going to happen.

RACHEL: The terrorists, they killed my son for God sake!

NAOMI: Here you kill yourself with time. Then they come for you and put you in that third elevator.

RACHEL: Yeah, the one that doesn't stop to pick up any passengers because it's express.

NAOMI: Straight to the basement.

RACHEL: Yeah, but I'm good at not seeing things.

NAOMI: Not *that* good. *(Pause.)* All right I'll shoot you for it.

RACHEL: You're crazy.

(They play the child's game of fingers called: odds/evens.)

NAOMI: Odds.

RACHEL: Okay, evens. *(She shoots. Naomi wins.)* Okay two out of three.

NAOMI: *(Shoots and wins.)* That's it. You coming!

RACHEL: What the hell. If you're gone, who would I talk to anyway? Naomi . . . a nice Jewish name.

(Mitch enters with guard.)

MITCH: So you mean there's no one on duty who can give her some help?

RACHEL: Oy, the Golem!

GUARD: What's the problem, Mrs. Pilgrim?

MITCH: She's acting very . . . strange.

NAOMI: Nothing, I want my son to take us out for ice cream. That's all.

GUARD: We have ice cream in the cafeteria.

NAOMI: Not the kind we want.

MITCH: Ice cream?

RACHEL: Some time it's hard to find just the right flavor. My son, Bobby, the soldier who never managed to kill anyone, except himself. *(Pause.)* He used to bring the most wonderful most magical ice cream. It's hard to find.

NAOMI: Not as hard as getting honey from the rock.

MITCH: Honey from the rock?

RACHEL: I remember a delicatessen somewhere on 72nd. The sweetest ice cream.

GUARD: Does this place have a name?

NAOMI: Rapture, I think.

RACHEL: Yeah, that was it, Rapture . . .

GUARD: They seem right enough to me. What's the matter, you don't like ice cream?

MITCH: Okay, okay, but just so we understand. Just ice cream.
GUARD: *(Whispers.)* Yeah, you know sometime when you get old all you got left's your taste.
RACHEL: If you're lucky. Some people never had it to begin with.
(They start to set out Rachel in her chair.)
GUARD: *(To Naomi.)* You're forgetting your walker.
NAOMI: It's all right my son will hold me up. Remember when I passed out that time in the house and you picked me up and carried me in your arms. I was so surprised. I never knew you were so strong, Mitch.
MITCH: Me either. Don't test me again though. Please.
NAOMI: You know Mitch, it's not your child that you don't like.
MITCH: No? What don't I like?
NAOMI: It's that thing you let them do to you.
MITCH: What's that?
NAOMI: Disappear you.
MITCH: You see you don't understand, by thirty I was going to own my own business.
NAOMI: And?
MITCH: Well . . . I didn't did I. I still don't have what I want really.
NAOMI: By forty you're suppose to own your mind. By then it's suppose to be yours, if not, something's wrong.
MITCH: And a house. I was going to get you a house.
NAOMI: I don't need a house, Mitch. I just need a door I can walk out of. You do that for me and we'll call it even, okay. You don't have to prove yourself for me. You were already a success long time ago.
(There's a sudden lighting change. Spotlight on Naomi and Mitch. All else is darkness.)
MITCH: Listen I . . . can't.
NAOMI: Can't what?
MITCH: Do this. It would be the end right now. I can't take you out of here. Let me talk to her and see. Maybe next week.
NAOMI: Next week? You like this. You like having me here where you don't have to worry.
MITCH: Yes.
NAOMI: You were just biding your time waiting to put me in here.
MITCH: No that's not true.
NAOMI: Put me in here where you know you can come cry about your life and leave. Drop off some flowers and leave.
MITCH: Next week, I promise. We'll talk. *(He kisses her quickly and runs off.)*

NAOMI: Wait, don't go, Mitch! *(Lighting returns to normal as Rachel enters singing.)*
RACHEL: *(Singing.)* On a wagon, bound for market
There's a calf with a mournful eye.
NAOMI: Mitch, you'll never ask.
RACHEL: *Up above him there's a swallow
Winging swiftly through the sky.*
NAOMI: You'll just let them erase you.
RACHEL: *(Sings.)* Calves are easily bound and slaughtered
never knowing the reason why.
But whoever treasures freedom
Like the swallow has learned to fly?
RACHEL: Okay I'm ready, how I look?
NAOMI: Forget it.
RACHEL: What do you mean forget it, where's Mitch?
NAOMI: He says he has to ask his wife?
RACHEL: About ice cream?
NAOMI: Forget it he never will. Our son Mitch. The good son.
RACHEL: Listen, it was a good idea but listen you got to kind of wonder about anybody his age who actually enjoys coming here to visit. If this is the high point of his week, you got to kind of think the boy's in trouble. Know what I mean?
NAOMI: Come on let's try.
(Guard enters and blocks path.)
GUARD: So, looks like no Rapture for you today after all, ladies.
NAOMI: Well we told you we'd be going for ice cream.
GUARD: Sorry, he didn't sign you out.
NAOMI: Look I'm a grown woman.
GUARD: He signed you in, he'll sign you out.
NAOMI: But . . .
GUARD: You know the rules. Listen . . . maybe you'd like me to get you a little something.
RACHEL: What did I tell you?
NAOMI: *(Steps away.)* No, never.
GUARD: Well you never know.
RACHEL: Leave her alone, Golem.
GUARD: Fair enough, I'll help you a little bit but I'm not losing my job for you two.
(He exits.)

NAOMI: Okay, we're going to have to do it ourselves.
RACHEL: Do what?
NAOMI: Bust out.
RACHEL: Now I know you're insane.
   (*Darkness.*)

SCENE FOUR

Naomi sneaks on stage wearing coat, checks passageway, and then summons Rachel.

NAOMI: Come on let's go.
RACHEL: Where the hell we going?
NAOMI: First we try the window, that's easiest.
RACHEL: You know now a days I have one lucid day a week. One lucid day . . .
NAOMI: Good, I'll make an appointment.
RACHEL: This ain't it. Why don't we wait until next week.
NAOMI: Because there might not be a next week, that's why.
RACHEL: There's always a next week.
NAOMI: Yeah but you might not be in it.
RACHEL: No such luck, I'll be here.
NAOMI: Well if you want to stay with the Pampers brigade, you stay. Me, I'm out. Bring your chair over here.
RACHEL: What for?
NAOMI: You hold it steady I'm going to try the window.
RACHEL: Try the window. What are we going to do?
NAOMI: Maybe lower ourselves down.
   (*Rachel starts laughing.*)
RACHEL: Next.
NAOMI: We wait here until morning.
RACHEL: You mean we won't sleep?
NAOMI: You said you don't sleep anyway.
RACHEL: But what are we going to do now that we don't have Mitch?
NAOMI: What is this, no Mitch no life?
RACHEL: Well?
NAOMI: He's more scared than we are.
RACHEL: Without him why bother? Face it we can't survive a week out there without him.

NAOMI: A day is all it would take to go *bungee jumping*.
(Rachel stares at her open-mouthed.)
NAOMI: Close your mouth you'll catch flies.
RACHEL: Bungee jumping, that's why you want to get out of here?
NAOMI: I always wanted to do that.
RACHEL: All the crazies, to me they come. Like moths to a flame.
NAOMI: Hey don't knock it. At least it's better than watching a television that's turned off.
RACHEL: Maybe.
NAOMI: So, do you think we can survive a day out there?
RACHEL: Yeah, maybe a day.
NAOMI: Well all a week is, is just seven days tied together real close. That's all.
RACHEL: Things sound easy when you say them.
NAOMI: It's how you look at it. We're not trying for a week just a day at a time.
RACHEL: You know what it's really all about don't you?
NAOMI: What?
RACHEL: They work so hard to come up with stuff to keep us alive and then they don't know what to do with us now they got us. They don't want us alive.
NAOMI: Yes they do because we're money.
RACHEL: Wow, you changed. Everyone was so nice, remember? *(Pause.)* We really going to sit here all night? Why can't we leave in the morning, first thing?
NAOMI: Because in the morning after we have our medication we're not going anywhere, that's why.
RACHEL: We got to stay awake like watchmen.
NAOMI: *(Sings.) Watchman, watchman, what is the hour of the night?*
RACHEL: It's one o'clock and all is well . . . I think. Why is it that it's always night we fear dying in?
NAOMI: Because it's dark and easy I guess.
RACHEL: Do we fear dying at night or *of* night?
NAOMI: I don't know, I guess we think that if we can see Him, we can duck Him. Sit up all night with a shotgun to drive Him off.
(They sit with their backs against each other and scan the stage for sign of the enemy.)
RACHEL: Hello operator, give me God. When dawn comes, it's safe to sleep. Right?
NAOMI: It's never safe.
RACHEL: But can't we at least stay for the pressure pill?
NAOMI: You can do without it.

RACHEL: And the green ones they're good for my nerves.
NAOMI: Tell you what, why don't we just take the whole pharmacy?
RACHEL: How we going to . . . oh, you're being sarcastic, right. Okay.
NAOMI: You know what I think? I think they have us so programmed that we just take drugs to forget time. I mean every hour they got us taking something.
RACHEL: Well they just keep us tranquilized so they don't have to deal with us. You can't blame them. Would you want to deal with this bunch all day long?
NAOMI: If it was me, I'd give them all the medication one time. BAM!
RACHEL: I don't like being programmed. So let's make our own. I'm still scared though.
NAOMI: You know what I hate most about this place, no pets. I mean what's life without something that's alive and ours?
RACHEL: They figure if you can't take care of yourself how the hell you going to care an animal. *(Laughs.)* Hell, we're the animals here.
NAOMI: No, the vegetables. Well, hell with that.
RACHEL: So how we going to get out the door?
NAOMI: Look what I got. *(Shows her shopping bag.)*
RACHEL: What's in there?
(Takes out pink uniform of a nurse's aide.)
NAOMI: A nurse's aide uniform, I got it from the pantry.
RACHEL: What can you do with this?
NAOMI: Walk right the hell out of here.
RACHEL: Won't they notice you?
NAOMI: A black nurse's aide? Please. You're invisible. Like magic.
RACHEL: Oh, I get you. But what about our wristbands?
NAOMI: *(Whips out scissors.)* I'll do you, you do me.
RACHEL: God, it's hard, they're so thick.
NAOMI: Not as thick as chains. What's the matter you weak? Let me do you. *(Cuts through.)* There.
RACHEL: Okay, okay give me a second. *(Struggles and finally cuts through.)* I know I'm not a complete spastic.
NAOMI: Did you say princess?
RACHEL: No, I said spastic. *(Pause.)* Wait, somebody's coming.
(Wingate enters.)
NAOMI: Wingate, what the hell is he doing, sleepwalking?
WINGATE: The cat. I feed her.
RACHEL: What cat, never knew there was a cat here.

WINGATE: I feed her.
NAOMI: Good for you. Go feed her. Go. *(Changing into uniform.)*
WINGATE: You going?
NAOMI: You, not going to tell are you?
WINGATE: I tell.
RACHEL: No you're not. *(Reaching in shopping bag.)* Two cans of Insure.
WINGATE: Three.
RACHEL: Yeah, all right, three.
WINGATE: Sweatshirt.
RACHEL: Yes, sweatshirt.
WINGATE: I come.
NAOMI: No, you don't come. Go feed your cat. Go!
WINGATE: Mickey Mouse?
NAOMI: *(To Rachel.)* Well, its dawn, you ready?
RACHEL: Naomi, outside they have terrorist.
NAOMI: And in here they have Mickey Mouse and medication. Well?
RACHEL: "I shall do the thing which goodness is." Maybe . . . Here.
   (She gives Wingate sweatshirt. Naomi pushes Rachel in wheelchair.)
RACHEL: *(Sings as lights dim.)* On a wagon, bound for market
   There's a calf with a mournful eye
   Up above him
   There's a swallow
   Winging swiftly through the sky.
NAOMI: Good-bye Wingate.
WINGATE: Good-bye . . . Mickey Mouse . . . Good-bye.
   (All the silence of the world. Curtain.)

END OF PLAY

COPYRIGHT INFORMATION

Skitaletz (The Wanderer) copyright © 2000 by Dmitry Lipkin. All inquiries should be addressed to John Buzzetti, The Gersh Agency, 130 West 42nd Street New York, NY 10036.

Boxcar copyright © 1999 by Silvia Gonzalez S. All inquiries should be addressed to New Dramatists, 424 West 44th Street, New York, NY 10036.

A Bicycle Country copyright © 2000 by Nilo Cruz. All inquiries should be addressed to Peregrine Whittlesey, 345 East 80th Street, New York, NY 10021. (212) 737-0153.

The Negro of Peter the Great copyright © 2001 by Carlyle Brown. Reprinted by permission of Cherylene Lee. All inquiries should be addressed to Bruce Ostler, Bret Adams Ltd. 448 West 44th Street, New York, NY 10036.

The Women of Lockerbie copyright © 2000 by Deborah Brevoort. All inquiries should be addressed to Helen Merrill Agency, 295 Lafayette Street Suite 915, New York, NY 10012. (212) 226-5016.

Millenium 7 copyright © 2000 by Edgar Nkosi White. All inquiries should be addressed to Morgan Jenness, Helen Merrill Agency, 295 Lafayette Street Suite 915, New York, NY 10012. (212) 226-5016.